# LIVINGSTONE'S HOSPITAL

# LIVINGSTONE'S HOSPITAL

## THE STORY OF CHITAMBO

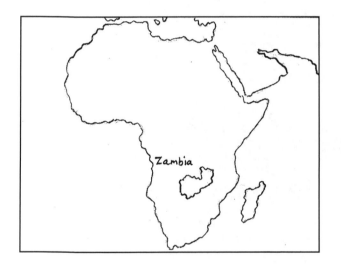

Marion A. Currie

authorHOUSE®

AuthorHouse™
1663 Liberty Drive
Bloomington, IN 47403
www.authorhouse.com
Phone: 1-800-839-8640

Published by AuthorHouse    06/25/2013

ISBN: 978-1-4567-9609-9 (sc)
ISBN: 978-1-4817-9054-3 (e)

# CONTENTS

# DEDICATION

In memory of my parents Nancy and Milton Currie and baby sister Catherine; my grandparents John and Jean Todd, and Hamilton and Isobel Currie, and to all who, like Livingstone, gave their hearts to Africa. To my brothers and sisters, for all our shared journeys.

**Do you carry out the work which I have begun? I leave it with you.**

David Livingstone, Cambridge, 4th Dec 1857

# ACKNOWLEDGEMENTS

My love and appreciation go to my two sisters—Jo and Zanna, for their company on not one but two return journeys to Chitambo, with Zanna's daughter Jasmine in 2003 and Jo's son Paul in 2008. These were journeys of the heart with many attendant joys and sorrows. Jasmine's fresh perspective and cheerfulness were delightful. Paul was a rock when he needed to be and an unapologetic adventurer when the occasion arose. Jo deserves a medal for her work with Penicuik for Africa, and on her own, in raising awareness and funds for the Chitambo Ambulance Appeal. *Mwawombeni mukwai!*\* She has become an integral part of the Scottish Zambian community and was rightly rewarded with a proud place at Kenneth Kaunda's dinner table in Edinburgh in July 2009.

I would like to pay special tribute to Margaret and Mary Ritchie who came on the second expedition. They were stalwart in the face of all the physical and emotional ups and downs of the journey. Margaret, ex Matron of Chitambo Hospital, gave me great help and encouragement in writing this book. I appreciated her sincerity, insight and humour. It became apparent while we were at Mwenzo that Margaret was significantly unwell, in spite of which she remained stoical for the rest of the journey. On returning to Scotland she bravely underwent treatment for cancer, and her death on 6<sup>th</sup> October 2009 was a great loss. Our hearts go out to Mary.

Thanks too to Marion Lacey (nee Martin) who also took her courage in both hands and returned with us to her childhood home at Mwenzo. I appreciated her love, support and relaxed approach.

Special thanks to Lily Musk who has provided me with a large chunk of written material and who has helped with editing. With Chad's untimely death in 2004 a great man was lost but his writings have been an invaluable part of the story and his humour shines through even in the worst of times.

It was Lily who gave me a copy of Alan Buckle's manuscript "*A History of the Serenje District*" which was my inspiration for starting this book.

Thank you to Alan and Gerie for allowing me to use this material and the photographs. I have appreciated their letters of encouragement. Sincere thanks to my librarian friend Sally Gale who helped enormously with the historical research, and the layout, and who kept appearing at just the right moment.

The Moffat families in Scotland, Zambia and New Zealand have been most helpful. Moffat hospitality is legendary, and David and Christine at Mkushi have kept the tradition alive. Malcolm Moffat in Edinburgh has been very generous in allowing me access to all his research on Moffat history. Thanks to Nancy Bollen (nee Moffat) and Geoff of Whangarei, New Zealand, for their hospitality and access to the family photo album.

Special thanks to David Livingstone's great grandson, Neil Wilson for the previously unpublished extracts from his father Hubert Wilson's letters, and for some priceless photos of early Chitambo.

To all those who have contributed to the book, heartfelt thanks. I know that it has not been easy to retell some of the Chitambo stories. Thanks to Jan Willem Briet, Daphne Robertson, and Frits van der Hoeven for their moving contributions. Thanks also to Hans Doornbos for the freshness of his perspective.

There are many people in Zambia who deserve my thanks: The Chileshes in Lusaka for their outstanding hospitality, Julie Limpic at Juls guest-house for making us so welcome, Justin Lubhezi for providing fine reliable vehicles, Rev. Gibson Chilongo for the warmth of his welcome, and his infectious good humour, Dr. Mufune, Medical Director of Serenje and Chitambo, with the District Health Management Team, for co-coordinating our visit to Chitambo, Rev. Mugala at Chitambo, Drs. Kanku and Nzinga at Chitambo, Chief Muchinka at Mabonde. Special gratitude to HRH Chief Chitambo IV, at Chipundu, for taking the time to listen to our story and for accompanying us to the Livingstone monument and the Lulimala River where David Livingstone emerged on his last journey.

To Kim and Edmund and all the camp staff of Kasanka Trust, we are still indebted for the wonderful hospitality and all the invaluable help with the ambulance project. We began to feel like part of the family!

Thanks to the World Vision team at Mwenzo, to Rev. and Mrs. Chulu, Dighton Sichalwe, and others for the warm welcome, hospitality and enthusiasm. The time at Mwenzo, though brief was very memorable.

Thanks to the WICHDA society who cherish the history of Mwenzo and with whom I remain in contact.

To all those whom I have not named, but who have played their part in this story *Mwawombeni bonse!*** While the Chitambo story goes on, it has become necessary to stop somewhere! I hope that this book will trigger more memories, and I welcome any amendments and further contributions.

I would like to acknowledge Getty Images and Corbis International for the use of photographs of the "Livingstone tree," and the photo of Livingstone with daughter Anna Mary, respectively. Acknowledgements are due to the Scottish National Library Trust for enabling the use of photos in their collection, and to Chief Chitambo IV for permission to use his photo. Gratitude to all those who appear in the photos and who have given their permission.

Finally to my husband Guy and sons Greg and Theo, who have patiently tolerated my obsession with Chitambo Hospital and David Livingstone for many years . . . . It's over.! *Or is it?*

*Well done, Madam! ** Well done all!*

# PROLOGUE AND PREFACE
# TO THE SECOND EDITION

The 200th anniversary of Livingstone's birth on March 19th, the wonderful progress made at Chitambo Hospital, and the feedback of many kind readers have impelled me to revise this book. My sincere thanks go to all those who have taken the time to read and respond to the Chitambo story, and to those who continue the good work at Chitambo Hospital.

This is the story as far as I know it. There are doubtless other versions, and others would have told it differently. Wherever possible I have tried to stick to historical fact but in places I have had to rely on eye-witness accounts, memories and speculation. My only regret is that I have not been able to include more voices, particularly those of the local Africans who made significant contributions to the founding and running of the hospital.

In places I have given my own interpretation of events and I may have taken some poetic license. For this I take full responsibility. Livingstone never founded a hospital. It was his wife's nephew, Malcolm Moffat who started the mission at Chitambo and Livingstone's grand-children who helped to get the hospital underway.

A hundred and five years later Chitambo hospital is thriving in spite of many constraints, and when I started writing this story, it was being run by a local Zambian doctor. For Livingstone I think this would have been one of his wildest dreams come true, and would have partly compensated for any sense of having failed in his quest for the Nile's source. I would like to dedicate this book to all who contributed to that dream, and to those who keep it alive today.

The following poem appeared in Punch magazine on April 25th 1874, the year of Livingstone's burial at Westminster Abbey:

"Open the Abbey door and bear him in
To sleep with king and statesman, chief and sage,
The missionary come of weaver kin,
But great by work that brooks no lower wage.
He needs no epitaph to guard his name,
Which men will prize while worthy work is known.
He lived and died for good, be that his fame;
Let marble crumble: this is **Living-stone.**"

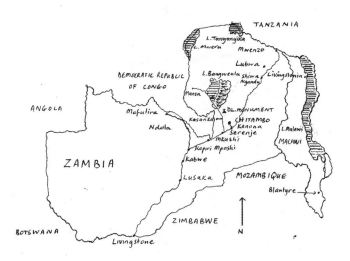

**Map of Zambia showing borders, not to scale**

**Map of Livingstone's last journey-from his book—Travels**

# CHAPTER 1

# JOURNEY TO THE HEART

## GOING BACK: 2003

A simple unadorned slab of cement marks Dad's grave in a clearing among the miombo trees. The gentle August sun and a light breeze set the leaves shimmering. A crowd has gathered in a semi-circle around the slab and the minister starts speaking softly in a sing-song voice. At the rise and fall of his mellifluous tones I start to recognize a few Lala words and it is as though they seep into some frozen corner of my heart and set it melting. Now the crowd is singing a hymn, their voices blending in effortless African harmony, and I find that I'm crying. Tears of joy and grief, wonder and gratitude trickle down my dusty cheeks. I no longer try to hide them. I can see others in the crowd wiping their eyes, which makes me cry all the harder. Jo places a small bouquet of wild-flowers at the head of the grave and then we walk back up the path to Chitambo with some of the local people who still remember him.

"I'm going back" announced Zanna, out of the blue in late 2002. "Whether any of the rest of you want to come or not." I felt anxious about letting her go on her own—my younger sister, a solitary red-head journeying into the wild heart of Zambia. Jo was uncertain, but she responded to the ultimatum. And so it was that my two sisters and I decided to return to our childhood home, thirty-something years on.

For my part the decision was not lightly made. There were the usual separation anxieties, my fear of flying, and uncertainty about security in Zambia. Well-meaning friends were suspicious of any African country beginning with Z, and we had no idea how we would be received after such a long absence.

Not knowing who was in charge at Chitambo I wrote to 'the Minister' and 'the Doctor-In-Charge', Chitambo, P.O. Kanona, and waited to see what would happen. I explained that our father, Dr. Hamilton Currie had lived and died there, in 1974, and that we would like to come back to visit the hospital and the church. Weeks passed and there was no reply. Then a letter bearing Zambian stamps arrived. Eyes prickling with tears, I read the following letter typed on United Church of Zambia headed notepaper:

*Dear Dr. Taylor,*

*In the name of our heavenly king I greet you all. I hope and believe you are all fine. Doctor I was more than the word happy when I received an unexpected letter from you, this is a wonderful and amazing thing.*

*Your request of visiting me, Chitambo mission, is greatly welcome, and the church members who used to worship with the late Dr. Currie are still alive and they will be very happy to see the children of our late beloved Dr. Currie who is buried here, and we shall even visit his grave.*

*I will organize church members to commit this day 17th August into prayer, so that God will continue nursing the soul of our late parent, and make good memories to him.*

*And please see me in the picture preaching to Chitambo congregation on one of the Sundays. I and my family would like to receive your photo soonest and please write to me as soon as possible.*

*Your God's servant,*
*Rev. G.A. Chilongo.*

Thus began my unusual correspondence with the Reverend, whose friendly letters were sometimes scented with after-shave. I duly dispatched a photo of the four of us: my husband and I, and two teenage sons in our New Zealand home. I applied for leave from my job as a G.P. in a Maori health centre. My Maori patients were very appreciative of my need to commune with my ancestors and they gave me their blessing. Zanna booked accommodation for us at Kasanka Game Park, a small conservation park 150 Km from Chitambo and about 50 km from the monument marking the site where David Livingstone died.

Fortified by a battery of vaccinations, and a week's worth of doxycycline as a precaution against malaria, I prepared to drive out of Wanganui in the middle of the night, 9th August 2003. Both boys were asleep, only their tousled heads visible from under their duvets. With a tight feeling in my throat and chest I kissed Guy goodbye and set off on this most uncertain of adventures. Wellington harbour glistened in the moonlight as I sped along the motorway towards the airport, and the Interisland ferry, all lit up, slid out to sea.

There was nothing unusual about the flight from Wellington to Sydney, but on checking into the departure lounge, bound for Johannesburg everything changed. There was an African vibe and a myriad of accents. There were 'coloured' ladies returning to Durban and thick-set white farmers bemoaning the way things are going these days. There were families of Indians, and solitary black businessmen. On the plane I sat next to Nene a young black geologist from Guinea. She had been to a conference in Papua New Guinea and was on her way home. I secretly regarded her as a Number One Lady Geologist.

Johannesburg airport was busy and crowded. I had to wrestle to keep my bag from over-eager porters in orange dungarees who would otherwise have whisked it away and set off at a running pace towards the bus-stop. A transit bus took me to the airport hotel, where a notice in the bedroom advised barricading oneself in for the night. Taking the advice, I spent a fitful night in a state of excitement and some trepidation. It was a relief to get up in the morning and check in to the flight to Lusaka.

This time I sat next to an American banker who was flying up to Lusaka for the day to wind up the bank's operations in Zambia. Jim was looking forward to retiring to an architect-designed house in Arizona. He had a careworn, crumpled look about him and was glad to be leaving Africa. He was cynical about Zambia and looked surprised and slightly wistful when I told him an abridged version of my story.

There was little to see of the vast land we were flying over, just a red-brown haze of scorched earth with occasional circles of irrigated land. But as we banked and turned to land at Lusaka it was the long dry grass lining the runway that suddenly took me back, and a great surge of childish excitement filled my stomach with butterflies. There's something magical about emerging into the warmth of Africa and climbing down the mobile steps to the heat-hazed tarmac. It's an old-fashioned feel, evoking memories of hanky-waving film stars or VIPs in black and white newsreels. In the cool of the airport building a visa officer refused my Scottish bank-note in favour of an English one. He looked too young to be interested in Zambia's Scottish heritage.

My sisters had arrived from Britain ahead of me and were already at the guest house. Having been pre-warned about taxi fares, I negotiated with a taxi driver to take me there. At first Fredson was unimpressed by my bargaining but soon we were deep in conversation. When I told him that I was returning to Zambia after thirty-two years he shrieked "Jesus Christ" over and over again, slapping his thigh and driving erratically. "But I was only two years old when you left!" he screeched. We passed the University of Zambia which was built during my school years in Lusaka and by the time we reached Jul's guest-house we were firm friends.

# MONUMENT

In a clearing among the mpundu trees stands a white cement-covered obelisk, topped by a small bronze cross. The monument marks the place where Scottish missionary/explorer David Livingstone died in 1873. It is a lonely spot in a remote corner of North-Eastern Zambia, about 30 kms off the Serenje-Samfiya highway, and close to the present-day Chief Chitambo's village. The site is not widely publicized and visitors are few. People who have been there describe it as an eerie place and they feel its pervasive sadness and desolation.

A bronze plaque on either side of the monument reads

**ERECTED BY HIS FRIENDS
TO THE MEMORY OF DAVID LIVINGSTONE,
MISSIONARY AND EXPLORER**
**HE DIED HERE MAY 1ˢᵗ 1873**

As children growing up in Zambia (then Northern Rhodesia) we accompanied our parents on pilgrimages there. There's a photo of my two older brothers, David and Douglas, and older sister, Jo, leaning against the monument, with Gran Todd and Mum in 1953, the year before I was born. Dad was a bush doctor based then at Mwenzo hospital in the far north of Zambia, and Mum had been a nurse until she had four of us in close succession. Both Mum and Dad were born in Malawi (then Nyasaland):Mum at **Livingstonia**, near the lakeshore, one of the first

Scottish missions in the region, and Dad at **Blantyre** mission (named after David Livingstone's birthplace, Blantyre, Scotland) at the southern end of the country. Grandpa Todd, Mum's father, was also a medical missionary, while Grandpa Currie, Dad's father, was a mission printer. So from the time before any of us were born, whether we liked it or not, we were already entangled in the web of Livingstone's legacy.

**Currie family with Gran Todd at the monument 1953**

# BEGINNINGS

According to legend, the first people in the Serenje-Chitambo district were certain 'small men', who may have been responsible for some of the earliest rock art. The Lala are thought to have come from the Luba country of the southern Congo around two hundred years ago. The earliest Europeans in the district are semi-mythical figures in the folk-tales of the Lala, and were probably Portuguese.

From the early 16th Century Portugal had established trading posts on the East African coast from Mombasa to Sofala, pushing the Arabs out to the north. Driven by tales of gold and silver mines in the interior they ventured inland. Many of their journeys began at Tete on the coast and headed to the kingdom of Kazembe, king of the Lunda people. Their mission was to establish trade and to lay the foundation for a treaty which could be used later to claim the land between their existing colonies of Angola and Mozambique.

One Silva Porto otherwise known as Francisco da Silva made several expeditions into the area, and met Livingstone in 1853. Livingstone described him as *'the chief of the Mambari'* (slave traders). At the time of their meeting Porto was trading in ivory. He was born in the town of Porto in Portugal in 1817. At the age of 12 he sailed to Brazil, and spent ten years learning the dynamics of coffee, trading and the slave market. He then moved to Luanda, the Angolan capital, from where over 4 million slaves would be shipped to the New World. Porto married a high ranking woman from the Bie kingdom of the Ovimbundu people, who were also prolific traders, and he acted as a sort of diplomat between the Ovimbundu and the Portuguese. Between 1853 and 1854 Porto attempted a transcontinental journey from west to east but became ill and had to be left behind. A group of his fellow 'Pombeiros' (slaving agents) passed through the present day Serenje district en route for the Rovuma River and the east coast. Their journals give some insight into the lives of the African people at the time. The area was referred to as Ilala.

By the 1850s this region was heavily populated. The men hunted with poisoned arrows and spears. They also cultivated large gardens. The women filed their teeth and braided their hair. Beer was brewed from locally grown grains, either maize or millet. Traditional religion was then and is still deeply rooted in the lives of the Lala people. It is animist, based on the attribution of life or consciousness to natural objects or phenomena, and includes the belief that the evil eye is responsible for all human miseries and failures in life. Intercession with a Supreme Being is possible through the ancestors. Physical or mental illnesses and death are often attributed to a spell or curse having been put on the sufferer. A traditional doctor or diviner is then required to hunt out the 'witch' and cure the victim.

In the 1880s Portugal attempted to make the land claim to the area between her two colonies, using the diaries of these early explorers as evidence but the British contested this. When Porto da Silva saw that the destruction of the Ovimbundu kingdom was inevitable he draped a Portuguese flag around his shoulders, sat himself on twelve barrels of gunpowder, and blew himself through the roof of his house.

The British were by no means innocent of involvement in the slave trade. Scots and English entrepreneurs began to purchase land in the West Indies and the east coast of America in the 1600s. The land was cleared for tobacco and sugar plantations. Following the Act of Union between Scotland and England in 1707 Scottish merchants joined the English trade routes including the 'triangular trade'-a process whereby cloth, copper and guns were shipped from Britain to Africa where they were sold or exchanged for slaves, who were transported to the West Indies and America. The slaves worked to produce sugar, rum, cotton and tobacco, which were shipped to Britain. Ironically (for Livingstone) the Scottish ports of Glasgow and Greenock became wealthy this way. By the late 1700s one third of Jamaican plantations were owned by Scots. Livingstone was aware of the abolition movement as the British act of 1807 made the purchase of new slaves illegal and that of 1833 outlawed slavery in the British Empire.

Slave trading by the Portuguese and Arabs continued unabated until well after Livingstone's death in 1873. It was not to be officially abolished in the United States until 1863 and in Cuba and Brazil until 1886 and 1888 respectively. The Arab world continued importing African slaves well into the 20th century. On the eve of the Second World War the British were negotiating with Arab leaders to put an end to the slave trade in their region once and for all. By this time the damage was done. The heart of Africa had been torn out.

# LIVINGSTONE BEFORE CHITAMBO

David Livingstone was born on March 19th 1813 in Blantyre, (Scotland), a small village 8 miles from Glasgow. The ancestral home of the Livingstones was the island of Ulva off the west coast of Scotland, but David's father had moved to Blantyre during the notorious Highland clearances, and found employment at the cotton mill. In Livingstone's own words: *Our ancestors were Roman Catholics, they were made Protestants by the laird coming round with a man having a yellow staff, which would seem to have attracted more attention than his teaching, for the new religion went long afterward, perhaps it does so still, by the name of "the religion of the yellow stick."* From the age of ten young David worked in the Blantyre mill and attended school in the evenings after work, so that he could gain entry to University. He was a voracious reader and enjoyed books about science and travel.

He was also fascinated by the natural world and spent a great deal of time in an old quarry near his home, hunting for fossils and rocks. He was described by village people as a loner, somewhat sulky, 'feckless' and ungainly. He was socially awkward, preferring his own company or a good book and he gained a reputation for stubbornness and tenacity.

As children we were brought up on tales of Livingstone's stamina, how he learned Latin from a book propped up next to his weaving loom, and how he survived being mauled by a lion thanks to the quick actions of one of his trusty followers. Visits to the tenement block where he was born, now the David Livingstone Centre, Blantyre, Scotland, reinforced these tales of his courage and perseverance.

**The David Livingstone Centre, Blantyre, Scotland**

While Livingstone was raised by devoutly Christian parents, he had some difficulty with religious dogma and doctrine. Although his father Neil Livingstone had already taken the bold step of leaving the Free Church of Scotland for an independent church, David and Neil disagreed about certain things including the role of science in modern life. David believed that science and Christianity were complementary while his father remained suspicious of all things scientific. All the same, David grew up a devout Christian and he resolved to devote his life to 'the alleviation of human misery.' Livingstone's ambition to become a doctor did not greatly impress his father, but when he expressed the wish to become a Medical Missionary, Neil could see the possibility of science and religion coming together for 'the greater good', and he relented.

Livingstone was remarkable in achieving an education at a time when less than ten percent of mill children became literate. In learning Latin, botany, simple mathematics and theology, he was quite unique. This he did while working from six in the morning until eight in the evening, six days a week. The work was exhausting, and the workplace hot, dusty and noisy. On top of all that he had to endure the taunts of his work-mates who must have regarded him as something of a freak.

In the autumn of 1836 he entered Anderson's College, a prominent medical school in Glasgow and boarded in Rotten Row, which he described as a *"mean locality."* He walked the 8 miles from Blantyre to Glasgow at the start of each week, turning down the offer of a lift from a friend of the family. In Glasgow he studied Theology, Greek and Medicine. One of his first medical texts was Culpeper's Herbal, and he spent some of his spare time collecting and studying medicinal herbs. The medical course at that time was basic. Surgery had to be performed at great speed, in the absence of anaesthetics. Little was known about the causes of most diseases and even the students' knowledge of anatomy was rudimentary, due to a scarcity of bodies for dissection. Livingstone, though not a high-flying academic, forged lifelong links with some of his Glasgow professors. He also befriended James Young, a chemist who went on to discover the process for making paraffin from shale. "Sir Paraffin" was to be a lifelong friend and benefactor.

At the end of his second year at University Livingstone offered his service to the London Missionary Society (LMS) as it accepted candidates from all Protestant denominations. Livingstone was unimpressed with the orthodox Calvinism of the day with its divine punishment and eternal damnation. And so he became a non-conformist. His application to the LMS was conditionally accepted in 1839 and he was sent to Chipping Ongar for probationary training under a Rev. Richard Cecil, who did not take to Livingstone. Under this critical tutor Livingstone did not blossom as a preacher. He was shy and awkward, and could sometimes be very blunt in his speech. On one occasion when required to give a sermon, he became paralyzed by stage-fright and had to leave the pulpit. He managed to scrape through the course but preaching was never his strong point and he did not go on to theological college.

Then followed a medical attachment in London. During this time Livingstone had the privilege to meet many of Britain's leading scientists whose support was immensely valuable to him in later years. Livingstone's dream was to go to China but entry into China at that time was prevented by the Opium War. He was offered a place in the West Indies but turned it down as he regarded it as a 'settled country'. A visitor to Livingstone's hostel in London was to change his life. Rev. Dr. Robert Moffat had worked for the London Missionary Society in South Africa since 1816. Also a Scot and an agriculturalist, he had founded the mission station at Kuruman (in what is now the North-East Cape area of South Africa). Moffat inspired Livingstone with his talk of '*the smoke of a thousand villages where the gospel has not been proclaimed*'. Shyly Livingstone asked Moffat if he '*would do for Africa*'. '*Yes*' replied Moffat, '*if you are prepared to leave occupied ground and push on to the North*'. This was exactly the kind of thing that Livingstone was prepared to do.

Livingstone returned to Glasgow to sit his final medical exams He had chosen to present a thesis on the use of the stethoscope. This recently invented instrument was still somewhat controversial and Livingstone became embroiled in an argument about it with his examiner. To his great relief he passed.

While at Chipping Ongar Livingstone had befriended two brothers called Prentice and a girl, Catherine Ridley, who were also planning to become missionaries in Africa. Livingstone was attracted to Catherine and when they parted they exchanged gifts. She was not in robust health, however, and Livingstone often wrote anxiously to Tom Prentice, enquiring after her. He wrote to Catherine too and he longed to hear from her. Catherine never made it to Africa. Sadly for Livingstone she married Tom Prentice and settled at home.

Livingstone was appointed to Kuruman by the LMS and was under instructions to wait there for Moffat's return from Britain. A last night was spent at the family home in Blantyre. In the morning father and son walked the eight miles to Glasgow where they parted never to meet again. Livingstone was ordained as a missionary in London and sailed on December 8th 1840 on board the George, bound for Cape Town, a voyage which took three months. The ship had to call in at Rio de Janeiro for repairs, and Livingstone took the opportunity to go on an exploratory walk into the jungle. He was delighted by the vegetation, the exotic insects and the hospitable people he met. Meanwhile his fellow travellers were worrying about his disappearance. It was the first of many such adventures. While on board the George, Livingstone befriended the captain who taught him some useful navigation skills.

Landing in Cape Town was a profound moment for Livingstone. He spent a month orientating with Dr. John Philip, the local head of the London Missionary Society. It was something of a shock to him to discover that many church members were unsympathetic to the black cause, and he spoke out against racism, immediately earning himself in white circles a reputation as something of a hot-head. It was a relief for him to leave the Cape colony with its prejudices and inequities.

The journey to Kuruman involved sailing to Algoa Bay, and then travelling by ox-wagon for 530 miles. Everything about the journey intrigued Livingstone, but Kuruman disappointed him. The mission itself was well established under Dr. Moffat's care, but the surrounding countryside was barren, and the tribes generally hostile. Livingstone noted the tensions amongst the missionaries and he made himself unpopular by suggesting that Africans could be trained to carry out some of the mission work.

Robert Moffat's return to Kuruman was delayed, and, in the meantime, Livingstone wasted no time in setting off on an exploratory journey to the north with a senior missionary, Roger Edwards. Their purpose was to find areas where missionaries could settle and carry out their work. Livingstone quickly became a keen explorer, an eagle-eyed observer and passionately interested in African culture and customs. By the end of 1843 he and Edwards had decided to found a new mission at Mabotsa, among the Bakhatla tribe with the approval of chief Moseealele.

On hearing of the Moffats' return, Livingstone rode to meet them, and accompanied them to Kuruman, where he stayed with them for two weeks. That was all the time he needed to notice Mary Moffat and to decide that she would be a suitable bride. Returning to Mabotsa, he decided to propose to Mary on his next visit to Kuruman. Mabotsa was plagued by lions which normally fed on the abundant game and left the villagers alone. One particular troop was making a nuisance of itself by mauling the village cattle. Livingstone was invited by some of the villagers to join a lion hunt. Having cornered the largest of the troop and fired, he was in the act of reloading his gun when the wounded lion sprang on him and caught him by the shoulder. "*Growling horribly*" wrote Livingstone "*he shook me as a terrier dog does a rat.*" The lion was momentarily distracted when one of the villagers, Mebalwe, fired at it. It dropped its prey and mauled Mebalwe, as well as injuring a third man. Finally the lion was shot and speared. Livingstone never regained full use of the left arm, as the fractured shaft of humerus failed to unite, leaving him with a 'false joint'. Although Livingstone made light of the injury, he had to supervise the setting of the broken limb himself, and was ill from the suppurating wounds for weeks. By July 1844 he was tired of bachelorhood and rough living, and he returned to Kuruman to convalesce for three weeks. He wasted no time in proposing to Mary under the fruit trees of Kuruman, and she wasted no time in accepting.

The Moffat parents were somewhat astonished but delighted, although Mrs. Moffat had some misgivings about Livingstone's domineering personality. According to Livingstone Mary was *"not romantic but a matter-of-fact lady, a little thick, black-haired girl, sturdy and all I want"*. Mary was the ideal wife for Livingstone. Born in 1821 in Griquatown (now Griekwastad) and raised at Kuruman she was fluent in Setswana. She was trained as a teacher, and could turn her hand to domestic work and nursing. Above all she knew how to be *useful*. They were married on 2nd Jan 1845. *"The woman"*, Livingstone wrote to a friend *"is the glory of the man. I am very contented and very happy in my connection"*.

Mary was happy at Mabotsa. She started an infant school, while Livingstone was busy with preaching and building. They had their own home and Mary was expecting their first child. But Livingstone was having difficulties with his missionary colleagues over ideas that he had for building a seminary. Livingstone's obstinate determination began to raise its head and he and Edwards began to irritate each other. This was the beginning of a lifetime of displacement for Mary, with great hardship and long separations from her husband. Livingstone went off scouting for a new place to start a station, while Mary waited anxiously for him to return. Fortunately he arrived back in time to deliver their first child, Robert.

The couple moved to Chonwane, north of Mabotsa. This was a dry and dusty place, and Mrs. Moffat was shocked at what she found when she visited. Mary was thin and baby Robert was ill. Mary was taken home to Kuruman for a rest, and for the birth of her second baby, Agnes. As soon as mother and baby were able, they moved again, this time to Kolobeng, where they began all over again. On leaving Chonwane Livingstone burnt their house to the ground to prevent the marauding Boers from using it. At Kolobeng, in their temporary shelter the wind blew hot or cold and irritated the children's eyes. Livingstone set about building a solid home and for the first time in their married life, the Livingstones now lived in relative comfort. But not for long. Livingstone spent long periods of time away from home exploring. On the occasion that he took the family along, to explore the region north of Lake Ngami the journey was gruelling, especially as Mary was expecting another baby. The plans had to be aborted as Mary and the children became ill, and they returned to Kolobeng in a bedraggled state. Baby Elizabeth was born sickly. Her low birth-weight and Mary's subsequent right sided weakness and slurred speech suggest that she had suffered from pre-eclampsia or raised blood pressure of pregnancy. Unsurprisingly baby Elizabeth succumbed and died aged six weeks.

Undeterred Livingstone set off again with a pregnant wife, much against the wishes of his mother-in-law, to the Chobe River, where Mary and the children had to be left while he and his hunter friend Oswell pressed on looking for a place to settle. This time the two men reached the Upper Zambezi in the company of Chief Sebetwane, who then became ill and died. Finally Livingstone realized that he needed to turn and head for home again, with a now heavily pregnant wife. Mary delivered one night in the ox-wagon, a son whom they named Oswell, after their travelling companion who had been completely unaware of the labour and birth!

Livingstone now decided that Mary and the four children should go to Scotland, so that the children could have a good education, and Mary a rest. Thus followed a four year separation during which time Mary missed her husband terribly. Mary, who had grown up in Africa, did not feel comfortable in the dour Livingstone home in Hamilton, near Glasgow. Young Robert was a very boisterous child and took a great deal of energy to control. Very quickly Mary had fallen out with her in-laws who found her plain, poor, difficult to understand and (perhaps worst of all) fond of a drink. She moved into a rented room, and had to beg Livingstone's friends and acquaintances for money.

Livingstone then set off across the Kalahari Desert to Linyanti with the intention of finding a potential route to the coast. He explored the difficult terrain from Linyanti to the west coast, and then the equally challenging route to the east coast. In so doing he walked right across Africa and "discovered" the Victoria Falls in the process. Husband and wife were re-united in 1856 when Livingstone returned home a hero. At last they had time together again as a family and enough money for some of life's small comforts.

A rare insight into the nature of Livingstone's medical work in Africa is gleaned from the minutes of the Edinburgh Medical Missionary Society in March 1857: *Dr. Livingstone mentioned that his operations had consisted almost entirely of the removal of tumours, which were invariably of a benign character, the only exception being one resembling melanosis; that he had never met with cancer or scrofula, calculous disorders or consumption. He observed that the natives make capital patients, never calling out under the knife as used to be the case in other countries before the days of chloroform. Their treatment of fractures is on the whole very successful. They use the bark of a tree for splints, and, as union is generally rapid, few subsequent deformities are met with. More than once Dr. Livingstone had noticed cases of dislocation which had escaped being reduced. He had not found occasion to perform any of the so-called capital operations of surgery, but among other minor operations he had cured one native lady of squint. Dr. Livingstone alluded with quiet humour to his behaviour towards other practitioners, never condemning their practice before the patient, but taking them aside, when he generally found them very ready to acquiesce in his views of treatment.*

*He also spoke of his fame as an obstetrician, in which branch he had no competitors, being decidedly at the top of the tree. He alluded to one case in which having cured a native lady of some complaint, he or his medicine got all the credit of a child which she bore fifteen months afterwards, so that the celebrity thus acquired was the source of no little inconvenience . . .*

*Dr. Livingstone thinks that although the native prescriptions are often sufficiently absurd, there is reason to believe in the efficacy of some from their being widely known among various tribes and over vast territories. He has no doubt that many medicines exist in these countries which may yet prove valuable additions to our materia medica. But in the management of febrile diseases the native doctors possess nothing equal to quinine. Dr. Livingstone was in the habit of combining it with an aperient in the form of a pill, which agreed so well with his patients, and became so famous, that had it been in this country it would have eclipsed even Morrison's pill*

In March 1858, following publication of the explorer's book 'Missionary Travels' husband and wife set off again, with their youngest son, Oswell. The other children were left with Livingstone's mother (his father having died before Livingstone's return to Britain). No longer employed by the London Missionary Society, he was now sponsored by the British government and his brief was to explore the valleys of the Zambezi and Shire. Livingstone had persuaded a rather reluctant British government and certain key British businessmen that the Zambezi River was probably navigable as far inland as the Batoka Plateau and that this would be an ideal area for large-scale production of crops such as cotton and sugar. He also implored the Foreign Secretary to put pressure on the Portuguese to allow him unhindered access to the Zambezi. This was part of Livingstone's own agenda to establish Commerce and Christianity in central Africa, and thereby deal a blow to the slave trade. Livingstone was now Her Majesty's Consul, in Portuguese East Africa, a sore point with the Portuguese government who were not yet prepared to relinquish their territory or their slave trading.

On the sea voyage to Cape Town aboard the Pearl, Mary was constantly sick, and to Livingstone's surprise and distress it turned out that she was pregnant again. This meant that she and Oswell would be left at the Cape, to be taken home to Kuruman by her parents, while Livingstone's expedition headed for the Zambezi. Robert Moffat, who met the Livingstones at the Cape, was not amused that Livingstone had left the service of the London Missionary Society and had persuaded Robert's son, John Moffat to do the same (for a period of five years). He was also upset that Livingstone was not accompanying a group of new missionaries to work among the Makololo. As it turned out seven of that party of nine missionaries died in the attempt to establish a mission. Livingstone was to be held partly responsible by some for this tragedy.

Baby Anna Mary was born at Kuruman in 1858, and Mary decided to return to Scotland to be reunited with her other children. Once again she was unhappy in Britain, and when Livingstone heard of this from others he summoned her to join him, leaving all the children in the care of relatives. Anna Mary was only eighteen months old when Mary tore herself away from the children and set sail in the company of a Dr. James Stewart of the Scottish Free Kirk. Stewart, a friend and confidant to Mary, was keen to meet Livingstone and to join in his expedition to find a suitable place for a mission.

From Cape Town Mary and Stewart joined a Universities Mission party including Bishop Mackenzie's sister. The Bishop, encouraged by Livingstone's enthusiasm, had already been accompanied by Livingstone to the Shire Highlands to found a mission in that somewhat unpromising area, and his sister was to join him. Also in the party was a Mrs. Burrup who was to join her missionary husband. The ladies sailed on board the Hetty Ellen to the mouth of the Zambezi where they met Livingstone's party aboard The Pioneer. They were to make their way up to Shupanga where Captain Wilson and Dr. Kirk, of Livingstone's party would take the two ladies to their destination. Mary, reunited with her husband, was in her element, but soon news came of the deaths of Bishop Mackenzie and Mr. Burrup en route for the Shire highlands. The distraught missionary ladies were taken back down the Zambezi to be put onto a ship for Cape Town.

On the return journey upriver to Shupanga Mary became unwell. Livingstone was anxious about her and gave her large doses of quinine. Mary had for some time been unsure about her religious faith and this deeply troubled Livingstone who put considerable energy into reading to and praying with her. She became feverish and jaundiced. Despite Livingstone's best efforts he could not save her and she died on 17th April 1862. Livingstone was inconsolable and wept uncontrollably. To his mother-in-law he wrote

*This unlooked for bereavement quite crushes and takes the heart out of me. Everything else that happened in my career only made the mind rise to overcome it. But this takes away all my strength. If you know how I loved and trusted her you may realise my loss . . . there are regrets which will follow me to my dying day. If I had done so and so—etc. etc.*

In his journal he wrote *For the first time in my life I feel willing to die.*

Also for the first time his fellow travellers noticed a vulnerability in Livingstone, a softening of his tough and stubborn demeanour. For a time the wind went out of his sails. The Zambezi expedition continued, however, for another two years, following which it was recalled with little to show for it, but a tantalizing glimpse of some of the great lakes of Central Africa. It had been Livingstone's hope to prevent slave traders from getting to the Shire Highlands by launching a gunboat on Lake Nyasa. Using 6000 pounds of his own savings he had a boat designed in England, named "The Lady Nyassa" and brought out to the Zambezi for this purpose. War, drought, famine and low morale in his party brought an end to this dream and Livingstone sailed home via India and Suez to face his motherless children in July 1864. Despairingly he wrote to his friend Waller *Why don't the very rocks groan on those beautiful hills? The lamp is flickering and soon enough it will be dark enough, aye, even for the Portuguese slave trade.*

# LIVINGSTONE—TOWARDS CHITAMBO

**Livingstone with youngest daughter Anna Mary**
**(Corbis International)**

Then came Livingstone's greatest challenge. After a satisfying period of time at home, the warm hospitality of friends and family, and the acknowledgement of his work, particularly against the slave trade, he was offered the opportunity to lead an expedition in search of the source of the Nile. The Royal Geographical Society and the British Foreign Office were jointly prepared to sponsor him. The race for the Nile's source was on. Explorers Burton, Speke and Baker were on the same quest.

The Greek historian Herodotus, in the 5th century BC had visited Egypt and had enquired about the source of the Nile. A scribe had told him that deep in the heart of Africa there were two hills with conical tops. Midway between the two hills were the 'fountains of the Nile'. The possibility of the existence of such fountains was to haunt Livingstone, and he interchanged the words 'Nile sources' and 'fountains' in his own writing.

For Livingstone there were probably several reasons to take up this challenge. He still felt that he had not made his mark. He needed to earn enough to have his children educated. The difficult and tragic Zambezi expedition had to be put behind him. There was, perhaps some atonement to be done for the cost in lives and resources, of his unsuccessful expeditions. There was another book to be written, and, if he were successful this time he might have more authority in the battle against the slave trade. *The Nile sources are valuable to me only as a means of opening my mouth with power* he wrote to his brother John. What's more he particularly detested Burton for his apparent immorality and his anti-missionary and anti-African stance.

Livingstone, while sometimes coming across as patronizing in his writing about Africans, was undoubtedly pro-African and he spoke out in favour of African resistance to European rule in the Cape area. His Glasgow upbringing had already brought him in contact with the anti-slavery movement. He believed that missionaries had a role to play in encouraging African empowerment, but his compatriots were not yet ready to hear this. He also felt that Africans would only be willing to accept Christianity if their social and economic conditions were better. Britain no doubt saw other economic opportunities following on from Livingstone's endeavours.

Telling his children that it would take him *about two years,* he set off again for Africa in 1865, aged 52. Sailing to Bombay, he was welcomed by the governor, Sir Bartle Frere, who gave him a ship which was to be handed over as a gift to the Sultan of Zanzibar. In India Livingstone recruited thirteen Sepoys of the marine battalion, nine Nassicks (freed African slaves) ten men from the island of Johanna, of whom Musa had already served with him on the Shire River, two men from Shupanga (Susi/ Souza and Amoda) and two Yao from northern Nyasaland, of whom one was Chuma.

Livingstone also gathered together an assortment of animals with which he wanted to experiment on his next journey. These were—camels, Indian water buffaloes, mules and donkeys. He hoped that the animals would withstand the tsetse fly, and that they could be introduced as an alternative to slave porters, thereby dealing another blow to the slave trade. The plan for the journey was to explore the Rovuma River and its relationship to Lake Nyasa, then to explore the territory between lakes Nyasa and Tanganyika. Finally he would search for the source of the Nile around Lakes Mweru and Bangweulu.

Nothing on this journey went according to plan. Although happy to be back in Africa, Livingstone had lost some of his previous vigour and he was plagued by ailments. Some of the porters were lazy, others dishonest, and many of the animals died. The most robust were the donkeys, but the majority of these died through neglect and abuse at the hands of their drivers. Everywhere the desecration caused by the slave trade was obvious. Food was scarce and there were hostile tribes. At the southern end of Lake Nyasa there were tales of terrible atrocities committed by the Mazitu (otherwise known as the Angoni/Ngoni). These were fierce hill people who would swoop down on the other tribes by the lakeshore and wreak havoc. Here the Johanna men, led by Musa, abandoned the expedition and took back to Zanzibar a fabricated tale of Livingstone's death and burial. The outside world mourned, but some of the men who had previously travelled with Livingstone were not convinced. The result was a rapidly mobilized expedition led by E.D. Young who had served on *The Pioneer* on the Zambezi expedition. They made their way in *The Search* up the Zambezi and the Shire and into Lake Nyasa. They were able to ascertain, by talking to villagers and looking at items left behind by Livingstone, that he was still alive and continuing his journey.

In the two years following Musa's desertion, Livingstone's caravan had grown smaller. He had a few porters, two faithful attendants, "Susi" and "Chuma", and a small herd of goats which provided milk. Heavy rain, hunger, the loss of his medicine chest, and further desertions added to his woes. At times like these only Livingstone's steadfast faith in his God carried him through. Ironically, when things were at their worst he was taken in and nursed back to health by slave traders, who supplied him with provisions and carried his mail to Zanzibar.

By 1871 Livingstone was 'lost' to the outside world, and again there were fears for his well-being. This time it was American journalist Henry Morton Stanley who went to the 'rescue'. The story of their famous meeting at Ujiji in November 1871 is imaginatively told in Martin Dugard's book *"Into Africa"*. The two men became firm friends in their months together and it was with a heavy heart that Stanley left Livingstone to pursue his quest. Livingstone could have saved himself and gone back with Stanley, but he was now totally at home in Africa and apart from concern for his children, there was nothing to go back for. A letter from his elder daughter Agnes reinforced this for him. *"Much as I wish you to come home"*, she wrote in January 1872 *"I would rather have you finish your work to your own satisfaction, than return merely to gratify me"*. It was seven years since he had seen her.

Livingstone recorded in his diary on 27th Jan 1872: *Vanity whispers loudly: 'she is a chip off the old block'. My blessing on her and all the rest. I propose to go from Unyanyembe to Fipa, then round the south end of Tanganyika, Tambete, or Mbete, then across the Chambeshi, round the south of Lake Bangweulu and due west to the ancient fountains, leaving the underground excavations till after visiting Katanga. This route will serve to certify that no other sources of the Nile can come from the south without being seen by me. No one will cut me out after this exploration has been accomplished, and may the good Lord of all help me to show myself His stout-hearted servant, an honour to my children, and perhaps, to my country and race.*

Stanley bade farewell at Unyanyembe where Livingstone picked up some supplies including four flannel shirts from Agnes and two fine pairs of English boots from his friend Waller. Stanley was to carry Livingstone's sealed journals back with him to the disbelieving world. Livingstone passed a weary six months waiting for porters promised by Stanley. A British search party, including Livingstone's son Oswell disbanded on hearing of Stanley's success. The officers in charge abandoned Oswell, who did not feel able to go on alone to meet his father.

In August 1872, the new porters arrived. One of them a 'Nassick' named Jacob Wainwright could speak a little English. The party set off towards Lake Tanganyika. Livingstone suffered from dysentery. The eastern edge of the lake was mountainous and the going was very tough. His instruments were damaged and the party sometimes lost their way. The mal-treatment and death from sleeping-sickness of the last remaining donkey was a blow. Once clear of Lake Tanganyika they travelled west and south towards Lake Bangweulu.

There are different translations of "Bangweulu". According to the missionary/explorer Dan Crawford who walked to the Bangweulu area from the west coast of Africa in 1889, the word means "where the water meets the sky", but this is a shortened version of the full name of the great lake—"Bangweuluwavikilwanshimangomwana", which means "the lake so stormy that it must be propitiated by the voyager and so wide that you must take provisions aboard for a trans-lake voyage." It is a shallow lake, rarely deeper than 6 metres, and usually calm. At the height of the rains it is about 75 km long and 35 km wide, with swamps to the south. The Unga and Lala people of the lake are expert canoeists and fishermen. Their canoes are made from single trees—small one-man dugouts or giants from the massive mofu tree. Legend has it that a monster, Chipekwe, inhabits the deepest part of the lake, and that anyone crossing the lake should do so in silence for fear of disturbing the beast which has a smooth, dark body and a single ivory horn. Such a creature has sometimes been depicted in rock paintings in the region.

The swampy terrain frustrated Livingstone who constantly had to negotiate with unreliable chiefs for the use of canoes. January 1873 was particularly wet. The last calf was killed on 1st Feb. and the last of the goats was slaughtered on 15th Feb. The camp was over-run one night by driver ants, and the men spent a wet, cold night fending them off. Did Livingstone lose heart? On 19th March 1873, his 60th birthday he wrote

*Thanks to the Almighty Preserver of men for sparing me thus far on the journey of life. Can I hope for ultimate success? So many obstacles have arisen. Let not Satan prevail over me, O my good Lord Jesus!* He spent his birthday in a spider infested hut, firing his pistol out of rage and frustration.

Hunger, cold and wet took its toll on the men, and Livingstone was weak with blood loss from his bowel. By 15th April he had to be carried some of the way. The distance travelled became less each day and Livingstone spent more time resting. The master of under-statement, he wrote on 19th April—*It is not all pleasure, this exploration.* He was finding it difficult to record any observations or even to hold a pencil. All the same, he asked the people of every village he entered whether they knew of a hill on which four rivers arose. He even wrote a dispatch for the British Foreign Secretary ready to send once he had found "the fountains." Only the date and geographical co-ordinates had to be included.

When he could no longer stand, his men carried him in a 'kitanda', or hammock slung on poles. On 27th April he wrote in his diary for the last time—*Knocked up quite and remain-recover—sent to buy milch goats. We are on the banks of the Molilamo. (Lulimalo?)*

No goats were found but the local chief was helpful and provided a hut for Livingstone. In the morning the doctor was unable to walk, and one wall of the hut was broken down so that he could be loaded into the kitanda. When the next river was reached he was placed in a canoe. On the other side of the stream was Chief Chitambo's village, also referred to later as Ilala.

Here a hut was quickly built and a rough bed made of sticks and grass. The chief came to meet him on 30th April but Livingstone was too ill to speak more than a few words. Some sixty years after Livingstone's death Chief Chitambo's nephew was to sign an affidavit to say that Livingstone was accompanied into the village by a half-caste boy who had come from Tabora with the porters, that this was Livingstone's son, who was also ill. There is no mention of such a child in Livingstone's diaries, and if he did accompany Livingstone on his last journey he vanishes without a trace. Livingstone biographer Tim Jeal has researched this possibility and been unable to find a shred of evidence for the existence of such a 'love child'.

# LUSAKA 2003

Juls guest house, off the Great East Road, was a walled compound comprising three separate buildings—Juls own house, a self-catering two bedroomed cottage, and a six-bedroomed apartment. A centrally placed swimming pool sparkled invitingly. We occupied the cottage, as a delegation from the WHO was in the apartment. Julie Limpic herself was a friendly and astute business lady, of African and European descent, who had grown up in Zambia's Eastern province. She was a fund of useful information about Lusaka.

With tears and hugs we greeted each other. Zanna had brought blonde thirteen year old Jasmine with her and we all delighted in seeing Zambia for the first time through her youthful eyes. We dumped our luggage in the homely and comfortable cottage, and over pots of tea and coffee we shared our travel stories. Since I had spent the night in Johannesburg and my sisters had slept reasonably well on their flight from London, we had the energy for a tour of Lusaka in search of our old boarding schools.

We piled into the black Delica van which Zanna had hired from Justin Lubezhi of Trust Car Hire, and set off round a very different Lusaka from that of our school days. The pavements thronged with smartly dressed citizens, many sporting shades and brief cases. Women were fashionably dressed and beautifully coiffed. A billboard near the local shopping mall advertised the latest in wigs and hair-pieces. Sometime after Zambian independence (24th October 1964), and during our secondary school years, there had been a backlash against all things 'western'. Wigs, jeans and mini-skirts were pronounced abhorrent. For a while bands of youths from (President) Dr. Kenneth Kaunda's United National Independence Party (UNIP) would harass young girls who flaunted the rules. The Society for the Re-Moralization of Zambia was formed, and membership soared as western films and fashion shows were 'censored' under its critical eye, and then censored again . . . and again.

On Independence Day Jo and I had marched with the rest of the boarders at Lusaka Girls' to wave our flags and watch the procession of dignitaries arriving for the celebrations. The diminutive Heile Selasse of Ethiopia went by, standing in the back of an open-topped limo in order to be seen. We waved for what felt like hours in the blazing October heat, aware that this was a turning point in African history and in our lives, for now the apartheid system would be no more. We would no longer be branded 'kaffir-lovers' by the less tolerant of our fellow-boarders. African girls would be able to attend our school, and we were to have a 'Zulu princess' in our hostel.

Dr. Kenneth Kaunda, Zambia's first President, was born at Lubwa mission in northern Zambia, some distance north of Chitambo. His father David was one of the first African ministers to be ordained by the Church of Scotland at Livingstonia in Malawi. The Scottish missionaries had been strong supporters of the independence movement and our grandfather, Dr. John Todd had been a friend and mentor of Kenneth Kaunda's. The icing on our cake was that our grandparents were invited out from Scotland to the independence celebrations and we were collected from the hostel in a chauffeur-driven limo for afternoon tea with the new President.

Now our quest was to find Lusaka Girls' School and Maxwell Hostel, and to thumb our noses at the many painful memories of those early boarding-school days. Miss Paterson, the Scottish headmistress was a femme formidable. Just the sheer bulk of her was enough to strike terror into our hearts. We ate, bathed, slept and did our homework to bells. The boarding 'matrons' were a tough bunch of ageing spinsters or divorcees who ensured that lockers were tidy, counterpanes straightened and shoes polished. Empathy was in short supply and generally only evident in times of illness. I seemed to be ill a lot. Our letters home were censored, lest we complain, so our parents never knew the full horror of the experience.

We found the school which appeared to be still functioning as a school. Maxwell Hostel was now the Ministry of Education headquarters and we were declined permission to go in and look around. All the same it had shrunk and had a shabby air about it. My inner child danced with glee. Oh how the mighty are fallen!

Our first secondary school had been the Jean Rennie. After independence it changed its name to Kabulonga Girls. It sat tantalizingly close to but separated from Kabulonga Boys. A patrolled fence and locked gates intervened, but love always found a way! The school had a good name in the early 1960s but standards started to slide in the late 60s and our parents transferred us to the Sacred Heart Convent. Of this our Protestant Irish grandmother was never told. We found Kabulonga looking much the same, and still thriving as a school. We were welcomed by groups of students who were sitting out enjoying the late afternoon sun. Somewhere in the hostel a choir was practising and their effortless African harmonizing provided just the right background music for our trip down memory lane.

## CHIEF CHITAMBO'S, 1873

Abdullah Susi (Souza) was the last person to talk to Livingstone. At 11pm on 3rd May 1873 Livingstone asked him how far it was to the Lualaba River. When he discovered it was about three days he said *Oh dear* and fell asleep again. Susi was summoned again about an hour later and asked to bring the medicine chest from which Livingstone, with great difficulty, helped himself to a dose of calomel (mercurous chloride). *All right you can go now* were the last words he was heard to speak.

A young man, Majwara, was put on guard duty at the door of the hut. According to one version of the telling of this story, during the night he peered into the hut and saw Livingstone on his knees by the 'bed'. Presuming him to be praying, he withdrew. Early the following morning when he looked in again, Livingstone was in the same position. He had died, it is thought, sometime in the early morning of 4th May 1873, although the exact date remains uncertain. Another account of Livingstone's death has him dying on the bed in a kneeling position, while a third version suggests he was found collapsed on the floor.

At first the men were afraid of Chief Chitambo's reaction to the death and tried to keep it from him. But the news leaked out and Chief Chitambo did everything he could to help. A stockade was built outside the village. There was great mourning for three days. Chief Chitambo wanted Livingstone to be buried at the village, but Susi, Chuma and Wainwright

25

knew that Livingstone would want to be returned to his homeland. One member of the party, Farijala, had been the servant of a Zanzibar surgeon (a Dr. James Christie). He conducted a skilled post-mortem, removing Livingstone's heart, lungs and intestines through a small abdominal incision. There was a large blood clot in the abdominal cavity. The shell of the body was then rubbed with salt, and brandy from Livingstone's medicine chest, and left in the sun to dry.

The internal organs were placed in a tin box and buried at the foot of a large mpundu tree. His body would return to his homeland, but his heart would remain forever in Africa. Jacob Wainwright read the burial service and carved the engraving on the tree, naming some of the people who were with him:

**Dr. Livingstone**
**May 4<sup>th</sup> 1873**
**Chuma, Souza, Mniasere**
**Vchopere**

**The Livingstone tree (Getty Images)**

**The tree and fence (Getty Images)**

His body, once dried, was bent at the knees, wrapped in bark, then bound in blue and white calico, and sailcloth. He was slung on a pole and carried, looking for all the world like a bundle of cloth, and so avoiding unwanted attention. Susi, Chuma and the rest of the party then set out on this last epic journey, of 1500 miles, taking six months. By coincidence at Tabora they encountered a party that had been sent to look for Livingstone. After a rest at Tabora, Susi and Chuma pressed on to Bagamoyo which they reached in February 1874. From Bagamoyo, Chuma sailed to Zanzibar aboard *HMS Vulture* to discover that the British Consul, Kirk was on leave. His deputy, Captain W.F. Prideaux, paid off the sixty men of the expedition, dismissed Susi and Chuma, and arranged for Livingstone to be shipped to London. Only Jacob Wainwright was allowed to accompany him. (The story surrounding this decision and the fate of the faithful Susi and Chuma is well told by Clare Pettit in *"Dr. Livingstone, I presume?*

*Missionaries, journalists, explorers & empire*") Livingstone's embalmed body was returned, aboard the *Malwa* to a Britain in mourning.

In London his remains were formally identified by Sir William Ferguson and five of Livingstone's friends at the Royal Geographic Society headquarters. This might have been difficult had it not been for the malunited left humerus. Livingstone was given a hero's funeral at Westminster Abbey on 18<sup>th</sup> April 1874. Among the pall-bearers were Kirk, Grant, E.D Young and Henry Morton Stanley. His coffin was lowered into a grave near that of the Unknown Warrior. The inscription on his stone reads

**Brought by faithful hands over land and sea here rests David Livingstone, missionary, traveler, philanthropist, born March 19, 1813, at Blantyre, Lanarkshire, died May 1, 1873 at Chitambo's village Ulala. For 30 years his life was spent in an unwearied effort to evangelize the native races, to explore the undiscovered secrets, to abolish the desolating slave trade of Central Africa, where with his last words he wrote, "All I can add in my solitude is, may Heaven's rich blessing come down on everyone, American, English or Turk, who will help heal this open sore of the world".**

## AFTER LIVINGSTONE

The first attempt at establishing Livingstone's dream of a mission in the Shire Highlands had ended in disaster, with the deaths of Bishop Mackenzie and Mr. Burrup of the Universities Mission. This had greatly saddened Livingstone, who was also openly critical of the withdrawal of the Universities Mission to Zanzibar. However, optimistic to the last he wrote *all will come right someday, though I may not live to participate in the joy or even see the commencement of better times.* Meanwhile young James Stewart, who had escorted Mary Livingstone to join her husband on the Zambezi, proposed to the Free Church of Scotland that they consider establishing a mission in the same area. Stewart went on to explore the area south of Lake Nyasa. He encountered the devastation caused by the slave trade, his funds ran out and he became ill. Dispirited he returned to Scotland, studied Medicine and was later posted to the Free Church mission at Lovedale in South Africa.

James Stewart was home on furlough from Lovedale when Livingstone's body arrived back in Britain. Standing by the grave in Westminster Abbey he was re-inspired to carry on Livingstone's work and after a night of debate and discussion with a group of like-minded friends he presented an idea to the Foreign Mission Committee of the General Assembly of the Free Church of Scotland. His idea was to found an institution in Central Africa, which might grow into a city, and become a centre of Commerce, Civilization and Christianity. *And this* he added *I would call Livingstonia.*

Then began the hard work of putting together the nuts and bolts of such an idea. A group of Glasgow businessmen, presided over by Mr. James White of Overtoun, formed a committee and raised the finances, while remaining accountable to the Free Church of Scotland. The Church of Scotland had its own plans for mission work but supplied a man for the expedition. The Reformed Presbyterian Church also aligned itself with the project. This collaboration of the Scottish churches would no doubt have pleased Livingstone.

One day in May 1874 a young Aberdonian medical student named Robert Laws picked up a copy of the Glasgow Herald in which Dr. Stewart's speech to the General Assembly was reported. The words sprang off the page at him. *That* he said to himself *is the very work I have been longing for and which for years I have been preparing for . . . . If only I were honoured to be the doctor of the expedition.* The stumbling block for Laws was that he belonged to the United Presbyterian Church which had no particular interest in Central Africa. The matter was resolved when Laws was able to talk to Dr. Stewart and the United Presbyterians agreed to "lend" Dr. Laws to the expedition. A Mr. James Thin, Edinburgh publisher and bookseller, of the Bristo Street United Presbyterian Church, gave financial backing.

Dr. Stewart was back at Lovedale, and unable to lead the expedition. There was only one other man in Britain who would do. This was Mr. E.D. Young who had served under Livingstone on the Zambezi and who had led the first search party for Livingstone after the fictitious tales of his death. When asked if he would take up the challenge the forty year old replied

*I can but try. I am long past the age when love of adventure would tempt me, but I will go as a matter of duty.*

A special steamer was designed by Messrs.' Yarrow and Headley of Milwall. It was 48 feet long and it could be taken apart so that every section of it comprised one man's load. It could manoeuver in 3 feet of water, and it had only one boiler instead of the usual two or three, as speed was not going to be an issue. A short maiden voyage was made with Miss

Mackenzie, sister of the late Bishop, on board. The steamer was named the *Ilala* after the area where Livingstone died.

The story of this remarkable expedition and its many ups and downs is beautifully told in W.P. Livingstone's book *"Laws of Livingstonia"*. The journey up the Shire and into Lake Nyasa and the subsequent settlements at Cape Maclear and later at Bandawe paved the way for the foundation of a permanent mission on the Nyika plateau. Dr. Laws became a legend through his patience, perseverance and great love of the African people. Through Dr. Laws' influence and vision, a large tract of land was made available by Cecil John Rhodes and it was here that *Livingstonia* was built.

Meanwhile there was interest in founding a mission near the spot where Livingstone had died. By 1876 the Church of Scotland had established a mission at the southern end of Lake Nyasa, and named it Blantyre. The United Free Church had missions at Bandawe, Livingstonia, and soon would open up Mwenzo and Lubwa. Chitambo represented a western extension of their territory. A young missionary at the Livingstonia mission seemed the ideal candidate for the job. He was Malcolm Moffat, grandson of the legendary Robert Moffat of Kuruman, nephew of Mary and David Livingstone. It would be hard to imagine anyone better suited to such a task.

# CHAPTER 2

# LAYING THE FOUNDATIONS

## SETTING OUT FOR CHITAMBO 2003

Preparing for our journey "upcountry" from Lusaka to Chitambo was far easier than it had ever been in our school days. We had the reliable and roomy Delica van, and petrol was readily available. All we had to do was fill up and go. After a hearty three course breakfast at Juls, we headed out to the Manda Hills shopping centre, as smart a mall as you might find anywhere. Security guards patrolled the car park while we used the ATM machine. Withdrawing a total of two million Kwacha between us, we hit the supermarket and stocked up on packets of pasta, rice, porridge, and maize meal (the local staple, "nsima"), tins of fish and fresh fruit and vegetables. If our supplies ran out we could fall back on the chocolate and muesli bars we had brought with us.

We left Lusaka via the northern roundabout and headed out on the Great North Road, a single strip of badly pot-holed tarmac. Smart blue mini-van taxis laboured up the hill ahead of us. Lopsided buses, loaded precariously with huge cloth bundles, furniture and bicycles belched out black smoke and ground their gears. The Spice Girls (Jasmine's choice) blared "if you wanna be my luver . . ." A billboard warned us to "Use condoms or die". Soon we were speeding along a better road, leaving the townships behind. Small mopane trees dotted the parched landscape. Groups of red-brown mud huts with traditional thatched roofs slid by. Corrugated iron replaced thatch in some villages. How did they withstand the summer heat? Huge electricity pylons bore cables across great swathes of deforested land.

There were several police road-blocks where very young-looking officers checked the van's papers, always with a smile and a friendly enquiry.

Equally friendly were the traffic police who pulled us up for speeding. We had been caught on the only speed camera in the country which was being trialled on a long, straight, empty stretch of road and none of us had registered a random 60 kph sign. The young police woman was apologetic as we handed over 67,000 Kwacha, about $10 US.

The Japanese government had helped Zambia upgrade its roads. Instead of simply donating funds the Japanese had provided the skilled labour force and equipment. They had done a superb job and most of the main highways were excellent—a far cry from the corrugated dirt roads of our childhood. The memory of the dreaded journey from Chitambo back to boarding school in Lusaka still makes me queasy. Tears, red dust, petrol fumes and the ubiquitous cheese and chutney sandwiches made for a long, uncomfortable day. I would usually start crying a week before the end of the school holidays. I would develop strange illnesses and odd itchy rashes. If these were not enough to delay the journey my misery would escalate to full-blown grief, which would only abate after waving goodbye to my parents and resigning myself to another term of incarceration. My only comfort was my big sister Jo.

The Great North Road links Lusaka with the towns of the Copperbelt. About half way is Kabwe, formerly Broken Hill, a mining town, since 1904, where lead and zinc had been scoured out of the red earth. Today it is a rather ugly sprawling town with a crowded main street. We filled the van with petrol there and pressed on. It was not until we reached the railway settlement at Kapiri Mposhi that we truly felt we were on our way. Kapiri is at the junction of the Great North and Tan-Zam roads. Shortly after turning north-east and leaving the chaos of Kapiri behind, we began to feel that we were on the home stretch. Suddenly the forest was thicker and the blue hills of Mkushi beckoned in the distance. We were invited for afternoon tea at the Moffats'.

**Zanna, Jasmine and Jo with the Delica van, 2003**

## MALCOLM MOFFAT'S EARLY LIFE

Robert Moffat established the mission at Kuruman in 1821. He was a pioneer in every sense of the word, turning his hand to building, agriculture, preaching and translating the Bible into Setswana. He and Mary had ten children, of whom three died in childhood. Mary, who married David Livingstone, was the eldest. John Smith Moffat, their seventh, was born in Kuruman in 1835. John became a missionary with the London Missionary Society and moved back to Kuruman in 1865 after a time in Matabeleland where he had been working in the territory of the Matabele chief Mzilikazi. John had married Emily Unwin, daughter of James Unwin, a Brighton tea merchant, in 1858. They had eleven children, of whom Malcolm was the tenth. It was in 1862 that John's sister Mary died at Shupanga, on the banks of the Zambezi. By 1870, three years before Livingstone's death, Robert was ready to go home, and John took over the running of the mission at Kuruman. On March 20th, 1870, when Malcolm was only two months old, his grandfather preached his last sermon in the massive stone church at Kuruman. Five days later, Robert and Mary climbed aboard an ox-wagon for their last 800 mile trek to Cape Town.

Two years later John and Emily trekked for a month from Kuruman to Port Elizabeth and sailed back to Britain, a voyage which took five weeks. The older children were at boarding school in England and had never met their three younger brothers. There was a happy re-union with Grandfather Robert, but sadly Grandma Mary had died in 1871. The family spent two years in Brighton, while John travelled up and down the country speaking at church meetings and raising money for the London Missionary Society. They left England again in February 1874, two months before Livingstone's funeral, and did not return for another ten years.

The outward journey was on board the Windsor Castle which ran into a terrific storm five days after they had set sail. The ship's steering gear was damaged and the cabins were flooded. Some of the luggage and livestock (which was to provide meat for the journey, in the absence of refrigeration) was washed overboard. Disaster was narrowly averted. Once they arrived at Port Elizabeth there were delays while their ox-wagon was repaired and oxen found to pull it. They arrived back in Kuruman in mid-June 1874 and remained there for three years.

During this time there were tensions between the missionaries at Kuruman. John was unhappy at what he saw as extravagant spending on the planned "Moffat Institute". When the opportunity came to move, John took charge of the mission at Molepolole when the Rev. Roger Price went on furlough. The Moffats were welcomed to Molepolole by Chief Sechele, of the Bakwena tribe, (referred to by Livingstone as 'the Bakwains') the same chief who had converted to Christianity under Livingstone's influence. The next three years were happier, although Emily found the heat oppressive.

When Malcolm was ten, John finally resigned from the London Missionary Society and once again the family packed up all their possessions into an ox-wagon for a two-month trek across country to Grahamstown—*"a pleasant and civilized town with good schools"* (according to Emily). Here Emily set up house and settled the youngest children in school, while John became Native Commissioner with the Transvaal administration in 1880. His work brought him into contact with the Boers who were suspicious of his motives. During the first Boer War he was threatened with death and kept as a prisoner in Zeerust. In a letter to his father-in-law in 1881 he wrote *I now represent a mere shadowy government which has been utterly discredited in the eyes of the natives by its broken promises to them.* Between 1882 and 1884 he was a magistrate in Basutoland, and from 1885 to 1887 he became the Resident Magistrate at Taungs in British Bechuanaland. In 1887 he became Assistant Commissioner for Bechuanaland and also the British Representative in Matabeleland. He now had the very delicate task of negotiating peace between the British colonial administration and Chief Lobengula. At the instigation of Cecil John Rhodes John Moffat was involved with the signing of the Rudd Concession with Lobengula. This treaty became the means for Rhodes and others to exploit mineral rights in Matabeleland, a fact which shocked and appalled John Moffat when he later discovered the extent of Rhodes' deception of Lobengula.

While Malcolm and his brothers attended school, their father was gone for months and years at a time, with only occasional short visits back to Grahamstown. We can only wonder at the quality of family life. In a poignant and prophetic letter John wrote *"As a family matter it bears a serious aspect. It means indefinite prolongation of a long life away from your mother and what is left of the household, but it seems likely that, like our progenitors, we shall scatter far and wide. We have had our ups and downs but it has been a happy family life and now it is vanishing away."*

In spite of the absence of their father, and to Emily's credit, the three younger sons did well at school. Howard became a farmer/politician and eventually Prime Minister of Southern Rhodesia. Alford became a respected surgeon in Cape Town. Older brother Robert became the first Chief Medical Officer of Uganda (and later his father's biographer—Moffat R. U. *John Smith Moffat)*. Malcolm's eldest brother Livingstone Moffat married into the Pringle farming family and settled in the Eastern Cape.

These were turbulent times with tensions between the British and Boers running high. In October 1887, when Malcolm, aged 17, had finished school, he accompanied his father on a visit to Bulawayo in Matabeleland, where they met Chief Lobengula.

Emily and young Alford moved from Grahamstown to Cape Town where they were briefly re-united with John at Christmas 1891. Malcolm, aged 21, was also in Cape Town training in agriculture with a view to taking up a post in the Cape colonial government. Then in 1894, when Malcolm was 24, everything changed. Dr. Robert Laws, missionary with the Free Church of Scotland was passing through Cape Town on his way back to Nyasaland, where missions were being founded on the shores of Lake Nyasa. He encouraged Malcolm to apply to the Livingstonia Committee in Edinburgh for employment as "agriculturalist and evangelist". In July a letter of appointment was sent to Malcolm from the mission secretary in Scotland together with instructions for him to sail from Cape Town to Chinde on the east coast of Mozambique. On 6th October 1894 Malcolm set sail aboard the *Mexicana,* thus embarking on his missionary career.

# MALCOLM MOFFAT AT LIVINGSTONIA

In 1891 Robert Laws was pleased to be returning to Nyasaland after his furlough. He was particularly pleased to have recruited some good people. In Scotland he had appointed Rev. A.G MacAlpine, Dr. Prentice, and the Rev. James Henderson. Rev. Henderson was to run the educational institute at the new Livingstonia site. A Miss Stewart of Aberdeen was to start work among the lakeshore women. Plans were also underway for another mission station at Mwenzo on the Nyasa-Tanganyika plateau. Meanwhile Dr. Elmslie was eagerly awaiting Dr. Laws' return to Bandawe on the lakeshore. The original Free Church mission had been at Cape Maclear near the southern end of the lake, but the heat and the prevalence of malaria had taken their toll. The mission moved further north to Bandawe, but this site also had its problems. Hostilities between the Tonga people of the lake shore and the war-like Ngoni from the highlands had made life very difficult for the missionaries, who tried to remain neutral.

The Nyika plateau promised to be a healthier site for a mission. The Ngoni were pleased that "Lobati" was going to settle among them. On 7th November 1894 Dr. and Mrs. Laws, and Mr. Murray, a carpenter and several Tonga porters, set out on the lake steamship—the *Ilala,* from Bandawe to Kondowe, where they landed on a narrow beach and clambered up the steep cliffs to the plateau. One of Dr. Laws' mission helpers—Yuraia, who had been recruited from Lovedale in South Africa, had already built a small house for the missionaries. Then followed the enormous task of dragging all their belongings, including a piano, up the steep slope. The first buildings were very basic and they were cold and damp in the rains but the climate was invigorating and the view out over the lake was spectacular.

Malcolm joined the mission in 1894 and at the end of a six month trial period the mission council agreed that this would be a suitable site. Malcolm settled into his work as agricultural missionary to the new "Overtoun Institute" (after Lord Overtoun of the Livingstonia Committee in Glasgow). James Henderson, ordained minister and teacher who had also studied medicine for two years, joined the mission in 1895, aged 28. He was reputed to have "a wonderful physique, one of the handsomest of men." He never seemed to know fatigue but was troubled by excruciating headaches which caused days of great distress. James Henderson shared a house with Malcolm. According to Henderson—in *Forerunners of Modern Malawi* by M Ballantyne and R Shepherd:

*I am living in a small reed and thatch house the other end of which is occupied by Mr. Moffat who is the agriculturalist of the mission. We have one room each and common one. We are having our meals together in Dr. Laws' house. Mrs. Laws makes us exceedingly comfortable and very kindly looks after our food. Mr. Moffat is expecting to grow a variety of foods as to make the mission as self-dependent as possible. At present we have plenty of milk, lemons, carrots, beetroot, arrowroot, peas, beans, leeks, onions and fowls. Some wheat has been sown as an experiment and good results are expected. Coffee trees are coming up and will be bearing in a year or two. There will be cape gooseberries and loquats besides other fruit. Potatoes, both English and sweet do well. Labour is fairly plentiful and cheap.* By Jan 1900 Malcolm was supplying food for 322 students.

Could there have been some rivalry between the two men? Henderson goes on to describe a hunting expedition on which he accompanied Malcolm. According to Henderson, Moffat reneged on his agreement to beat around a patch of bush to drive out guinea-fowl or partridges. Then, just as Henderson had a fine buck in his sights, Moffat appeared at the other side of it *walking along at a terrific pace as is his wont and never thinking once about game, and coming straight towards the beast.* When Moffat finally saw the buck He brought his shotgun up and *somehow made a beautiful miss.*

Henderson was so incensed at this that he stomped off to another area of bush. Irritated by the dense undergrowth he started setting fire to the grass. The fire then raged all night. *All night long the fire burned and spread, burning back against the wind and forward before it forming by and by a ring of light. It was really grand beyond description and by a long way the best fire we had seen around here this season.* By the next day it was threatening nearby villages as well as Moffat's mission gardens. Eventually, even though it was the Sabbath, boys and men were called to help put out the blaze. Moffat saved the day with his knowledge of bush fires and Henderson grudgingly admitted *Mr. Moffat knows about fires. We have agreed to call that day 'the broken Sabbath'.*

By April 1897 The Livingstonia Committee of the Free Church of Scotland was looking for someone to take over Miss Stewart's work so that she could go on leave. A member of Trinity Free Church in Glasgow wrote to the committee

*I think I can mention a lady in every way suitable for Livingstonia—Miss Jackson, nurse in Ward 10 at the Glasgow Royal Infirmary. She is 28 years of age, exceedingly pleasant in manner and appearance, and looks the picture of health. She has been five years a nurse and leaves the Royal Infirmary on Monday first as a fully qualified and certified nurse. She has arranged to take three months in the maternity hospital finishing in July. She is an earnest Christian and was actively engaged in Sabbath School teaching and Christian work before she became a nurse. She is a member of the Trinity Free Church of Glasgow and was brought to the truth under the Ministry of JJ Mackay, now of Hull. Her father married a second time and she is the only child of the first marriage, and there are no children of the second marriage. Her father has long made up his mind to let her carry out her cherished purpose of being a missionary. So far as I can see her temperament combines earnestness and brightness. She has got a good English education and with her experience as a Christian worker and through professional training as a nurse I am pretty certain she is the very person you are now in search for.*

When approached for a reference the Rev. J.J. Mackay wrote *I suppose I have known her for about ten years. Her mother was a Romanial (Roman Catholic). She herself was partly educated in "some convent or Roman Catholic seminary." She was induced to attend Trinity a few times during my ministry there and was converted. She began at once to do Christian work, becoming a Sunday school teacher, secretary of the YWCA and a hearty helper in many departments. She has since then become a qualified nurse. From all I know of Miss Jackson I can very heartily recommend her, and feel sure she will be a real acquisition to the mission. She is strong physically and mentally and spiritually. She is also sympathetic and kindly in disposition. If she accepts she will not disappoint you.*

Maria Jackson had some misgivings about the prospect of being appointed to replace Miss Stewart who was a teacher, but was reassured that she "would go out to make Miss Stewart's furlough less of a strain upon the mission and the variety of work is such that she would soon get into the duties that best suited her experience, gifts and aptitudes." The arrival of Miss Jackson on the scene was to change Malcolm's life.

Maria first appears in her letters to a Mr. Smith at the Foreign Mission Headquarters, 121 George Street. (In our childhood "121" seemed to cast something of an ominous shadow, as the parent body of the missions!) Her letter captures a sense of freshness and wonder at her new life.

8/11/97

*Dear Mr. Smith,*

*We arrived here yesterday in perfect health. It was the Communion Sabbath and Rev. J. Henderson was down from Kondowe (Livingstonia). We did not get ashore until the service was over, but we were in time for the afternoon meeting. It was held in the open air and I am not sure I can trust myself to write about it. Reading accounts of the work can never give any idea of what it really is. The number of people was so large, they all looked so earnest and some of them spoke so well. Forty-three children were baptised, a large number of people had been baptised in the morning. As the meeting went on I began to get afraid of the work, and when it was over I said to Miss McCallum that I almost wished I had not come out. The whole work looked so immense, the numbers so overwhelming. I have not been 24 hours here so I am giving my very first impression and that is astonishment at the large number of people here to work among. It has been decided for the present that both Miss McCallum and I proceed to Kondowe. Everybody says it is a splendid place, but just now we both feel intensely interested in Bandawe. The women here do not keep so much in the background. Yesterday they surrounded me, hundreds of them, all looking so pleased and good-natured and striving to shake hands with me. It was the strangest scene I ever took part in, and the warmest welcome I ever received anywhere in all my life. We saw Miss Stewart at Mandala (the shop); she certainly looked very much in need of a holiday. She watched us start for Matope and she said she would very much like to come back with us.*

*Dr. Fletcher, Miss McCallum and I have been perfectly well all the way out. Mr. Moir was very ill indeed on board the Sir Harry Johnstone and Mrs. Moir fell and hurt her knee badly the very night he turned ill, so Miss McCallum and I did the nursing. Captain Moncur of the Sir Harry had fever too, so the dining saloon on deck was given up to the invalids because the cabins were so hot.*

*The heat is really very great out here, but they say this is about the hottest season just now. It is very comforting to know that there is nothing worse to stand in the way of heat. I will not send you any description of the country or my impression of it, you must have read plenty of that sort of thing before, and kind friends have warned me before coming out not to "pad" my letters. One thing I cannot help mentioning is the exceeding kindness of everybody here. All are so willing to help you in any way. I am afraid "donnas" run a great risk of being spoiled. Miss McCallum and I are very pleased at the prospect of being together; we have mutually agreed to look after each other and warn each other when we see symptoms of becoming exacting or of our tempers being affected by the climate, or anything of this description setting in. We will soon be at work now and the prospect is a very pleasant and happy one. The nearer I draw to my work the less I dread it. The Master who has guided so well in the past, who has taken care of and blessed us with such good health on the way out will surely supply our need . . .*

*I remain*

*Yours sincerely,*
*Maria Jackson*

In the event Miss McCallum went on to Kondowe but *Miss Jackson remained a month at Bandawe to help with 'a severe case' there.* This may have been the African Transcontinental Telegraph official who was badly mauled by a lion and sent to Bandawe for treatment.

We know very little of the meeting of Malcolm and Maria, but Malcolm wasted no time in proposing. Maria however was at the beginning of a three year contract, while Malcolm was coming to the end of his. Malcolm was thus entitled to a return trip to Britain while Maria was not. Malcolm, who was already experiencing some frustrations at the mission, reached a compromise whereby he would stay an extra six months, while Maria would shorten her tour of duty.

Malcolm was planning to continue at Livingstonia but, in Dr. Laws' absence he had a major disagreement with Dr. Elmslie who was acting superintendent, over the terms of his re-appointment. Malcolm wished to have greater responsibility for the supervision of the agricultural students at the Institute. James Henderson, the Head of the Institute, had other ideas. It would seem that Malcolm felt that James was overstepping the boundaries and interfering with Malcolm's work. In a letter home in March 1898 Henderson further criticized Moffat for not managing to secure a supply of grain for the Institute. A significant proportion of the crops grown at Livingstonia had been eaten by locusts. The lack of food required the schools to be closed prematurely and the pupils sent home. Malcolm had also asked Dr. Laws to relieve him of the task of book-keeping for the mission. Dr. Laws had agreed to this but Dr. Elmslie objected on the grounds that Malcolm was asserting "unacceptable independence."

The couple left to get married, but under a cloud. Dr. Elmslie refused them any furlough allowance and Maria was not granted a passage back to Britain. In fact she was required to pay for her outward ticket. The journey to Cape Town took a month. Malcolm left Maria with her prospective in-laws and he sailed for Britain alone. He was warmly welcomed at Mission Headquarters in Edinburgh and the terms of his new contract were agreed. Maria's fare was refunded, and the couple would now be employed from Scotland rather than from Livingstonia. Malcolm returned to Cape Town in November and on 29th December 1900 he and Maria were married in the Claremont Congregational church.

Malcolm had planned that they would spend their honeymoon at Quagga's Kerk, the farm in the Eastern Cape belonging to his older brother Livingstone Moffat. The trip was delayed because *"The country is in such an unsettled state owing to the Boer invasion"*. Dr. Laws had passed through Cape Town on his furlough and was invited to lunch with Cecil Rhodes. When Dr. Laws arrived for the lunch he was advised that his host had made a quick exit on a train to Kimberley. Kruger had issued an ultimatum and the Boer War had begun. Malcolm was eventually able to obtain a military pass and the couple proceeded on their honeymoon. After a further month in Cape Town they sailed for Chinde and Livingstonia.

To Mr. Smith at Mission Headquarters Malcolm wrote on 8/1/01

*I am so glad to have had this furlough—It does one good to view the work from a distance and we will both go back much refreshed and encouraged. Mrs. Moffat sends her thanks to you for your good wishes—you seem to have a special interest in and regard for her; and of this I am of course, not at all surprised. I can quite endorse what you said to me in your office in Edinburgh viz. that I have got the best of the bargain. I do hope that we may be spared, given the help and more important still, the grace to spend useful lives together in the Master's service in Livingstonia. That we will be happy I have not the least doubt. That we will be good and faithful servants is our one desire and prayer. With many thanks to you for your good wishes and kind interest, believe me.*

*Sincerely. MM*

We do not know what the couple's reception at Livingstonia was like but not long after their return Rev. James Henderson sent this letter dated 21/3/01 to HQ

*"I came out here appointed as a colleague to Dr. Laws, and with the say in mission policy which membership of the mission council conferred. But since then control of the Institution has passed out of the hands of the mission council and I do not know exactly where I am. The immediate cause of my writing is that I have just heard from Home indirectly that Dr. Laws is making arrangements relative to the educational work here which overturns an organization entered upon after much consideration and carried out with much pains and acknowledged success, arrangements which, in my opinion, and I think Dr. Elmslie would agree with me, are at present unnecessary, which do not in any way relieve the great pressure on this department and which will take up immediately a salary much required otherwise. I cannot protest against it except to Dr. Laws himself who will as in all or nearly all previous cases agree with what I say entirely but follow quite another course. The conditions under which the work is at present carried out are utterly disheartening, and, are such, and affect me so deeply that, as I intimated at the last Council meeting, I fear very much I shall not be able to continue until the end of this term.*

*Yours sincerely,*
*James Henderson.*

In 1901 Malcolm and Maria had a son, Unwin Jackson Moffat. The work continued. In addition to the obvious tensions in working relationships there were other hardships as evidenced by this letter from Rev. James Fairley Daly at Mission HQ in 1903:

*20/11/03*

*"Dear Mr. and Mrs. Moffat,*

*A letter from Dr. Laws and the new issue of "the Aurora" have just come telling us of the loss you have sustained in the death of your little twin infants. Allow me for myself and my wife to express our deepest sympathy with you. I trust Mrs. Moffat has been quite restored to health and strength again. By the time you receive this Dr. Elmslie and party will likely be amongst us and we shall hear from them how you all are and how things are progressing at Livingstonia. We trust that soon comfortable houses and other buildings will be provided for you all.*

*Yours very truly,*
*J.Fairley Daly*

By the end of 1904 it was obvious that Malcolm did not want to continue at Livingstonia. A visit from his father may have helped Malcolm to look at all the options. John S. Moffat enjoyed his visit to Livingstonia, taking Livingstone's route up the Zambezi and stopping to visit his sister Mary's grave at Shupanga. Certainly John was no stranger to the frustrations of mission life and no doubt he was able to advise his son accordingly.

J.Fairley Daly wrote to Malcolm on 23/12/04

*We were quite distressed to hear from the Minute of the Mission Council that you have sent in your resignation and proposed leaving the mission. We trust that some arrangement may be made which will permit of your continuing the good services you have rendered to the mission for some time yet. We understand that you and Mrs. Moffat have agreed to take the place of Dr. and Mrs. Chisholm at Mwenzo Mission while they are at home on furlough. Perhaps after their return the developments of mission work and the rearrangements of staff may permit of some arrangement being made which will make it possible for you to remain connected with us. Of course I am writing simply as an individual expressing my own feelings but I know that the committee highly appreciate your work and would regret very much your leaving the mission. Remember me very kindly to your wife who I trust continues to enjoy good health and strength.*

*With kind regards to you both,*

*Yours very truly,*
*J Fairley Daly.*

In 1905 their second son John Smith Moffat was born at Livingstonia and the Moffats moved west to Mwenzo Mission. The late Rev. Fergus Macpherson in his book *North of the Zambezi* gave the meaning of

Mwenzo in Cinamwanga as *'heart'* or *'of one's own free will'*. He goes on to say that it also carries a challenge of *'who can hinder me?'* The Namwanga trace their history back to a man called Musyani who came into the Mwenzo area several hundred years ago. He impressed the people with his skills and knowledge, and settled among them to become their Chief. The present day Winamwanga Cultural Heritage and Development Association (WICHDA) are of the opinion that Mwenzo means *'definitely'* or *'deliberately'* in relation to Musyani's arrival.

The Moffats' move was to be a temporary one, a stepping stone to a proposed new mission site near Chief Chitambo's village, the site of Livingstone's death. In his letter of congratulations J. Fairley Daly of Mission HQ writes

*I hear there is talk of your settling at Chitambo or one of the new stations in the West.*

*For this your past experience has well fitted you and the committee at home will have every confidence that all that can be done for the success of the work, and done well, you and your wife will do. The visit of your father (Rev John S. Moffat) to Livingstonia was, from all I hear, much appreciated. His help and council were most useful and to you his visit must have been a special pleasure. His last journey through Central Africa must have been especially interesting, and added greatly to his experience of Africa and African missions.*

*Yours very truly,*
*J.Fairley Daly.*

## CHURCH AND MISSION 1906

David Livingstone wrote home to his family in 1850:

*I am a missionary, heart and soul. God had only one son and He was a missionary and a physician. I am a poor, poor imitation of Him, or wish to be. In this service I hope to live, in it I wish to die. I am immortal till my work is accomplished and although I see few results future missionaries will see conversions after every sermon. May they not forget the pioneers who worked in the thick gloom with few rays to cheer, except such as flow from faith in the precious promises of God's word.*

While God is said to move in mysterious ways, the newly-formed United Free Church of Scotland was moving in very definite ways, as indicated in this report from Lord Overtoun the Chairman of the Livingstonia Committee written in 1906-

*Thirty-two years have passed since, worn out with exposure and fatigue, David Livingstone died on his knees in Ilala at Chitambo's village, about a day's journey south-east of Lake Bangweolo. An obelisk now marks the spot where his heart is buried, while his body, carried by loving hands, rests amid the mighty dead in Westminster Abbey. He thus took possession of Central Africa for Christ, and like those who followed him in proclaiming to dark Africa the glorious gospel laid deep the foundations of the native Christian Church, which today, after thirty years, has over three thousand members, and is beginning to cover the land.*

*The first ten years' labour of the Livingstonia Mission, which was organized to commemorate Livingstone, though it brought few converts, saw the formation of a chain of stations extending for some four hundred miles along the western shores of Lake Nyasa. During the next decade some of the devoted band of missionaries, moving sixty miles westward, settled among the wild Ngoni and other upland tribes, forming the beginnings of a second chain of stations parallel to the first. At these stations the four methods of the mission—evangelistic, educational, medical, and industrial—were prosecuted on a continually increasing scale. Under the influence of a spiritual movement, which has now prevailed in the field for many years, the native agency began to assume great importance. For the training of these native leaders, the Overtoun Institution was founded, on an elevated, healthy plateau, at Kondowi, which is now called Livingstonia. By means of the teachers and other mission workers trained there and at the stations, the missionaries became able to multiply their influence nearly a hundredfold.*

*The whole territory occupied having been divided into districts commanded by stations, the missionaries at the stations set themselves to cover the whole of their districts with a network of their school-church system, holding it as their policy that within their districts no collection of people, however numerically insignificant, was to be neglected. The result of this was that towards the middle of the third decade most of the districts were completely covered, and the missionaries began to find themselves in possession of a staff of native workers experienced in pioneering, for the utilization of which they had to look beyond their allotted spheres into the heathen lands of the west.*

*The native church, from the beginning, had a missionary spirit, which grew in intensity in response to the calls of the European leaders. The heathen hinterland began to possess the minds of the missionaries and their people, and presently became a great and general motive power. An advance was begun westwards by parties of preachers and teachers from the stations, and by volunteer vacation bands of students from the institution, which pushed out the frontier of the land in which the gospel was known further and further. These enterprises culminated last year in a great simultaneous evangelistic movement, in which parties from all the nations of the mission were engaged and acting in concert, carried the gospel to nearly all the villages open to the mission across the basin of the Loangwa River, which is the source of the Congo. By this advance the spheres of the stations were immensely increased, the institution having one (sphere) that took from twelve to fourteen days to cross.*

## MALCOLM MOFFAT AT CHITAMBO

Thus Malcolm and Maria (who now signed herself 'Marie') were appointed to found the mission at Chitambo. Before going on furlough to Scotland, Malcolm was among a group to be ordained as ministers, at Livingstonia. Another member of the group was one David Kaunda, father of Zambia's future first president. It was 1906. In the same year James Henderson transferred to the Lovedale Institute in South Africa to become the Principal. Malcolm and Marie spent their furlough in Glasgow, where Malcolm took courses in building and architecture.

The family set out again for Africa in 1907 aboard the Kinfauns Castle. The boys, Unwin and John, were six and two years old. This time they sailed to Cape Town and then took the train from Cape Town to Broken Hill in Northern Rhodesia. This was a new route for missionary travel and a relatively expensive one.

The family camped at Broken Hill, (now Kabwe) the lead and zinc mining town, where Malcolm's brother Howard was the mine manager. The Moffats stocked up with provisions at the Mandala stores (Mandala meaning 'things reflected in water', the name given by the lakeshore people of Nyasaland to Mr. Moir, one of the original founders of the Lakes Trading Company, on account of his glasses. The chain of stores spread throughout southern Africa.)

The next part of the journey was on foot and it took two weeks. The children were carried in a *machila*, or Portuguese hammock. Seventy porters carried the family's possessions, and game was hunted for food on the journey. The route took them through the fertile plains adjacent to the Mkushi River, across the river and through Chief Chibale's area. According to Malcolm the journey was sometimes interesting, sometimes monotonous. They reached Serenje *boma* (Portuguese for 'administrative outpost') on 16/5/07. The plan was that they would use Serenje as a base while searching for a suitable site for the new Chitambo Mission. The original idea had been to build a mission at the exact spot where David Livingstone had died, but Old Chitambo, as it was soon to be called, was close to the Bangweulu swamps and was unhealthy on account of malaria and sleeping sickness.

The Moffats had only been at their new home for a few months when a man named Filemon Kamanga arrived, with a letter from Rev. D.R. Mackenzie of Livingstonia, recommending him as a gardener and general worker. He and his wife Estere Nyankata had made the 300 mile journey from Livingstonia on foot, because they wanted to help at the new mission. Kamanga began his service on the brickfield, and was the first to start work at what was to become the Chitambo Mission Station. It was he who helped put up the temporary huts when the site of the station was decided upon. He and his wife Estere were baptized at the first baptismal service in the Chitambo district.

There were local people who came forward to help. One of the first schools in the district was at Chimponda. Here a young man called Sabune (soap) distinguished himself in literacy classes, in being able to read the Sermon on the Mount—the first scripture portion printed in Chi Bisa-Lala. When the building work began at Chitambo he volunteered for work, and he later became the overseer of the agricultural work. He too was baptized and became an elder in the church.

**The original church at Chitambo, about 1909 (National Library of Scotland)**

# MKUSHI 2003

David Moffat, (son of Unwin and therefore Malcolm's grandson) and his wife Christine continue to run a farm at Mkushi. They have also played a substantial part in setting up Chengelo School—a private boarding school patronized by many of Zambia's influential families. We had sometimes stayed with David's parents Unwin and Sheila on our many long trips from Lusaka to Chitambo. To us children the farm was a magical oasis of tranquillity. Doves cooed in the surrounding woods and soft-nosed cows provided cream for our wheat porridge. Trees groaned under the weight of avocados, guavas and oranges. There were irrigation systems and soft green lawns, not to mention that luxury of all luxuries to a parched bunch of missionary kids—a swimming pool. Unwin was an agriculturalist while his brother John had been a District Commissioner. John later became influential in helping Northern Rhodesia move through the transition to independence in 1964. For this he was knighted. Sir John and his family ran a farm at Mkushi for many years before emigrating to New Zealand.

Turning off the main highway onto the gravel road to the Moffats' farm was, for us, like travelling back in time. The road was a dusty red swathe through leafy forest. Ladies wrapped in brightly coloured *citenges* (traditional cloths) carried ungainly bundles of firewood on their heads. Startled by the noise of the vehicle they would jump to the side of the road and then gingerly twist their laden heads round, grinning. We gave a lift to a group who were going to church. We never established how far they were planning to go, as we reached the turnoff to the farm and we let them out there amidst a round of curtsying and hand-clapping in thanks for the lift.

The farm-house, built in 1952 was a low brick building with a tiled roof. A sprinkler played over a green lawn, and water gurgled invitingly in the swimming pool. We parked under a large cedrella tree, whose huge seed pods cracked and exploded, from time to time, shedding their coin-sized seeds. David and Christine welcomed us and we stepped into the kitchen of so many African childhoods—a wood-burning stove, a water filter, a meat 'safe', avocadoes ripening on the window-ledges, and a fly-paper sporting its latest victims. We had tea and scones in the living-room where David Shepherd's elephants looked down on us from one wall and a photo of Livingstone himself, with youngest daughter Anna Mary at his knee regarded us coolly from the other.

Catching up with thirty years of news was clearly going to take some time, so we accepted the Moffats' offer of staying overnight on the return journey and we pressed on towards Serenje, where we would fill up with petrol. The sun began its slide towards the horizon, and for part of the Serenje run we were caught in its coppery glow. Then suddenly it was gone. The Serenje petrol station was at the road end, so we were able to fill up without going to the Boma (business centre). The pump attendants quizzed us about our journey and Jo bargained with a basket-seller.

In the old days, African journeys always seemed to end in the dark. That was part of the magic. Huge insects would flutter into the car headlights and small game such as wild-cats, deer and rabbits would scamper off into the night. North of Serenje we turned north-west onto the Mansa road, and it was only another half hour to the turn-off for Kasanka national park. We had to rouse the gate attendant who had hunkered down for the night. There was form-filling and payment of camp fees, and the painstaking writing of receipts before he swung the pole barrier up for us to go through. A single-track dirt road over tree roots and dry stream beds, took us the last 14 km to the main camp. We were met by a small group of camp staff bearing hurricane lamps. A camp-fire crackled invitingly in the back-ground and we were shown to our thatched 'rondavels'. We stepped through an invisible portal into the homecoming of so many pasts.

# MONUMENT 1890-1906

Livingstone's heart lay undisturbed at the foot of the old mpundu tree. A prospector, J.M. Thomson, who passed near the site in 1890 while seeking to obtain mineral rights from local chiefs, reported that the inscription on the tree was still visible. According to the Northern Rhodesia Journal (1950) Thomson himself did not visit the site as he was *unable to leave his plague-ridden caravan.* He sent a trusted headman to visit the spot. The headman came back with the news that the tree was still there and the inscription, which was cut deeply into the wood, was still visible and largely intact. To prove this he had carved out one of the letters, and brought with it a few leaves and a fragment of an old box! The letter was given to Livingstone's older daughter Mrs. Agnes Bruce.

In 1892 Captain Bia and Lieutenant Franqui of an Anglo-Belgian expedition visited Chitambo's village. Bia was the leader of the second Belgian Congo Expedition which was sent out by the newly formed Katanga Company to explore the region. Mrs. Bruce had sent a commemorative plaque which she wished to have placed on the tree. The Royal Geographical Society also sent a present of cloth and other objects to Chief Chitambo in recognition of his services to David Livingstone. The tablet and gifts had been entrusted to a Scottish Plymouth Brethren missionary, FS Arnot, who handed them on to Captain Bia. Bia and Franqui reached the area on 6th July 1892. The village was now deserted due to raids from neighbouring tribes. The old chief had died not long after Livingstone and he lay buried under the same tree. The Bia expedition could not find the tree, but they found Chief Chitambo's 17 year old son and successor, Piana Chitambo and older cousin Mwege Chitambo. They handed over the gifts and the plaque was attached to a tree in Chitambo's village. In order to prove that they had been to the area, they left a signed document with Chief Chitambo. On the return journey to Katanga Captain Bia died at Tenke and Franqui took over command of the expedition.

The next European to visit the site was Mr. E.T Glave, special correspondent of the New York Century Magazine, on 13th July 1894.

The village where Bia and Franqui had met Chitambo was deserted, on accounts of slaving raids on the "Awemba" (Bemba). The plate on the tree had been stolen by a slave caravan which had left the country between the River Mapula and Lake Bangweulu about eighteen months previously. The caravan was led by two Swahili slavers, Kasaki and Karuma who knew that the plaque had been stolen and who were heard boasting that they had robbed a white man's grave. Kasaki and Karuma had for many months been raiding the Bemba country, and when a large batch of slaves was collected they put them in chains and slave forks and took them to Nyungwe on the Zambezi.

ET Glave writes *I have visited the exact spot where the heart of Dr. Livingstone is buried and have a photo of the tree, with the inscription by Jacob Wainwright. The tree is situated about five miles South West of the village of Karonga on the river Lulimala.*

Big game hunter and explorer Mr. Poulett-Weatherley visited the place in 1896. He wrote: *You have no idea of the utter desolation and absence of natives round the old Mpundu tree. Chitambo's village was a good sized one, but on his death his people dispersed and wandered far away. I doubt if they will ever collect again.* Poulett-Weatherley cleared an avenue to the tree and photographed the inscription. He also mentioned 'the visitors' book'—another young mpundu tree forty-one yards to the east. Presumably some of the travellers had left their autographs here!

On 31st July 1897 the tree was visited by Rev. Dan and Mrs. Crawford, Scottish Plymouth Brethren missionaries, based in the Luapula area. Dan Crawford erected a fence around the tree and took photographs of it. He later supplied the information that the stolen brass tablet was melted down and moulded into bullets!

Another visitor, in 1898 was Mr. Hugo Gentle. He described Crawford's fence as *a strong ornamental palisade or fence.* He also recorded that the inscription on the tree read

**Dr. Livingstone**
**May 4th 1873**
**MA SUZA MNIASERE**
**VCHOPERE**

It was because of his report on the general state of the tree, which was under attack by rot and borers, that the Royal Geographical Society decided to remove the inscribed portion of the tree while there was still time, and to erect a more lasting monument. The help of Sir Herbert

M. Stanley, inaugural governor of Northern Rhodesia, was sought. He proposed a hollow bronze column, transported in pieces and screwed together at the site, then filled with cement. The estimated cost of this was about five thousand pounds. Sir Alfred Sharpe, the British Commissioner in Nyasaland took on responsibility on behalf of the Royal Geographical Society and commissioned Robert Codrington to carry out the practical task of saving the inscription. So, fittingly, in May 1899 Codrington (Deputy Administrator of Northern Rhodesia) was dispatched from Fort Jameson in the south eastern province of Northern Rhodesia to visit the site. The party set out from Fort Jameson carrying, amongst other things, a folding metal boat and a metal telegraph pole. Codrington wrote

*On the morning of May 10<sup>th</sup> we travelled 13.5 miles east-south-east from Chitambo's present village, and reached the site of Old Chitambo on the Lulimala stream. The trees have long since grown up all over the site of the old village, and, except for a small clearing and a low fence around it, there was nothing to distinguish the Livingstone tree, which was of a variety common to all the high country of British Central Africa. The inscription is, however, very well and deeply cut, the bark having been removed for the purpose, and shows that the boys who carved it took a great deal of pains to make the inscription as permanent as possible. The bark has grown over part of the "E" in Livingstone and part of the "3" in 1873. Borers were fast destroying the lettering, which is, however, still distinct, with the exception of the last two lines, in which the first letters of the names of the followers have disappeared . . . The tree itself, was hollow, and the rot was eating through into the inscription and would soon have destroyed it completely. The inscription was, therefore, not cut out a day too soon, as its existence was threatened by rot from one side and borers from the other, and any violent storm would have endangered the whole tree. There was also the risk of the inscription being carried away by private persons for the sake of speculation, one scheme of this sort, at least, being frustrated by my action.*

*Having taken steps to preserve the inscription from damage I immediately cut down the tree, and sawed it off above and below the inscription. When this was done its weight was so great that it was impossible for two men to lift it; and as there were several hundred miles of land transport to be accomplished before it could reach the ocean, I was obliged to take steps to bring it down to a reasonable weight. For three days my boys were engaged in carefully adzing out the inside of the section, until as much had been cut away as was consistent with the necessity of leaving a sound and durable piece of timber. Carefully packed with a quantity of naphthalene to destroy the borers, the section was sewn in canvas and slung on a strong pole but it was a heavy and inconvenient load, weighing about 200 pounds, and requiring at least twenty-five carriers; had it not been for our folding boat, I doubt if we should have got it across the large rivers which flowed between us and the Tanganyika plateau.*

*I had brought from Fort Jameson one of the iron poles of the Trans-Continental Telegraph, and this I firmly planted in the very heart of the tree-stump, where it will serve to mark the exact spot for many years if necessary, until some more elaborate monument is erected . . . . A large clearing was made and a strong fence built around the tree-stump. On May 14th, everything being completed we left Old Chitambo and travelled 3.5 miles to the Lulimala River, which we crossed in the folding boat, assisted by a few canoes from the large village on the river-bank.*

The section of the tree bearing the inscriptions now rests in the Royal Geographical Society rooms in London. In the absence of suitable stone in the region where Livingstone died, the RGS raised money for a permanent memorial of bricks and cement. By 1900 sufficient funds had been raised for the project. In 1902 Mr. Owen Stroud, with some African artisans was sent up from Fort Jameson to erect the memorial. Mr. Stroud dug out and cut up the tree stump, two portions of which are now in the national museum—The Rhodes-Livingstone Museum in the town of Livingstone. One of these portions bears the following note: *I certify that this piece of wood was cut down by me on 7th August 1902 and is part of the tree under which Dr. David Livingstone's heart etc. was buried. Signed Owen Stroud.*

The building of the monument was slightly different from the original plan. Instead of cement blocks, the monument was built with burnt bricks, and plastered with cement to give a smooth finish. The bricks for the monument were made and fired on the spot, and some of those that were unused could be seen at the site for many years to follow. The monument was surrounded by four concrete and brick posts supporting three iron rails and one wooden rail. Stroud also planted some wattle and blue-gum seedlings near the monument but these have not survived.

Two brass plaques, sent from the RGS in London, with separate brass letters soldered onto the plates, were attached, one on the east and one on the west side of the monument, reading-

**This monument
occupies the spot
where formerly stood the tree
at the foot of which
Livingstone's heart was buried
by his faithful native followers
on the trunk was carved
the following inscription
David Livingstone died May 4<sup>th</sup> 1873
Chuma, Souza, Mniasere, Vchopere**

**ERECTED BY HIS FRIENDS
TO THE MEMORY OF DAVID LIVINGSTONE MISSIONARY
AND EXPLORER
HE DIED HERE MAY 4th 1873**

The first plate bears the slight inaccuracy in that it misquotes the words originally carved on the tree. There is also a discrepancy regarding the actual date of Livingstone's death. The last entry in his diary was April 27th. According to Souza (Susi) and Chuma the death occurred in the early hours of May 1st and this date has been accepted by most authorities. Biographer R.J. Campbell states that on the 30th April, Chief Chitambo called on Livingstone, and the next day the explorer was dead. One of Livingstone's biographers, Waller, notes that at the time of meeting HM Stanley, and in spite of his attention to detail, Livingstone had got fourteen days behind the calendar, so it is likely that Jacob Wainright's date of 4th May was inaccurate.

Explorer J.E. Hughes, author of *Eighteen Years on Lake Bangweulu*, visited Old Chitambo's on 7th May 1904 and took with him cypress seedlings to plant round the monument. These were given to him by Sir Hector Croad. Some of the seedlings were flattened overnight by a charging rhinoceros, but some survived until 1948. Afterwards Hughes conceded—*There is no need, however, for any more trees to be planted at this place. The forest itself in which it stands, is full of splendid indigenous trees than which nothing could be more suitable and around the little clearing there is a magnificent natural park waiting to be laid out. The surroundings of the monument are still those of solitude and silence and not so long ago of big game in plenty.* As well as the rhinoceros encountered on this trip Hughes mentioned lion and sable antelope.

**The Livingstone monument, Chipundu.**

## CHITAMBO 1907

On Thursday 16th May 1907 Malcolm and Marie reached the Kombe River and after a long rest, according to Malcolm, *we started the ascent up and onto the plateau on which Serenje stands. It took us two hours. Mr. Croad, the Native Commissioner, met us and took us over to the house which the mission council had bought from Mr. Wenham. It is a nice little two-roomed wattle and daub house, with outside kitchen and two small verandahs with little storage places. Mr. Croad has very kindly had the whole place cleaned up and whitewashed, so it was awaiting us in beautiful order. Serenje is 4,850 feet above sea-level according to my aneroid.*

Shortly after their arrival the Moffats were joined by Dr. Alexander Brown of Aberdeen, who went by the Nyasa route. Dr. Brown was born in Aberdeen in October 1872, the year before Livingstone died. Like Livingstone he came from a poor family and like Livingstone he started out as a labourer, (making ropes in the ship-yard,) and he attended night school to learn Latin. He graduated in Medicine from Aberdeen University in 1905 at the age of 33. On graduating he went on to Liverpool where he took the Diploma in Tropical Medicine. He spent a little time orientating at Bandawe on the shores of Lake Nyasa prior to his arrival at Chitambo. One of the first things that he and Moffat did was to visit the Livingstone monument.

**Malcolm Moffat and Alexander Brown, Chitambo**
**(National Library of Scotland)**

Malcolm wrote on 27/6/ 07-*Dr. Brown and I had a most interesting and encouraging tour through the central portion of our district. We visited Chitambo and shall never forget our three days' sojourn at that quiet solemn spot away there on the banks of the Liluwe stream or marsh. To fully take in the greatness of Livingstone's life-work and the triumph of his death, one must visit that lonely spot where he breathed his last.*

*The place was all overgrown with weeds and long grass. The only signs of life to be seen were the fresh footprints of eland and buffalo all around the monument. There are no villages very near. Chitambo, the son of Old Chitambo who used to live here when Livingstone was carried into his village, lives away about 8 miles to the south west on the Misumba stream. So the monument stands there month after month without being looked upon by man. 'He died here' the inscription decidedly affirms. To every visitor to the spot the truth is vividly brought home that he as certainly lives here. The memory of Livingstone is treasured by his fellow Scots. The story of Engelesa (Livingstone), the kind one, the good man who came here and died in Chitambo's village and whose heart was buried on one side of the mpundu tree, the other side of which had been buried Chitambo Mukulu (Chitambo the Great), is told and retold among these dark-skinned Africans . . . And it was the actual sight of this spot away in "Wisaland" (the natives call it Chipundu) which brings home to one, as nothing else could the great triumph of his missionary life. Dr. Livingstone speaks and inspires at Chipundu as nowhere else.*

*It was a great privilege which Dr. Brown and I enjoyed, and we moved slowly away on Monday afternoon, after spending a quiet Sabbath there and a busy Monday forenoon cleaning up the place, inspired with fresh hope and confidence. Dr. Livingstone has indeed opened up the way. As a mission we must follow hard and strong.*

On the same date Dr. Brown wrote *This is a magnificent country. Leaving out of account the gigantic mountains round about Kondowe, I have not yet seen a bit of the country to equal it for hill and dale, distant mountain and level plateau, stony kopjes and grass-covered hills which, all lying under the haze of a glaring tropical sun, combine to make up a landscape charming and beautiful. The people are Awisa, are not numerous and are widely scattered. They are shy. They are the ordinary type of African workers—some do as little as they can get off with, some are willing to learn.*

From Mission HQ James Fairley Daly wrote to Malcolm Moffat on 9/10/07

*Your letter of 27 June giving an account of your first visit to Chitambo with Dr. Brown and including your interview with Old Chitambo's son I felt to be so interesting that I published it in the Scotsman and the Herald. It created a great deal of interest and in order to make it permanent we have printed it in the Letters for the Third Quarter of this year which you will have received ere this reaches you. We shall be glad to hear from you as you come to know more and more of the district and what kind of people you are working amongst, and if you are likely to have anything of a population in the midst of which to establish the station and set up the schools. It almost seems from what you say as if the population in the district was rather sparse and made up of small villages than of populous centres.*

*I hope Mrs. Moffat and the children continue to enjoy good health and strength. She must be at present the only European lady in your whole district, situated many days' journey from any other mission station or European family. We often think of you in your solitude and pray that you may enjoy much of the presence and power of God in your work, and realise that indeed you are not alone, for He is with you.*

**Moffat family picnic, Chitambo**

**Welcome dance, Chitambo**

# CHITAMBO MISSION ESTABLISHED 1908

The period of "observation" was completed by the end of 1908 and in January 1909 a letter from Mission HQ read *It is satisfactory to learn that you are all agreed that the site on the Mawonde stream is the best and promises to be a good missionary centre.*

Malcolm and Dr. Brown then set about the business of establishing the mission.

**The Moffats' first house at Chitambo (National Library of Scotland)**

On 30th June the accounts for the mission were opened and in July of that year the first school began. By the end of the year there were three schools with five teachers and 120 pupils. By August a book-store was opened and in October a general store followed—selling calico, slates, pencils, readers, hymnaries and bibles, though none in the local language (Chi Bisa-Lala). By 1910 the store's stock list included beads, soap, salt, scarves, thread, twill, blankets and a suit.

Meanwhile trouble was brewing on a distant front. The idea of establishing a commemorative mission close to the site of Old Chitambo was occurring to other denominations, most notably the Universities Mission (UM)—inspired by Livingstone's famous address to students in Cambridge in 1857. The UM was planning to establish itself right at the site of the monument.

An astounded James Fairley Daly of Mission HQ had this to say to Malcolm Moffat:

*I am sending you by this post a copy of a magazine of the Universities Mission called "Central Africa" which contains an extraordinary article saying that they wish to extend their work westwards in N.E. Rhodesia to the borders of the Congo territory. They speak of it as establishing a third Diocese in Central Africa and ask their friends to help them raise eleven thousand pound. They express the desire to settle at the spot where David Livingstone died and never mention the fact that another mission is already working there. A large information meeting was held in Cambridge last night addressed by the Archbishop of Canterbury and three other bishops to inaugurate the new scheme and plead for money. Lord Overtoun is writing to the Archbishop and the director of the Universities Mission protesting against their coming into your sphere and also to Mr. Codrington. You may see Mr. Codrington or his successor for we understand he has been changed to NW Rhodesia and so talk over the matter. Remind them of their invitation to us to enter in and possess the land, I mean to start a mission there. We have done so and spent already good large sums and appointed you and Dr. Brown. We have raised money to build houses, school and hospital, and will be spending nearly one thousand pounds a year on the work. All this we did believing that the NE Rhodesian administration kept that district for the Presbyterian mission and allocate to other missions other districts where the work would not clash. It would be a thousand pities if our mission and the Universities Mission found starting work in the same district . . . energetically opposing one another . . .* the rest of the text is indistinct but the happy outcome was for the UM to back down and allow the United Free Church of Scotland to forge ahead, perhaps to the "skirling" of bagpipes!

**Carpenters at work at Chitambo about 1910**

The first solid house to be built at Chitambo was the Moffats' at a cost of 270 pounds. The house—a large, brick building with a verandah on three sides, is on the right of the road into Chitambo station, although now in a state of disrepair. Dr. Brown stayed at Chitambo from the end of 1906 until 1912. He and Malcolm built his house of bricks and timber. The bricks were made in local kilns and timber came from nearby forests. Saw pits had to be dug before any construction could start. No cement was used in the building. The original roof was flat but not surprisingly it leaked and the house had to be re-roofed with galvanized iron. Dr. Brown's house, completed in 1910, was the first on the left as one entered the mission and it remained the doctor's house for the next eighty years. It is now completely in ruins. John Howie, a joiner, farmer and dispatch rider, previously at Livingstonia, helped with the building of the first houses.

Food supplies were precarious in those early days. Cattle were ordered for the mission but they had to be herded across the Luangwa Valley from Fort Jameson in the south-east of the country. In the meantime milk was bought from the District Commissioner in Serenje. The Nyasaland-based African Lakes Trading Company supplied provisions. Flour was imported in sealed tins from England, and rice was procured from the nearby Luangwa Valley. In the wet season a charcoal-burning brazier was kept going in the store to prevent provisions from becoming damp.

The medical work was initially rather unsatisfying for Dr. Brown, owing to the sparse population and the lack of trust in *musungu* medicine. Dr. Brown felt under-employed in the clinic and busied himself with other issues such as investigating an outbreak of the dreaded sleeping-sickness. He longed for a busier medical life and this became the subject of some pointed exchanges between himself and mission HQ.

James Fairley Daly wrote on 23/2/12

*Dear Dr. Brown,*

*Your letter about Chitambo and especially your last letter desiring to resign from the Livingstonia Mission and if possible to be transferred to an Indian mission was a great surprise. Dr. Elmslie (of Livingstonia itself) tells us that almost all the medical missionaries in Livingstonia pass through what he calls "the medical fever of disappointment" at the limited amount of medical practice a pioneer missionary experiences. Your early experience at Bandawe where mission work had long been established did not give you the usual experience our medical men have passed through during their first years in Africa. When therefore you left Bandawe to pioneer in Rhodesia you naturally must have felt keenly the difference between busy Bandawe and sparsely populated Chitambo. Chitambo, however, when it becomes more established and a better known mission centre will likely draw to itself a larger population or attract to itself medical cases from a distance when its hospital and medical missionary become better known . . . We suggest that you should arrange to attend the Council and talk over both the future of Chitambo and its work and your own connection with the mission, with your brethren before finally deciding to send in your resignation. Could you not take counsel by correspondence with men like Dr. Elmslie, Dr. Laws and Dr. Innes before coming to a final decision? We are strongly of the opinion that you should remain at Chitambo until the return of Mr. Moffat from his furlough which is now due.*

Dr. Brown wrote to Dr. Laws and received a reply. The contents of that letter are unknown but a sharp response is drawn from James Fairley Daly at Mission HQ-

*In writing that letter Dr. Laws, you must remember, was simply giving you frankly his own opinion and perhaps you will find some others agree with him. Anyhow it is hardly what you call 'a series of charges more or less grave against a mission worker' . . .*

Dr. Brown upheld his decision to resign in June 1912 and was posted to Kalna in Bengal in March 1913. He served as a Lieutenant in the R.A.M.C. in Mesopotamia during the First World War. He met his future wife, Helen Youngson, daughter of a Rev. John White Youngson in India. They married in 1917 at Sialkot in the Punjab. The Browns returned to Aberdeen in 1920 and Dr. Brown went into General Practice there until he retired in 1938. He died in 1954. His son, Professor Alexander (Sandy) Youngson (Brown) was Vice Principal of Edinburgh University from 1970 to 1974.

By 1912 Chitambo hospital had three beds, but up to 2,500 people were being treated a year. By 1919 there were ten beds and 3,800 out-patients. The majority of the patients were local Lala people. But one was an unfortunate European man by the name of Captain Kelsey in 1913 or 1914. He was attempting to drive from Cairo to the Cape long before the roads were suitable for even the most robust of cars. This captain of the Suffolk Regiment had shot and wounded a leopard. In order to finish it off he had followed it into the long grass. According to one story he was killed and his body was buried "near Luputa, just south of the Great North road." Another account has the man treated by "the widow of Rev. Malcolm Moffat, in 1914". This hardly seems possible, as Malcolm Moffat died in 1939! Further confusion may have arisen because a Captain Everett of the Anglo-Belgian Border Commission died near Chitambo in 1911.

In 1913 a printing press was established at Chitambo. The type and press came by rail to Broken Hill and then by road. On arrival it was broken and the repairs took some time. By 1919 the 'Everett Press' had printed 500 copies of the four gospels in Chi Bisa-Lala, as well as a Chi Bisa-Lala dictionary and grammar. The whole of the New Testament was eventually printed, the translation having been done by Malcolm Moffat. Miss Irvine revised it later, when she was living at Kalwa. Dr. Hubert Wilson (Livingstone's grandson) contributed by translating the First Epistle of John. He had started language classes on the boat to Africa with a Mr. Charles Stuart. All the school books needed in the district were printed at Chitambo.

Malcolm and Marie lost no time in getting to know the local people. Marie describes a visit to the village of a chiefteness in 1914-

*In one of the villages in the district of Chitambo there is a woman chief, the first I have known in these parts. During a recent visit of examination to some of our out-schools Mr. Moffat and I entered the village. We were received by a number of women, with what I call "the steam-whistle" greeting, a shrill scream they utter when they are pleased about something. We sat down on a mat in the shade of one of the huts. Our two children were with us.*

*Eight old ladies came and sat down at my side, and a crowd of young folk gathered in front. One man sat apart and answered Mr. Moffat's questions, and gave us the general news of the village. After a little more talk he and Bartomeya, the teacher, went to look at the school, and I chatted with the eight old ladies. While we were talking another old dame came along, sat down and greeted me. She joined in the conversation, and said, like the others that she was glad we had come. I liked her face which was benign and capable, and I began to wonder if this were Nanzala. When Mr. Moffat returned he noticed this person, and asked in English if I thought she were Nanzala. The man who had done all the talking did not understand but he caught the word Nanzala and said at once "Yes this is she." We sat down again and Mr. Moffat asked if she were pleased with the teachers. "Yes" she replied heartily and he went on to say he was glad her people were being taught to read God's word and that they now met together on the Lord's Day to worship him. Nanzala clapped her hands and agreed that it was all very good.*

*While Mr. Moffat had been talking, a great commotion had been going on at the other end of the village, and I wondered if all the fowls were rushing about hither and thither, but when we were leaving, a boy came and gave us a fowl as a parting gift. We accepted it and said "Goodbye".*

*Some of the young folks came with us, and a little way out of the village I heard somebody behind me say "Go safely, go safely." I turned, and there was Nanzala bowing and clapping her hands and beaming good-bye.*

*This visitation of the schools was done in October, the hottest month of the year. From the beginning of April to the end of October no rain falls, and one wonders how anything can live through the long burning days, but the trees put forth their young leaves and lovely flowers spring up before a drop of rain falls. The fresh leaves are all shades of red and brown and yellow, the autumn tints at home. They turn to green when the rains come.*

*Here is a specimen day. We left at 8 am, the children in hammocks and Mr. Moffat and I walking. We had to stop during the hottest part of the day. In the sun it was like walking beside a hot oven. When we reached camp about 3 pm, Mr. Moffat drank five big breakfast cups of tea right off! Nothing is so good as tea when one has a real African thirst. After tea we went to a school. The people are keen on learning and they have made much progress. Six years ago there was no written language; the people had no idea of reading or writing; now there are numbers in all the villages around who can read the four Gospels in their own language. Counting in the very simplest form, they find very difficult. I watched a class struggling to add together 12,16,4. The figures were on their slates and one boy of about 14 had "12" for an answer.*

*After the classes were examined, they gathered together for Scripture. They had been learning the 23$^{rd}$ Psalm and it was a pleasure to listen to them repeating it. They knew it by heart, for there was nothing here to perplex their minds—like the white man's way of counting.*

An early visitor to the new Chitambo station was the Rev. J.H Morrison, author of *"On the Trail of the Pioneers"*. He describes Chitambo in 1914:

*The site chosen is on the very summit of the watershed, where the nights are cool and there is an exhilarating sense of space and air. From the roof of the mission house a wide view is obtained over a sparsely wooded country. Five miles away is Moir's Lake,* (later known as Lake Lusiwasi) *most irresolute of waters, named after the most resolute of men (the Moir brothers who started the Lakes Trading Company in Nyasaland). So nicely is it poised on the broad watershed that it oozes out at one end to the Zambezi and at the other end to the Congo.*

*The progress achieved in a few years at the mission is astonishing. A more capable pioneer it would have been impossible to find than Mr. Moffat both by natural relationship as the nephew of Mrs. Livingstone and the grandson of Robert Moffat, as well as by lifelong experience of African life. The plan of the mission station is on bold and ample lines. The various buildings are grouped irregularly. The mission house faces the school and the teachers' huts; behind these are the store and the printing press; to the left the doctor's house and the new hospital. Broad roads lead off in every direction through fields of 'milesi' and 'amasaka', while down by the stream is a carefully irrigated garden. The whole might well have stood for a lifetime of labour, and it supplies a striking illustration of what one capable and vigorous man can do to make the wilderness blossom as the rose.*

*To us at least Chitambo appeared a veritable oasis in the desert, a home of rest for wayworn travellers. Our march had been long and weary, through a fly-infested and hungry land. Often did we think with longing of the brimming pots of milk in the villages around Mwenzo. Food for the carriers was scarce, and our own supplies ran short. Milesi porridge with milk is palatable enough, but when the meal is ground by a native woman at the door of her hut and swept up off the clay floor, it cannot be over-clean, and served with sugar, and-when sugar failed, with marmalade, was anything but appetizing. After these experiences came Chitambo, where we rested under a hospitable roof and enjoyed again the luxury of fresh milk.*

Rev. Morrison goes on to describe his visit to the Livingstone Monument in 1914; Malcolm lent him a bicycle, a guide and a rifle, with instructions on what to do in case of a lion attack!

*"Chipundu! Exclaimed little Irak suddenly, as we struggled up out of a swamp on the east side of Lake Bangweulu. We had just reached the edge of the forest and, passing under a single line of trees, I found myself face to face with the monument. It stands in the centre of a square clearing, the four sides of which, about a hundred yards in length, are marked off with an edging of bricks. The square is hoed clean, and the firm grey soil has the general appearance of fine gravel. The line of squares is broken on the middle of the east side where a broad hoed road, running straight back into the forest for*

200 yards, leads to a little cottage, built as a rest-house for any visitor to the grave. Beside the rest-house are a few native huts for the accommodation of carriers, but they are now half in ruins.

I had no time to take in all this, however, for the moment I stepped into the square with head uncovered, I was furiously set upon by swarms of tsetse fly. I had previously passed through several fly areas, but for rash and fury I had encountered nothing like the flies at the monument. In vain we thrashed about us with leafy branches. They swarmed on us like bees and we were compelled to beat a hasty retreat to the cottage and slam the door. One might write a volume on the plague and peril of the tsetse. Without doubt it is man's deadliest enemy in Central Africa, more hurtful and horrible by far than all the varied tribes of beasts of prey. The tsetse has the persistence of the midge, the gluttony of the bluebottle, the lightning of the cleg, the diabolical ingenuity of the mosquito, with a catalogue of devilish qualities of its own. And now, as the convicted carrier of sleeping sickness, it has been branded with its last title of horror. When will the laggard government sign the warrant for its extermination? When will the preservation of Big Game cease to take precedence over the preservation of human life?

It is the presence of the tsetse that has determined the site of our Chitambo Mission. Reverence for the memory of the dead would have suggested that the mission should be planted near the monument, but regard for the health of the living has led to its being put on the watershed, fifty miles away and a thousand feet higher up. There, on a broad breezy upland, the industry of Mr. Moffat has created at the new Chitambo a thriving missionary centre, which is the real memorial of David Livingstone.

This has led to certain confusion on the map at least. An African village has no permanent site. The so-called Old Chitambo where Livingstone died does not now exist. The chief and his people migrated to the west, and no trace of their village now remains. To the natives this spot is known as Chipundu, and no fitter name could be given, for the tree under which Livingstone's heart was buried, commonly called an 'mvula' tree, is, in the language of the Ilala, a 'chipundu'.

It was late in the afternoon of the second day that we reached Chipundu. The first day was easy-going, for me at least who could pedal for long stretches on the forest path, which went winding steadily downhill. But on the second day we had a weary wrestle through the swamp, where the long grass, as stiff as canes, met over our heads and often completely blocked the way.

*It may have been the fatigue of the journey, or perhaps the sad associations of the place, but as I sat in the cottage, I thought I had never seen the twilight fall so mournfully. Perhaps it was in such twilight that Livingstone wrote in his diary near the end "Nothing earthly shall make me give up my work in despair". One thought of the awful crawl of his last week which brought to a close his mighty wanderings. "April 22<sup>nd</sup>—2 hrs. 23<sup>rd</sup>—1&1/2 hrs. 24<sup>th</sup>—1 hr.; 25<sup>th</sup>—1hr; 26<sup>th</sup>—2&1/2 hrs." A total of 8&1/2 hrs. Less than we had done that day!—Each of these swampy hollows a day's journey.*

*After sunset the young moon silvered the treetops and gleamed on the monument at the far end of the glade. It was interesting to find from the 'Last Journals' that the same crescent moon was looking down on the world the night he died. As the tsetse by this time had retired, I proposed to the carrier boys a moonlight visit to the grave. It was plain the suggestion had no attractions for them. Besides being wholly unromantic, they were tired and nervous too, for lions had recently been troublesome in the neighbourhood, and had mauled a man in broad daylight, not far from the monument. Gallant little Irak, however, took his spear—the same that is now standing in the corner of my study. My faithful Jumari lit the lamp—which he had now carried after me for 800 miles, and with one of the carriers following us, we strolled down the glade. To occupy their minds I began a very round-about paraphrase of the lines—"If thou wouldst view fair Melrose aright, go visit it by the pale moonlight."*

*And certainly the words may be applied with equal truth to Chipundu. The pyramid gleaming like white marble above the dark surrounding cypresses, the still solemnity of the encircling forest, the crescent moon sailing overhead, made an utterly unique and unforgettable picture.*

*It was a perfect night when one would fain have strolled for miles through the dim forest, but the pleasure of a moonlight walk would have been bought at too terrible a risk. In Central Africa night always brings the lurking dread of beasts of prey. So we returned to the cottage, where the boys were already stretched on the floor in sleep.*

*Opening the window I leaned out for a long while, drinking in the cool night air and letting the stillness and vast solitude wrap me round. Just on such a night as this he died. These half-ruined huts, dimly seen in the moonlight might be the very huts built by his men. With but little imagination one could repeople them. Among the dim shadows of the trees a figure moves about, touching one and another into wakefulness, as they lie round the embers of the watch-fires. Then sit up and talk in hurried whispers; they gather about the hut door; fearfully they stoop down and peer in. Alas, it is true! Their great leader is dead. At that moment a light breeze touches the treetops like the passing mutter of an angel's wing. It sends a far-heard whisper through the forest, and one wakens as from a dream. Did ever a human soul pass upward to God out of so vast and terrible solitude?*

*Next morning we were all astir at dawn, and, as the tsetse gives little trouble til towards the heat of the day, we had a delightful half-hour at the monument. Irak, with his spear beside him, conducted the service and acted as interpreter. The service at dawn. "Let us with a gladsome mind Praise the Lord, for he is kind"—which we sang in ChiWisa to the old familiar tune. I loved that boy for the choice of his hymns. Then he prayed. After that I told as simply as I could the story of Livingstone's death, and of his faithful followers; also Scotland's love to Africa and the debt she owed. One could not help but feel a thrill in saying "They buried his heart just here".*

*The little group of carriers sat crouching in front of me very quiet and motionless. How much of the story was penetrating their minds it would be impossible to say, but there were two bright-eyed little lads there, Changwe and Chikumbe, who had followed their fathers on this trip just for the fun of the thing, and had come in, the night before, limping badly but still game and smiling. I am sure when they get home again they would have something to tell.*

*For my own part in the service I sang some verses of the hymn "For all the saints who from their labours rest", explaining it as a hymn which we in Scotland sing when we give thanks for David Livingstone and all such faithful servants of God. Then I closed our little meeting with a prayer. A few moments more and the carriers had shouldered their loads and were striding off, for we had a long day before us. From the edge of the clearing I turned and took a last look. In half a dozen paces the long grass of the swamp had shut out the monument from our sight, but left it, in mind at least, a most holy and imperishable memory.*

*In the cottage I left a book in which the rare visitor to the grave might inscribe his name, a sheet of paper which had previously done duty for a visitor's book, and which contained some interesting names, having unfortunately been destroyed. It is with the utmost pleasure that I have learned, since coming home, that the first names to be inscribed in the book were those of Livingstone's own grandchildren—Dr. and Miss Wilson.*

# CHAPTER 3

# BUILDING ON THE FOUNDATIONS

## KASANKA 2003

The dawn chorus began very early at Kasanka and the first choristers were the hippos. Their sonorous low-pitched grunts and snorts sounded deceptively close. As the sun crept up over Lake Wasa it seemed to thaw the voices of a myriad of colourful birds. It was impossible not to get up and climb the wooden ladder to the camp's viewing platform, to look out over the rooftops to the water's edge for anything that might be moving. The August air was chilly and we were glad of our winter fleeces. From the platform we also had a bird's eye view of the camp staff carrying large buckets of hot water from the 'Rhodesian boiler' to each individual rondavel. One diminutive man would steady the ladder while the other climbed up to empty the water into a yellow plastic tank on the roof, ready for the resident's quick but refreshing shower.

Breakfast was served on the verandah of the lodge, looking out at the lake. Here we met our hostess, Kim Farmer, an Australian radiographer who had worked at Serenje Hospital before she met Edmund, the park manager-cum-pilot and tour-guide. Edmund had flown a tour group to the Luangwa Valley and so Kim was holding the fort. Kim had often visited Chitambo as a radiographer and was able to update us on the situation there. Over Scottish-style oat porridge, we plied Kim with questions about Chitambo.

Since we were not expected there until Sunday 17th August, we decided to spend a few days relaxing, game-viewing and enjoying being together again on Zambian soil. Our game guides were amused by our enthusiasm for the insect life and the familiar fruit-bearing trees. As children we had spent our school holidays roaming the bush around Chitambo and we knew all the wild fruits—such as *masuku, mpundu,* and *yunga.* We 'hunted' ant-lions and kept chameleons as pets (much to the horror of our Zambian friends who regard the chameleon as an evil harbinger!) The 'chongololo' was a large shiny black centipede which seemed to be abundant in the rainy season. There were trap-door spiders, stick insects, stink-bugs, dung-beetles and all sorts of ants. The memories came tumbling over each other, and so did the Lala/Bemba words of our childhood—most importantly the greetings for different times of the day, small exclamations and words of praise or encouragement. The most frequently used greeting—*Mutende* means 'peace be with you.' In making the greeting to someone you meet along the path, you clap your cupped hands together and, if you are a woman, give a little curtsy. Then you make enquiries about the other person's health and that of their children, before parting with more hand clapping and curtsying. It's a friendly society.

We drove out in the Delica van on a morning's game-viewing, forgetting about the dreaded tsetse fly which has a particular predilection for black vehicles. Every time we opened the van door a swarm of the beasts would pour in and then settle near the floor where they would bite our ankles. Fortunately only one in about six million carries the sleeping-sickness parasite. At Fibwe hide we climbed a very long ladder, much to Jasmine's horror, to a viewing platform from which we could see the rare sitatungwe, a small, woolly-coated water-loving antelope. Kudu, eland, impala, reedbuck, and warthogs were abundant. The handiwork of elephants was everywhere, but luckily we did not meet the small and angry herd that was roaming the park terrorizing young German volunteers by stomping past their tents at night and uprooting small trees. An armed guard had been posted at their camp for protection.

On the following day we took a picnic to Lake Waka Waka, in the company of Bethsheba, Kim's young Zambian administrative assistant. She had befriended Jasmine, and plaited her blonde hair Zambian-style. Bethsheba was bored by the camp routine and keen for a change. She persuaded Kim to let her have a day out by offering to 'guide' us.

The road to Waka Waka was a dirt track, but quite passable. It led us tantalizingly past a sign to Chief Chitambo IV's village and the turn-off to the Livingstone Monument. Sadly we had only enough fuel to get to the lake and back, with a little left over for the excursion to Kundalila

Falls the next day. I found this deeply disappointing and would have to wait another five years to visit the monument. Lake Waka Waka was a natural, clean lake free from crocodiles and the scourge of bilharzia, or so we were told. Two young men attended the camp site and kept the place immaculate. There were changing rooms and sheltered picnic areas, and a rowing boat to take us to the other side of the lake. Bethsheba, free of the inhibitions of her ancestors, stripped down to her undies and plunged in to the lake. We splashed and swam, and made garlands of water lilies. Hosts of tiny blue butterflies hovered at the water's edge.

After the picnic we climbed the hill behind the lake and enjoyed the peaceful view. On the return journey Zanna and I decided to walk ahead of the van, while Jo, Jasmine and Bethsheba came along behind us. It was early evening and as the shadows lengthened we became a little anxious about where the others had got to. In the silence of the bush thoughts of leopards flitted through my mind. After what had seemed a long time we heard the welcome sound of the van. At dusk, on our way back into Kasanka something spotted and hairy flashed past the window—probably one of the wild-cat family, a large *civet* or *genet*.

Round the camp fire that evening we exchanged stories with a group from the south of Zambia. Some of them ran a crocodile farm, and were enjoying a much-needed break. Farming in Zambia was a tough way to earn a living. They were lean, leathery and somewhat jaded. A very large moon slid up into the black sky and glimmered on the lake. The dawn chorus was replaced by a cacophony of crickets and frogs. We planned to visit some of our old childhood haunts—Nsalu Caves and Kundalila Falls the following day.

## THE WILSON ERA AT CHITAMBO

From 1912 to 1914, after Dr. Brown's departure, there was no doctor at Chitambo and then two of David Livingstone's grandchildren arrived—Dr. Hubert Wilson and his sister Ruth Mary Wilson. Their appointment, by the Livingstonia Committee of the United Free Church of Scotland on 18th March 1913 coincided with the centenary of Livingstone's birth.

Hubert and Ruth were the children of Livingstone's youngest daughter, Anna Mary. Like his grandfather, Dr. Wilson finished his medical training at Glasgow Royal Infirmary and then took courses at the Eye Infirmary and the Tropical Diseases hospital in Liverpool. Ruth trained in Edinburgh as a nurse and midwife. On one occasion in 1909, in the spirit of his grandfather, Hubert had walked the 44 miles from Glasgow to Edinburgh to visit Ruth. They came to Africa by the 'old' route, setting sail aboard the *Llanstephen Castle* on 14/2/14, down the east coast to Chinde, then up the Zambezi and Shire Rivers to Nyasaland. From Blantyre mission they travelled north to Bandawe, and then to Fort Jameson before crossing the Luangwa Valley to Serenje. While travelling through southern Nyasaland, they met a young school-boy called Hastings Banda—who was later to train as a doctor and become the first President of independent Malawi. The Luangwa crossing was risky on account of malaria, sleeping sickness and possible attack by wild animals. Of the herd of cattle that accompanied them on this journey, all but a few died of sleeping sickness.

Soon after their arrival at Chitambo they were out and about in the district on *ulendo*—visiting neighbouring villages and overseeing the schools.

Dr. Hubert Wilson wrote on 29/12/14 with reference to the *ulendo*-

*It has proved to be unusually pleasant and unusually tiring. Unusually pleasant because we have been in a country of mountains which were meat indeed to the soul, and of rivers, cool, clear and deep which will be a memory that will fade not away for a refreshment for body as well as soul. The work too has been interesting and it has been pleasant to see "ken't faces" in the teachers we found in all the villages. On the other hand the weather has been until today distinctly hot. There seems to be a wide difference in opinion here as to which is the hottest month of the year and I think there are at least 8 in the running for that distinction; But from my experience, I must decide in favour of October (the first of the eight). The heat was accentuated by the complete absence of shade in the villages—so that a midday rest was a season apart in a tent like a baker's oven, lying on a bed in a general sweat. Then we made several early starts, rising at 5.0 a.m. in order to be off by sunrise and these were a tiring beginning to a hot day, lastly to be besieged by crowds of candidates for medicine and then to spend a couple of hours at sundown going after game—well that was the tiring side. We are now landed at a village perched on the brow of a hill with a view like that from Rigg's Hotel at Windermere. The clearing round the school forms a terrace from which one can enjoy by the hour a prospect of mountains far and near—rugged and rounded—all sorts and sizes, and in almost all directions—but as it so happens we have not the leisure to do it.* (Did exploration beckon to Dr. Wilson as it did to his grandfather?)

**What you (AMLW) are to look for out of the fly window as you drive up from the station in April! From N.E.**

### What you (AMLW) are to look for

*We left our last camp at 6.15 this morning, planning to see Mtenje school at 7.0 or thereabouts and come on here (half an hour) to breakfast. However at Mtenje the scholars came out in swarms to welcome us and carry our Machila. The chief and his headmen were posted by the roadside. Then two blocks of women and when we arrived at the school there must have been two or three hundred people as excited as they could be. It was 7.30 so we decided to breakfast after school; Ruth to examine and treat the sick while I examined the sound. We brought a senior teacher from the last village—Jonah by name and he helped me—finally we got through—meantime Ruth had one can hardly say how many patients. However we had to clear them off and sat down to porridge in a quite exhausted condition about 9.0. The next thing was to see a boy with a bad big ulcer on his leg and to wait a quarter of an hour in persuading his papa and mama to send or bring him to the mission. Then the headman wanted us to see yet another case and this we decided to operate on in the afternoon—thinking the next village would be quieter!*

*However, most of Mtenje escorted us up here (about 1 ½ or 2 miles) carrying Ruth in her Machila and such a reception from the Chisaka people. Irak the teacher is clean and smart as a butterfly, and about 20 water pots filled with clean water—and a present for Ruth (from the lady scholars) of flour, about 30lbs and later to me half as much again with beans and peas—and ten eggs from the Headman and more from the teacher and crowds to watch us whether we wrote or washed or cooked or sewed!—And all—fancy this—under a heavily overcloudy sky with a fresh "Zephyr" blowing from the hills: we could go about or write without hats on and what a relief after the heat of the last week.*

*Now I am called to go out hunting as we want to give the people of these two villages a good present of meat.*

Ruth continued-

*I think little work was done in either of these villages yesterday—and in the afternoon we sent the Machila for the patient who came up and had quite a big operation under the eaves of a hut and removed a sarcoma (or cancer) and found things much worse than expected—the immediate operation was very successful and of vast interest to all the village, needless to say! But the low grey clouds were very home-like and refreshing. I think I healed single-handed 50 patients in each village.*

On 10/1/15 Hubert Wilson wrote (to his mother Anna Mary Wilson,) as the First World War began to have its insane effect on southern Africa:

*Our latest guest is a Mr. Gray, who visited us before as a Wesleyan missionary in September. You will hardly recollect our mentioning him: he joined a Mobile Column of Europeans as Chaplain and Ambulance, but was told when they left Broken Hill that he was a rifleman! The column reached to within 10 miles of us last night, their approach having been heralded by a letter from their Intelligence Officer (a Northumbrian Farmer from near Kashitu, called Stephenson) asking us to get 150 fowls and 500 pumpkins, as well as many potatoes, onions, eggs etc. etc. etc. as we could procure. I think exceptional efforts produced 14 fowls, and the pumpkins are not yet "in" being too early in the season. Stephenson turned up himself to lunch with the Moffats and at night having returned to the camp brought back a Corporal Moore (clerk in a mine) and the said militant Gray for the night. We took Gray, clothed him in flannels and set him to a roast leg of reed buck: ma'conscience the man's appetite were 'prodigious', meat tatties, soup, bread, jam and butter fled in such quantities down his receptive throat that had I not been his host I should have felt bound to ask where he concealed it all!*

*There are 105 of them—all whites with 16 spans of 6-18 oxen in each (yes work it out tomorrow morning.) They have each a personal boy, but do all their own road-making, tree-cutting and even water-drawing to the amazement of the natives who see their 'bwanas' doing jobs they never thought a'Mzungu' could or would attempt. They go 10 miles a day and follow the Traction Engines road; tomorrow (or this afternoon) they expect to reach Chanza and we hope to go up and see them there. Major Boyd Cunninghame is in command and seems a fine man and a disciplinarian. The Column is composed of planters, mine men, surveyors, doctors, clerks and a few broken-down wanderers, such as an ex-Mayor of Bulawayo who once possessed thousands of pounds. They sleep in tents or under the wagons.*

*We have been lifting potatoes this week and got some 20 stones. We are giving 5 stones to the Column and the Moffats are giving another couple of stones, as well as a bath of vegetables. Marie (Moffat) has made 10lbs of butter into 19 packets for the 19 messes into which they are divided. They also wanted a milk cow, but neither Malcolm nor I have one that will last more than 6 to 8 weeks.*

*My Fort Jamieson herd, by the way, is now nearly three weeks on the road and we expect them any day. One cow calved the day before leaving, which is unfortunate as it may lose its calf. I hope they will escape the (tsetse) fly and other plagues as they have cost 60 pounds which I cannot afford to lose. 4 others we will make the hospital buy, in order to feed the patients. At present we do it as regards milk . . . of our bounty. Now I finish (this letter) on Monday after visiting Chanza and seeing the sights.*

In Feb 1915 Dr. Hubert Wilson wrote again to his mother, Anna Mary, who was planning to visit Chitambo. He warned her about the culinary delights in store.

11/2/15

*We look to do our best for you in the meat line, but until August shooting is poor owing to the long grass in the dambos. It is quite 6 weeks since I shot anything, but the deaths of our lamented cows have supplied us with a species of beef while an odd duck and a piece of sheep have all helped to keep us in meat in an extraordinary way. Meat is difficult to keep at this time of year and while 'high' game is, to a certain extent, fitting and proper, high braxy beef is less enticing. If you come prepared for every hardship in the gastronomic line, you will, I hope, be agreeably surprised, but if you come anticipating a regular line of butcher meat meals, you will realize with a shock how different is the life of those who have neither shop nor farm at hand to supply their wants.*

*We have had 3 nice inches of rain this week and now the days are cool and breezy, suggesting white-topped waves on the ocean, and a dash of surf on the beach. When I think of these things as I am too apt to do, I decide that my friends must just be content to spend my furlough with me here, for ravishing as would be a visit to Scotland, to leave it again would be impossible!*

*I have been fairly occupied this week paying off the teachers, as they dribbled in from their schools, and taking the fees they had taken from their village scholars. I also gave an hour and a quarter to the Boarders school each forenoon, giving a lecture on the earth, sun, moon and map making. They were surprised to know that the sun and moon were spheres and not circular discs; also that the sun was burning, although at once volunteering that all the moon's light came from the sun. They did not appear to have seen a lunar eclipse but that I suppose is due to their being generally asleep when the phenomenon was in progress. On Thursday, as it was fine and sunny, we went to Chanza with our lunch and shot a single duck, after much wading in the thigh-deep lake. The birds were scarce and shy and my marksmanship poor. Four of the boarders came with us to carry our basket, kettle, gun and waterproof sheet. Since last Sabbath we have had no more deaths among the cattle—for which all thanks—but as one of those I bought from Malcolm is sick, I have enjoyed all the anxieties attendant on these misfortunes and I fear, if we were to be writing for next week, that it would be to chronicle her loss too; she is a nice old thing and somewhat of a pet, loving to have her head and neck scratched and stroked!*

*Ruth is doing famously with the fowls. She lost a nest full of '18 day' English eggs, through a fight among the hens and this was disappointing, but they seem to be laying well now, if eccentrically: an egg is found on the hospital mantelpiece, half a dozen in a seldom-used and nameless apartment and one on the laundry floor. Nothing like variety is their motto I suppose. And we do not object, always we can follow the working of their fancies and recover the eggs.*

Hubert Wilson prepared for his mother Anna Mary's arrival and wrote on 28/3/15

*My Dear Mother,*

*This is to meet you at Cape Town and need not leave for a couple of weeks but next week will be a very busy one with examinations in school and Preparatory services for the Communion added to the usual occupations, and the week after that I start for the Luangwa valley, there to open a school for the teachers in that part of the district, and to try introducing medical work. I shall return in time for Ruth to get off to meet you, at Broken Hill; we have discussed it all ways and this course seems the best. The schools are on in the villages in April and May and as I have introduced a number of changes, to make the work more efficient it would be a most unfortunate session to miss. At the same time if the irregularities of the sailings and trains throws you later than the date we are working for it would (according to their existing plans) mean I would be away from the station (meeting you) when Malcolm had gone to take Marie and the boys down to their train, and this at a time when teachers will be coming in after schools to be paid off etc.etc.*

*In addition there is the domestic side of it, that, inefficient as I am—to leave the house alone-Ruth will be able to make you vastly more comfortable-(in the cooking line especially!), on ulendo, and for me to set off on a 4 weeks trek would prevent the Luangwa journey which is an important one. If I go not Malcolm must and it is hard to ask him to leave his wife and family for ten days or a fortnight so near parting from them for a year or two, especially as the parting is largely on our account. As the Sole charge of the station, if he took furlough now would be a heavy responsibility to us. And so you see there are as many threads interwoven as in a web of tweed and that in a simple life like ours, where, one would have said, one could make (and adhere to) arrangements a year in advance! However I am to take you down when you return—you by that time being so accustomed to the hardships of travelling as to be in no need of extra care! Indeed able to manage for yourself and a linguist without doubt! Ruth will come with 50 men: a reliable Capitao, or responsible one, a capable houseboy with some English, and a stout heart. I will get over as many schools as possible so as not to need to run off when you arrive.*

*This letter should have commenced with a welcome to your own Continent after 56 (is it?) years of absence: no I forgot, Sierra Leone is in the same continent, but in a neglected corner. I am writing to Uncle John*

(John Moffat—Mary Livingstone's brother*) to ask him to advise you as to Cape Town hotels, if you need advice. So if you have not seen him yet, or made your decision, treat him as a papa, for he won't know if he ought to recommend something very cheap or something on Aunt Agnes' scale!* (Agnes was Livingstone's eldest daughter). *And if you are catching a train under his care keep a shrewd eye on your watch! The Moffats have a family disregard for the details of time and Uncle John ran us very close for our boat, so that we had to end in a taxi. You may remember us speaking of it. And do not let him tire you out if you can help it!!*

Anna Mary, born at Kuruman and raised in Scotland, was two and a half years old when her mother left her in the care of relatives and set sail to join the father Anna Mary had never met. She would meet him after the tragic Zambezi expedition but she did not take readily to the strange man with the moustache, nor did she like the black doll he gave her. She would have preferred a white one. She must have had mixed feelings to be finally making this pilgrimage.

Part of our ulendo on Ruth's birthday.
Bath ahead, then tent - taken in part of
the big Lusiwasi dambo. See small ant
hills in process of formation.

**Part of our ulendo on Ruth's birthday**

Anna Mary Wilson duly arrived at Chitambo and was installed in the guest house, later known as 'the cottage'—a single-storey brick house near the hospital. This house was later occupied by many missionaries including my grandparents the Todds, and my family, the Curries, while a new house was being built for us.

**Granny Currie, Gran Todd, Mum with baby Jo, Dad, Grandpa John Todd, Dave and Doug on the steps of 'The Cottage' Chitambo 1953**

It was from the bottom step of the cottage that our grandfather John Todd's dog was snatched one evening by a leopard, while John stood at the top of the steps.

"Missionary Record" of 1915 records the following account of the Wilsons' visit to the Livingstone monument. The piece is entitled *"A Family Gathering at Livingstone's Grave"*.

*As David Livingstone was painfully carried from the Rukara River to Chitambo's village, how great a comfort would it have been to him in his loneliness had he known that his youngest daughter, (Anna Mary) whom he had left at home a little girl, would one day visit the spot in which he was so soon to die, and count it a high privilege reverently to trace his steps and gaze on the scenes which passed unnoticed before his glazing eyes.*

*During the month of July last his grandson, Dr. Wilson, made his headquarters in the rest-house at the monument, having with him eight native teachers whom he was instructing in a senior teachers' school. Part of each day was spent, with the assistance of local workers, in building four huts to replace those fallen into disrepair, digging a well, cutting a road to Chitono's village, and clearing away the bush around the monument. It is of interest, with a view to the ultimate improvement of conditions in the sleeping sickness area, to note that the tsetse flies which swarm in vast numbers round the monument were effectively banished from its immediate neighbourhood by thoroughly clearing a broad belt of 50 yards round about. People coming in from the bush still brought a few flies with them, but they ceased to be the same unbearable nuisance as before.*

*About a dozen villages are accessible from the monument. These were visited at the week-ends and services held by the teachers, while Dr. Wilson gave attention to the sick. On 4th June, Mrs. A.M. Livingstone Wilson arrived at Chitambo Mission Station and in the last week of July she took the opportunity of visiting the place where her father died. Travelling with her daughter (Ruth), she was met by her son at Mulungu on the Lulimala. Those who are familiar with the story of Livingstone's last days will remember that Mulungu is one of the villages mentioned by Susi and Chuma as having been visited for the purpose of securing a canoe and some milk goats for the dying traveller's use.*

*Together the family paid a visit to Chiunda, some 12 miles further upstream, where the Sabbath was spent in attending to the numerous tropical ulcers that abound in the village, holding worship among the people, and resting after four days of tiring travel. Monday night was spent at Chimesi where it is probable that the doctor rested when he wrote the last entry in his daily journal; and on Tuesday morning the Lulimala was crossed, where native testimony agrees that he made the crossing. Two hours later the monument at Old Chitambo's was reached.*

*Surely it was a notable occurrence. Men die in the fond hope that they will be laid with kindred dust, and that some who love them will stand beside their grave and bring them to remembrance. No such hope could have cheered the dying hours of Livingstone. Sundered from his wife's grave by half a continent, and from his family by half the circle of the globe, if he thought about it, he must have concluded that his grave in the depths of the dim forest would be forever unknown to his friends and be trodden down by the careless foot of wild beast . . . Yet the spot has become one of the earth's sacred places, and after nearly half a century his family come to visit and tend it with pious care.*

*The night was spent in the rest-house, and on the following morning Chitono, the headman of the village nearest the monument, came with Chisira, the toothless old blacksmith, to tell what they remembered having seen as young lads, forty-two years ago. They were accompanied by the son and nephew of old Chitambo, but these were too young to have any recollections of the great traveller who died in their village, although they could tell of various interesting visits that had been paid to the old tree before it was replaced by the monument. Old Chitono can be as blank as a stone wall when he chooses. Only last year the writer of these lines vainly questioned him about Livingstone, but his one answer was that he was too young to know anything, while in his wily old head he was saying "why should he give himself away to a mere stranger". And the toothless blacksmith will hardly speak when spoken to, but grimly puffs his goat's skin bellows, while the boys play 'chisolo' beside his forge. But today their hearts were opened and their tongues unloosed. They told the whole story as they had seen it, pointed out the forest paths, showed the site of the hut, and made the whole scene live again.*

*One wonders what passed through these old men's minds as they told their story. Forty-two years ago they were boys, looking with boys' idle curiosity on an old man, spent with travel and sick unto death. Now they are old themselves and see his children's children coming to live among them, full of youth and hope and ardour, and the promise of a lifetime of service. Did they wonder at the magnetic power of that lone grave and the strange things that have come to pass by the dying of him whose heart lies buried there? And did they, perhaps, have some dim and flickering vision of defeat turned to victory and of a spirit triumphant over death? Who can tell?*

**Dr. Hubert Wilson (seated) with the Unwin and John Moffat,
and the Chitambo cowherd**

The Wilsons had barely started work at Chitambo when the First World War broke out. Ruth was the first to be called up, to serve in East Africa while Hubert chose to serve with the Royal Army Medical Corps in Italy and France. The Committee at Mission HQ did not feel quite as certain that he would be serving a more useful purpose, but they did not stand in his way, and so he left Chitambo in 1916 not to return until his demobilization in 1919. This he did with a Military Cross. After the war, in 1920, Ruth married Private Alexander Macdonald, who had arrived at Chitambo shortly after the Wilsons. The couple moved away to the other side of the Luangwa Valley.

The war years were hard for the mission. In 1914 there were 112 teachers in 43 schools. By 1918 there were only 41 teachers with 28 schools. The educational work slumped, but it did continue, thanks to the foresight of Malcolm Moffat who had trained 'monitors' to go back and teach in the villages. Later a further 'brain drain' was caused by the drift of local people to the mines in the Copperbelt. While Chitambo escaped any direct harm from the war, Mwenzo Mission which was close to German-occupied Tanzania was attacked. The story is told of Dr. Chisholm's little daughter, Maisie going missing when people were evacuated from Mwenzo. She was found unharmed in a nearby village where she had been carried by the villagers and looked after until her parents' arrival. Meanwhile a proposal to build another mission named "Ilala" about 60 miles south-west of Chitambo, using funds from a bequest (from Peter McKinnon), foundered, as the funds were needed elsewhere and the area was not considered populous enough.

The First World War stimulated the building of a telegraph system to the north of the country. The wires were simply tacked onto trees, and it seemed to work well enough. An army signal and telegraph post was established at Chansa. The first operator, "Chapman of Chansa" became renowned for his speed and efficiency in sending messages up and down the wire under the most difficult of circumstances. Chitambo Hospital made a bicycle available at Chansa so that anyone needing to get to the hospital in a hurry could cycle that last four miles down the Chansa road!

One of the greatest difficulties for the hospital staff was to get patients to come early enough for treatment. Most people came when they had tried everything else, and when it was too late. This must only have confirmed the impression of the hospital as a place to die. In order to prove that the hospital was not a place of death, Dr. Wilson, on his return from war service, had an idea. He found a boy who had an ulcer on his leg and offered him a shirt if he would come into the hospital to have it treated. This was a great offer as very few other boys owned a shirt, and so the boy came. However, he was frightened at night and told the staff that there were spirits in the hospital, and that he wanted to leave. When Dr. Wilson investigated he found that it was the reflection of the lamp-light in the windows that was frightening the boy. The 'spirits' were banished by pasting The Glasgow Herald over the windows. The boy's ulcer healed and he became one of the hospital's first satisfied in-patients. Ulcers were sometimes treated by means of a simple skin-graft and in time these 'patches' became quite popular.

The 'hospital' was still very basic. One room in a house built for a teacher, was used as a simple operating theatre. Another room was used as a dispensary. A third room was used as a consultation room and a fourth as an isolation ward. In the winter a fire was lit on the floor in the centre of the ward. Glass bottles for medicines and for patients' drinking water were in short supply, and were procured from any passers-by.

Goitre (enlarged thyroid gland) was treated with iodine water, which was given to the patient to take home. The iodine was often passed around the village, and instead of curing the patient, it often created more patients. Malaria and malnutrition were common conditions. The latter was helped with milk from the mission cows. Agriculture and husbandry had been given high priority from the start. The mission herds had been started in 1907 with five cows and two calves. By 1914 there were 35 cows, 13 heifers, 16 calves, 6 bullocks and 26 oxen. There was a bull called Roman, and his offspring were invaluable for pulling ploughs and carrying loads. Mission gardens were planted near the Mabonde stream. Lemon, mango and coffee trees were planted. Pigs and chickens were kept. Mrs. Moffat turned some of the milk into butter. Later on she turned her hand to making cheese as well. The finished cheeses were placed in tins which were weighted down and left on the verandah. On one occasion the cheese was stolen by hyenas amidst a great commotion of clattering tins. Beans were also grown at Chitambo and people brought their millet to Chitambo for grinding. Beans, millet and wheat flour were sold throughout the district, producing a small profit which was used for school uniforms, new buildings and for running the printing press.

The medical work at this time was covered by a grant of 25 pounds a year, with the addition of occasional donations. Dr. Wilson was able to supplement the grant by making visits to Serenje Boma at the request of the District Commissioner to hold outpatient clinics and to treat prisoners.

Building costs were rising. The third house (Anna Mary Wilson's cottage) had cost 500 pounds—a hundred percent rise from the original Moffat house. In spite of all the money-raising schemes, including Malcolm's sale of animal skins, and donations from other stations, times were hard. The mission headquarters could not provide any more assistance as they had extended their activities to the limit and beyond. Internationally the parent church had 18 areas of mission activity on 3 continents, and all of these had more than one station with many outstations.

The building of the church was a major undertaking. Malcolm had been keen to build it since his arrival at Chitambo but had been discouraged by the Foreign Mission Committee who had felt in 1911 that "*The Church and School are not yet approved and sanctioned by the Mission Council and there is a serious difference of opinion as to the wisdom of spending 700 pounds upon a Church at Chitambo Station. This means going against the whole policy of the Mission that the native churches should be built not with the money of the committee but with the gifts of the natives themselves.*" Building was not started until 1919. Malcolm Moffat had trained as a builder at Milngavie in Scotland and he drew upon this course to the full, creating a typically Scottish 'Kirk', with local materials and the labour of the African people. Malcolm often located suitable timber when on *ulendo*. A large saw-pit was dug, where the wood was cut into 60 pound loads to be carried to the building site. The bricks were made and burnt at Chitambo.

**Chitambo church built 1919**

The church still stands today (2013). The original high, tiled roof has been replaced by galvanized iron, and the interior has been painted many times. It is currently bright blue and white. Above the altar a frieze of Jesus and the disciples at the last supper has been painted, but Peter's head is obscured by a large red-rimmed clock. Some of the roof beams look perilously close to collapsing. Bats cling to the highest beams and their squeaks, and the faint smell of bat prevail during church services as they did in our childhood.

The mail came from Broken Hill, (now Kabwe) and was brought by postmen on bicycles—a distance of about 300 km (about 230 miles). The postmen were sometimes attacked and killed by lions. The mail was often badly mutilated as well. In these early days there was a lot of game in the Chitambo district including leopards, lions and hyenas. The mission staff carried guns with them when they visited each other's houses at night for this reason. When they went on *ulendo*, they hunted game for meat for themselves and their porters. These early journeys were usually on foot, or by bicycle, and were great opportunities for learning the language and customs of the people.

During 1920 a pride of lions caused a great deal of trouble by killing cattle. A trap was set by connecting a trip-wire to the trigger of a gun and tempting the lions into the right position by tying up a live goat. This method killed one lion on the first night and a second lion set off the device by knocking it with his tail when he jumped over his dead companion. Two more were killed and another wounded in this way. It was thought that Chitambo was on a migration route for lions making their way to the Luangwa Valley.

Dr. Wilson was the first person to bring a motor car to the mission. In order to collect his car from the settlement of Chifwefwe, down the Great North Road, he was given a lift by a Peter Stephenson, the brother of local legend Chirupula Stephenson, kindly and eccentric administrator of the Mkushi district and builder of roads. Born in Sunderland and trained as a telegraphist, Chirupula Stephenson had arrived in Blantyre, Nyasaland, via Kimberley and Bulawayo. He met his first wife, Loti, of the Ngoni tribe, in Blantyre. He paid ten shillings for her. He had many wives from different tribes, including the daughter of a Lala chief, and some of his children attended school at Chitambo, while he and his wives kept the hospital busy.

Dr. Hubert Wilson gives an account of life and work at Chitambo in "Driving in the Wedge at Chitambo—a Medical Mission sketch"-

*The sun is baking the station until the houses shimmer and quiver in the bright light. The calves have sought what shade the small trees afford, and the young cow-herd is fast asleep nearby, while the fowls are entrenched in dusty holes under the coffee trees round the house. Everything is very still, for it is the hour of noonday.*

*Suddenly there sounds out the distant notes of the school bell warning the boys of the approach of two o'clock, when, hoe in hand, they must go out to their afternoon's manual work; And as if it were a summons to announce to visitors our re-awakening, it is no sooner sounded than a little cavalcade appears wearily coming up the straight, hot sandy road. Something is being carried by two men at a slow jog-trot. What is it? Meat shot by someone, sent into the station? Is it a double load finishing its long journey up from the railway? No it looks more like a human being, and the carriers appear to be strangers. Between them is a pole, supported on their shoulders, from which is slung a rough net of bark-rope containing a huddled black figure.*

*As they turn up towards the verandah, the dog, galvanized into activity springs to her feet to bark out a sharp alarm, and before the burden is laid down we are going down the verandah steps to see who it is that has come. It is an old man, thin, skinny and no longer comely. A tuft of hair on his chin is whitening with age, and his wrinkled brow betokens a long and weary struggle—a life of fear and trouble.* He looks up with a supplicating gesture, in which fear and something approaching dislike are mingled with mute entreaty, but in a moment the shifty dark eyes moved away and turned to his leg, the lower half of which is covered with a most objectionable piece of ancient blue calico.

His two carriers—nephews, they tell us—having wiped off the sweat with which they are bedewed, and drunk a calabash of water obtained from our houseboys, assume the role of showmen, and, mingled with pride and solicitude, untie the fibre string . . . . The flies are brushed aside, and there is exposed a large dry leaf covering an irregular, ugly hole in the old man's leg, to which it is stuck by a mixture of dear knows what concoction of native medicine and cow's dung.

He is a patient from a village on the outskirts of the district away over the Congo Border. For five and a half days the two nephews have carried him, impelled less by the love for their relative, be it understood, than by fear of what might be murmured against them by ill-wishers if he were to die on their hands.

The hospital is already full. The ten beds with which it is accredited in the Annual Report have been made to accommodate twice as many patients, for such elasticity is easy in a country where the sick prefer in many cases to lie on mats under rather than on the bedsteads! An orderly has removed the outer coverings of the ulcer all neatly arranged about him on old pages of the Glasgow Herald. Gently he begins to soften the caked mass, and how patiently those fingers work! By degrees the ulcer becomes visible, and in time it is thoroughly cleaned, and covered up with an antiseptic dressing (for it is 1920 and antibiotics are not yet invented). *The foul old rubbish is then picked up between two sticks and carried over to be burnt in a pit nearby. The proceeding has been watched by an observant group of boys all in hospital, also on account of ulcers, which are now healing and painless. Sitting round in a circle, they follow each step of the operation with whispered comments, or loud reasonings with the new patient if he complains or looks afraid.*

Outside, under a shelter in the sunshine, sits a little group of decrepit men who make no effort to join their fellows because they are lepers. Hopeless cases they would have been a few years ago. Recent discoveries have altered their outlook, and now, amazingly improved, they look at life in a changed light. We could fill our hospital with such cases but the treatment is costly *and we cannot use up our entire yearly grant on one little section of suffering humanity.*

*Meantime on the verandah of the women's ward, a lively colloquy is in progress, for the lady patients are entertaining the old man's wife to a fire of questions about her journey and her husband's sore, and much else to which we cannot listen. To all of which she replies with dull monotonous apathy, for life is a drab affair to her, and besides she is weary and has a headache, for which she has bound a fibre cord around her brow. Presently she will ask 'Mr. James' (medical orderly) to give her some medicine and he will come up to the house to report that she has a temperature of 103 degrees and that he wants to know what to give to her.*

*Tomorrow she will be better and will be sitting outside again, preparing, for her husband's delectation, some leaves which she has collected, and which when boiled, he will enjoy with porridge. Maybe she has recognized in them a plant with what she has heard has healing virtues. She thinks it will do the old man no harm to have the benefit of it, in addition to the white medicine. For it seems strange to her that the European doctor, who is accredited with amazing powers of driving evil spirits out of the sick, has never given her man anything to swallow for this purpose. And were he not to improve very soon, these thoughts would germinate into questionings, doubt, distrust, even dislike and she might eventually infect his mind with her forebodings, so that they would disappear one morning, believing that the white man's heart has not been good towards them and that he had failed to do all that he could have done to drive out the evil spirit that had caused the disease.*

John Howie was responsible for constructing the water supply for Chitambo. At first water had been brought from the river by two small boys carrying drums. Howie built 'the furrow' from the Mabonde Stream to channel water into the Chitambo mission. He started farming classes and he tried to introduce a new type of hoe, which was not very popular. He was a rather dour man, and it was said that he deliberately kept the road from Chitambo to Chansa on the Great North Road in poor condition to discourage visitors. Dr. Wilson, on the other hand, had many visitors, including family members and friends from other parts of the country. Members of the Moffat family were welcome visitors, and there were fleeting visits from Sir Stewart Gore-Brown of Shiwa Ngandu (described in Christina Lamb's Book *The Africa House*). Sir Stewart was reputed to be 'always in hurry.'

The Moffats had employed a young boy named Duncan as a 'houseboy' in 1920. He was one of six staff—*house-boy, bed boy, cook, kitchen boy and two garden boys*—according to Duncan. One of his main tasks in those days was to fetch water from the Mabonde stream, a journey of about half a mile each way. He usually made six trips a day. By 1925 an ox-drawn cart was introduced for carrying drums of water. After the Moffats' retirement, Duncan stayed on, working for many of the other doctors.

Dr. Hubert Wilson went home to Scotland in 1922, married and came back with his wife, Rhoda (nee Mackie) in 1923. Mrs. Wilson started a primary school on the verandah of their house and helped with the Sunday school. Two of their children—David and Elspeth were born at Chitambo in 1925 and 1927 respectively. In 1927 the family returned to Scotland to be close to his mother Anna Mary, and Dr. Hubert Wilson worked as a GP in Dundee for the next 20 years, while writing a biography of his grandfather.

## MALCOLM MOFFAT'S RETIREMENT

Malcolm Moffat, pioneer, missionary and minister, who never gained the fame or notoriety of Chirupula Stephenson, quietly worked away at Chitambo, and was made President of the National Missionary Conference in 1927. He retired from the mission in 1930 but he moved only a short distance away to the farm at Kalwa, where he continued to grow crops and exert a peaceful influence

Sir Herbert Stanley, the first governor of Northern Rhodesia had once stayed with the Moffats at Chitambo, on his way up the Great North Road, in the 1920's, when Malcolm was beginning to think of retirement. Malcolm had considered retiring to Scotland, but he was persuaded by the local people to settle among them. He decided to find a small piece of land where he could farm and also continue some missionary work. Sir Herbert Stanley instructed the Director of Lands to grant to Malcolm "such lands as were necessary". A long journey was undertaken to look for a suitable place and eventually a site on the Kalwa River was chosen. "Kalwa" became the Moffat farm.

Clearing of the site started in 1928. Bricks and tiles were made and burnt locally, and mortar was made from mud and sand. Local trees provided the timber. The house had a spacious verandah at the front and an enclosed courtyard at the back. Separate buildings housed the farm machinery, and the workers had the best housing of its time in Northern Rhodesia. The Moffats lived at Kalwa from 1931, their main house being completed in 1934, and a small church completed in 1936.

**Malcolm and Marie Moffat 1931**

Marie continued making butter and cheese, while Malcolm kept cattle and planted orchards of guava, lemon, orange, tangerine, pomegranates, paw-paw and banana trees. He grew strawberries, grapes, cypress trees and great clumps of bamboo, alongside Old English roses. Water was brought to the house by a furrow from the Bucheche River, a tributary of the Kalwa. The furrow then ran on to irrigate the farm.

Proximity to the Great North Road meant that there were plenty of visitors, and Moffat hospitality became widely known. Enigmatic lady doctor Hope Trant, who intrigued us as children with her collection of somewhat aggressive colobus monkeys, was travelling north to Mbeya when her car broke a spring. The Moffats entertained her for two days while Malcolm repaired the broken spring. Buses and lorries from Kitwe to Abercorn sometimes stopped at Kalwa, and the passengers were refreshed by tea and buns from the Moffats.

Malcolm continued to teach farming methods to local people, and to encourage other local industries. He tried to improve housing and to encourage co-operation in all areas of life. His youngest son Robert was married to Margaret in the church at Kalwa on 2nd June 1939 with Malcolm officiating. When Malcolm Moffat died on Christmas Eve 1939, at the age of 69, he was mourned by many. He was buried a hundred yards from the house, on the banks of the Bucheche River. It was said of him by the local people, after his death *"He was a saint"* and *"He brought us the light".* After his death Miss Irvine lived at Kalwa for a year while revising the Chi Bisa-Lala New Testament.

There are six graves at Kalwa-

1. Malcolm Moffat
2. Marie Elizabeth(4/1/34, daughter of Sir John and Lady Peggy Moffat, aged 2)
3. Marie Moffat, Malcolm's wife
4. Malcolm and Marie's eldest son, Unwin together with his wife Sheila
5. Malcolm and Marie's youngest son, Rob Moffat together with his wife Margaret
6. One of the Moffats' faithful workers ba-Jonathan Nyirenda

For a while Kalwa was used by the Ministry of Agriculture for various projects, including growing coffee. It stood empty for several years but was used by friends for holidays, or as a retreat centre. Later still it was used as a conference centre for staff or students of the Malcolm Moffat teacher training college at Serenje. Finally in 1971 it was given to the Baptist Mission of Zambia and renovated by Rev. T. Waddill who came from the U.S.A. The intention was to restore it as a mission and agricultural centre. When it was taken over by the Waddills, old Peter Mupeta, a former employee of Malcolm Moffat still guarded the house and the memory. The fabric of the house has deteriorated and the furnishings have long since been removed, but the memory of Malcolm Moffat has not faded.

At Christmas 2012 a stone was erected at Kalwa to the memory of Malcolm and Marie's second son Sir John and his wife Lady Peggy Moffat who died and are buried in New Zealand.

## CHITAMBO 1930-1950

After Malcolm's retirement, John Howie returned to take charge of the mission. This responsibility was shared with Miss Irvine, the mission teacher. She ran the girls' school and she taught Chi-Lala to new missionaries. She had started out at Kondowe in 1907 and was fluent in Chi-Tumbuka. Her task as language teacher was not an easy one, but it was crucial, as the early missionaries were obliged to spend a concentrated period of time in language study before starting any other work.

By 1928 the Everett Press began to publish a tri-monthly newspaper known as 'Ilyashi' (meaning talk, chit-chat, rumour gossip or conversation). The editor was Rev. Hewitt of the Anglican mission at Fiwila, in the Mkushi District, but the printing was done at Chitambo, in a spirit of inter-denominational co-operation that would have pleased Livingstone. Ilyashi, in fact, had a wide circulation including the Roman Catholic 'White Fathers', and the Dutch Reformed Church of Broken Hill. The first printing went to a thousand copies and in November 1928 1,209 copies were produced. After this the circulation began to fall and by January 1930 only 596 copies were printed. After 1931 it disappeared into oblivion. Its demise was thought to be due partly to its cost and to the limited number of literate people remaining in the district. The Press then moved to Mwenzo where it was used to produce hymn books and a Bemba grammar. From Mwenzo it moved to the Malcolm Moffat Teacher Training College at Serenje where it was used for letter-heads and other administrative items. A national paper, 'Mutende' (meaning 'good health', and 'peace') was on sale at Serenje Boma from 1935, and continued to be published until 1952.

By the 1930s there was a motorable road from Broken Hill to the Tanzanian border, and a hotel at Mpika, a little further north east from Chitambo. The mission had a Ford V 8 and most of the sisters had bicycles. The hospital now had 20 beds and was treating up to 17,000 patients a year.

Dr. Beveridge ran the hospital until 1935. Born at Roseneath in Dunbartonshire, Scotland, on 3rd March 1906 to Rev. and Dr. Beveridge, he made up his mind at an early age to follow in his mother's footsteps. He was educated at George Watson's College in Edinburgh and graduated from Edinburgh University in 1929. After a housemanship in Barnsley and a short stint in Glasgow he set sail for Africa as a medical missionary. The Beveridges are mentioned in a letter by Herbert Gerrard, missionary in Zambia and then Kenya. He and his wife Doris called in at Chitambo in June 1934. In his book *"Africa Calling"* their son, John Gerrard writes of his parents *After breakfast with Dr. and Mrs. Beveridge they were shown round the mission comprising a girls' school with dormitories, a church and a hospital—all of brick with tiled roofs. Wherever they went they noted that Scottish missionaries were very good builders.* Dr. Beveridge resigned from the mission field in 1935 and went back to Scotland where he took his Diploma in Public Health in Glasgow. He returned to work in the City Health Department in Salisbury, Southern Rhodesia. In 1937 he submitted the following Chitambo case history to the British Medical Journal:

### Puerperal Inversion of the Uterus

*Sir,—I was greatly interested to read in the Journal in January 30 (P 220) of a case of actual puerperal inversion.*

*In my practice as a medical missionary in Northern Rhodesia I was called, in December 1933, to see a patient—an African native woman of 19 years of age. Eight hours before I saw her she had been delivered of a 6 lb. male child; this was her second baby, her first being eighteen months of age. I strongly suspected that the placenta had been delivered by traction on the cord, although the native midwife strenuously denied this, rather too strenuously in my opinion.*

*When I saw the patient she was suffering from a very mild degree of shock and from slight haemorrhage. The uterus was completely inverted; the fundus presented outside the vulva, and the cervix was low down in the vagina. That portion of the uterus lying outside the vulva was caked with dust from the mud floor of her hut. Under chloroform anaesthesia the uterus was thoroughly cleansed and well swabbed with iodine, and was then gradually, and with extreme gentleness, reduced. No further treatment was given and, unfortunately I was prevented from seeing her the next day. Forty hours after the operation of reduction I was more than a little surprised to see her standing on my veranda. She had walked twelve miles to thank me for curing her. There were no signs of sepsis, temperature 97.8F, pulse 72 and the uterus was felt by abdominal palpation to be in the normal position. From the time when the inversion of the uterus had been rectified she had a perfectly normal puerperium. Nine and a half months later she delivered a full time child, the confinement being, in every respect normal.*

*The most striking points in this case were the comparatively slight amount of haemorrhage and shock and the complete absence of sepsis. Incidentally, in my four and a half years' experience among the natives of Northern Rhodesia I have never come across any puerperal sepsis.—I am etc.*

*T. Morris Beveridge.*

Then for five years there was no doctor at Chitambo until the arrival of Dr. Cohen in 1940.

Dr. Joseph Cohen was born in London. As a young man he worked for three years as a missionary with the Barbican mission to the Jews in London. He studied Medicine in Edinburgh, graduating in 1938. He worked as a resident house officer at the Western General Hospital in Edinburgh and at the Livingstone Dispensary, in the Cowgate, Edinburgh. This Dispensary, set up in 1890 as a medical tribute to the work of David Livingstone, was a training ground particularly for doctors who were planning to work overseas or in poor communities. Incidentally the Livingstone Dispensary later became incorporated into the first University General Practice teaching unit in Britain. In 1939 Joseph married Maybeth Leyden at Rosewell parish church near Edinburgh. Maybeth had trained as a nurse at the Edinburgh Royal Infirmary, completing her training in 1937.

They offered their services to The United Church of Scotland and must have been posted to Chitambo in about 1940, although the records are scanty. The birth of their first son was announced in the Scotsman newspaper dated September 13th 1941: At Chitambo, North Rhodesia, to Dr. and Mrs. Cohen (Maybeth Leyden) a son, both well. Subsequently Dr. Cohen disappears from the records, but reappears as Dr. Collins, practising at Roan Antelope Hospital in Luanshya in the Copperbelt. Perhaps the Chitambo life was too isolating, or the mine hospital lured him with a better salary. Maybe it was easier to create a new identity in a larger town.

The spiritual side of the mission was still flourishing, with 17 evangelists, 12 elders, and over a thousand church members, under the watchful eye of Rev. John Howie. Miss Irvine and Rev. Howie worked together for nine years until Miss Irvine's departure in 1945.

Further north at Lubwa mission David Kaunda and his wife Ellen were involved in missionary work. David had trained as a minister at Livingstonia at the same time as Malcolm Moffat. After David's death in 1932 his wife Ellen was sent as the missionary representative to the national conference. In this way the Church of Scotland prepared to hand over responsibility to local people.

Their son Kenneth was born and educated at Lubwa mission school (although the Mwenzo people claim him as theirs!) Of his childhood, Kenneth Kaunda later wrote *"My parents gave me the name Buchizya", meaning "the unexpected one", for I was born in the 20th year of their marriage, the eighth in the line of children, three of whom died young. I was born in 1924 at Lubwa in the hills of the watershed between the great Luangwa and Chambezi rivers. My father David Kaunda was the first African missionary to be sent by the Livingstonia Mission of Nyasaland in 1904 to the Bemba-speaking people of the Chinsali district of Northern Rhodesia."*

Another example of African progress into responsible positions was seen in the person of Simon Vibeti, who had been trained at Loudon mission in Nyasaland and had worked as a teacher in the days of Malcolm Moffat. By 1938 he held the position of school supervisor and earned a salary of 30 pounds a year, which was more than double the wage earned by most Africans at that time.

Less encouraging was the closure of the boys' school at Chitambo because of discipline problems, and the temporary closure of the girls' school due to the frequent illness of the missionary teacher, Mrs. McCullough, who had to go home in 1936. From 1931 Chitambo had been authorized to conduct weddings. The first European wedding there was between a Miss Robertson and a Mr. Lowndes. In 1936 Malcolm Moffat officiated at the wedding of a Miss Ross and a Mr. Burnett.

In 1945, two years after Penicillin had been launched on the world market, Dr. Cohen was replaced by Dr. Mackay—who was the best student of his year in Glasgow. A keen academic, he was also a writer of articles to the British Medical Journal and had his case studies published.

Here he writes, in 1948, about a distressing condition:

## Cancrum Oris among African Natives

The classical description of Cancrum Oris as given by Christian (1938) is that of a rapidly progressive gangrenous stomatitis in a child already debilitated by another disease, usually one of the exanthemata. Varying treatments are advised but the prognosis is regarded as hopeless, though Thomson and Findlay (1933) state that occasional recovery does take place. Tidy (1939) states that death is almost invariable. All authorities seem agreed that the probable cause is a combination of organisms similar to that found in Vincent's angina—i.e. spirochaetes and fusiform bacilli. The fact is stressed by all writers that that cancrum oris is essentially a rare disease, though I have been unable to find any actual incidence figures.

## Observations in Africa

During the years spent as a student, house surgeon and general practitioner I did not encounter a single case of cancrum oris in Britain, despite the fact that the whole of this period was spent in a highly industrialized area where the children were often poorly nourished and often lived in unhygienic conditions. In contrast, in less than three years in the Serenje District of Northern Rhodesia we have come across no fewer than five cases. In the years 1945-7 cancrum oris patients constituted 0.7% of admissions. In no case has there been a previous history of a specific illness. It would seem, therefore that the main aetiological factors responsible for this comparatively high incidence are the bad diet of the African native and his unhygienic mode of life.

It is also worthy of note that the probable causal organisms of cancrum oris are similar to those which are almost invariably found in tropical ulcer, a disease that is always present among the people of this district. Of the five cases seen three were fatal. Of the two who recovered one was treated by extensive resection of the gangrenous area, followed by plastic repair; the other was treated with Penicillin. As favourable results were obtained by Penicillin therapy in cases of Vincent's angina it seemed natural to hope that similar results might follow the use of penicillin in cancrum oris. The rarity of the disease, however, seems to have made it difficult to procure reliable information. The Chitambo case indicates that cancrum oris should join the group of conditions classed as highly responsive to penicillin therapy. It was astonishing to see a condition *so notoriously fatal, and which had already killed one member of the family, respond so rapidly to Penicillin, supported only by the simplest local measures.*

The new doctor stayed just three years. In 1948 he resigned from mission service and went to Barotseland and then Pakistan. In 1973 he became deputy director of the Ross Institute of Tropical Hygiene in London. He died in office, aged 61 in 1981. Interestingly, his obituary in the British Medical Journal states that he was a Roman Catholic. This did not appear to impede his appointment to Chitambo.

Another period without a doctor followed. Then in 1949 a Malawian Medical Assistant by the name of Grant M'Kandawire arrived from a much more lucrative post in Tanganyika. He was to be a very long-serving and valuable member of hospital staff, staying on until the late 1960's. Also in 1949 Chitambo acquired Miss Agnes Campbell, from Lubwa, as Matron of the hospital. The minister in charge at Chitambo from 1948 was the Rev. Bill Bonomy. He took responsibility for the educational and pastoral work, taking over the latter from Revds. Siwale and Mushindo. In the late 1940s a secondary school was started. There were now a total of 33 schools, with 74 teachers and over 3,000 pupils.

The Church of Scotland Foreign Mission Committee (FMC) was now involved in some heated discussions with the missionaries of Northern Rhodesia about consolidating the medical work. The church was having difficulty with the running costs of hospitals, and the FMC suggested choosing one mission hospital in NE Northern Rhodesia for upgrading. While these deliberations were going on my grandfather, Dr. John Todd had started work at Lubwa. Inspired by the example of old Dr. Laws, he had originally been a missionary doctor at Livingstonia, in Nyasaland, where his two children, Nancy (my mother) and Bill were born. Sadly his wife (Jean Whyte Barclay) developed breast cancer in her early thirties and they returned to Scotland, where she died in 1937.

In 1938 he remarried—to Jean Welch, who was working as his practice receptionist in Renfrew. Nancy was training as a nurse at Glasgow's Victoria Infirmary when the Todds invited a Dr. Hamilton Currie to tea. 'Milton' Currie was completing his medical training at the Glasgow Royal Infirmary. Having been born in Blantyre, Nyasaland, where his father was a mission printer, Milton was keen to return to Africa. To the shy young doctor Nancy appeared as *a 'vision of loveliness'*, and after his posting to South Africa he courted her for three years by letter before proposing. In

1948 the Todds sailed for South Africa with Nancy on board, to meet Milton and to see whether she truly wanted to marry him.

The wedding was held in Umtata, in the Transkei, South Africa. The Todds left Nancy at her new home at Sulenkama mission hospital, and travelled north to Lubwa, where John helped re-design the hospital and start a training school for medical orderlies. This was Jean Todd's first taste of Africa and she rose to the challenge, assisting John in whatever way she was required.

Of their journey John wrote *From Sulenkama we travel about 1600 miles north into the Northern Province of Northern Rhodesia to our station and hospital at Lubwa. Lubwa is about 450 miles from Broken Hill where we leave the train, buy a car and travel the 450 miles under our own steam. Broken Hill is also our shopping centre for the next three years. Lubwa first received the gospel in 1905 when an African missionary David Kaunda crossed the dangerous Luangwa Valley from Nyasaland. In 1913 Lubwa was started as a mission station by Mr. McMinn. Lubwa is a beautiful station with a large school (primary to teacher training), a beautiful church and hospital, and splendid houses, mostly built by the Rev. Dr. D.M. Brown. Our houses are on the side of a hill 80 feet up and overlooking the treetops away into the dim distance-over the Chambesi Valley. The doctor has to be physician and surgeon, plumber, engineer, architect and builder . . ."* John Todd turned his hand to all these skills, and more. He was no stranger to hard work and improvisation. His grandfather had been a coach builder and his father a chemist. John had an aptitude for mechanical tasks as well as medicine. His years in the Royal Flying Corps in the First World War, as one of Scotland's ACE pilots, had tested his skills to the limit.

The Todds' time at Lubwa was formative in many ways. Jean learned the art of being a missionary wife. There were many lessons to be learned from the way "Ma Brown" did things. Scones, for example were made 'just so' and the ingredients were carried out on *ulendo* along with an iron griddle that could be placed over the camp fire. Another *ulendo* luxury was a wooden 'throne' which was placed over the camp long-drop to allow a modicum of dignity while in the field. John carried a gun and shot game meat for the porters in the tradition of all the earlier missionaries. Jean was made Scout Mistress for the Luangwa region—a vast wilderness encompassing much of the present-day game reserve. She could also help out at the hospital if called upon, and she was quick to learn the skills of nursing and medical assisting. The people of Lubwa gained confidence in the '*dear old man*' (so named on account of his hair having turned prematurely white) and they begged the Todds to return after their first tour of duty.

In a letter addressed to The Regional Secretary of the Church of Scotland, the Lubwa training School Staff wrote "Sir, *we most humbly ask you if you are as we perceive at the helm of the Committee, to steer to us our Dr. Todd once more. If it is possible, let him when it is that he must find his last resting place, find it here! During these few years that he has stayed with us here, he has effected great reforms. More than we can explain in words, there is the hospital itself self-explaining our request. He has transformed the whole hospital—it is now our Eden. More important than the outward appearance, the rate of deaths has amazingly decreased, and because of that the number of patients is increasing daily which is a very important effect on our people because they have through his services realized the goodness of the hospitals. Serious cases have come from far and near leaving many of the government hospitals.*"

But Mission HQ had other plans. The Todds were needed at Chitambo.

**John and Jean Todd on their way to Chitambo**

# THE ROAD TO CHITAMBO 2003

Having had a few days of relaxation at Wasa camp we were keen to spread our wings and venture further afield in the Chitambo area. Packing a picnic and donning shorts, *'tackies'* (trainers) and sunhats we set out in the van, with the intention of heading up the Great North Road to Nsalu Caves and then south east again to the Kundalila Falls. We were light-hearted and confident now that our trip was shaping up as well as, or better than we had expected.

Before we reached the Chitambo turn-off we passed the one-roomed post-office at Kanona, the relay station for all incoming mail to Chitambo, all those Christmas and birthday gifts of long ago, not to mention the eagerly-awaited letters from far-flung people of the opposite gender. A large canvas bag of mail would be delivered to Chitambo on a Wednesday afternoon and would be sorted on our living-room floor. Then the lucky recipients would retreat behind closed doors to savour their booty. Even now I can think of few pleasures as great as receiving a letter bearing foreign stamps.

And then we were at Chansa, the little settlement before the Chitambo turn-off. There was a small shop here—stuffed with everything from bicycle inner-tubes to sacks of mealie-meal, flour, batteries, and rolls of brightly-coloured *citenge* material. In front of the shop were stalls where women sold bundles of sweet potatoes, pumpkins, tomatoes and hands of green bananas. Feeling self-conscious in our shorts, we emerged from the van with our swimming-towels wrapped around our waists, and greeted the stall-holders. A lively conversation ensued when it was discovered that we were 'the ones' that the minister was expecting on the following Sunday. A young man told us that he would send a message to Rev. Chilongo to tell him that we had indeed arrived and that we would be at Chitambo on 17th August.

Now we had at least to look at the turn-off, and so it was that we found ourselves, towel-wrapped and wind-blown standing by a rusting and battered sign 'Chitambo Hospital, Ministry of Health, 7 km'. Tantalizingly close to but in no way prepared for visiting Chitambo we decided to spend the day at Kundalila (Cooing Dove) Falls. The Nsalu Caves were further north and we were unsure how far our petrol would take us. The nearest filling station was at Serenje, 150 km away.

The Falls were clearly signposted and we turned east, off the Great North Road onto the familiar single-track dirt road which led past a village, towards the edge of the great Luangwa Valley. Our arrival at the turn-off was noticed by the villagers, and it was here that we encountered the only unfriendliness of our stay in Zambia. A young boy aged around 11 pulled down his trousers and 'flashed' at us amidst a group of giggling children shouting taunts. The road took a direct route over undulating countryside, and sometimes we were driving on granite, then sand. At the tops of the hills there were views out across the valley to the distant haze. So far nothing had changed in the time we'd been gone, but we expected to find the Falls 'spoiled'.

We reached a wooden barrier and a gate-keeper's hut. A middle-aged man dressed in a National Parks uniform emerged from the hut. There was form-filling and the issuing of tickets. A tiny sum of money changed hands, then the gate swung open and we were in the familiar parking and camping area. There were no other cars, but two young boys hovered nearby and asked if they could 'look after' the van. We decided that this might be a good idea, and they took up their positions. We unloaded the picnic bag and set off down the path towards a foot-bridge across the river. The bridge looked recently—made of slender trees lashed together. Butterflies hovered in the spray of the rushing water. The falls rumbled in the back-ground. We squealed and hooted, dancing crazily across the bridge.

The scene that met us was unbelievable. Nothing had changed at Kundalila, save the appearance of a thatched and discretely screened pit latrine. The natural deep, clear pool in a bend in the river beckoned. Water-lilies bobbed near the opposite bank. Out on the plains beyond the pool stood the familiar cluster of palm trees, planted perhaps by Arab slave traders of long ago. We egged each other on to take the first plunge. Even in the late morning sun the water was breath-stoppingly cold. Soon we were all in and time seemed to stand still.

**L to R: Zanna, Marion, Jasmine and Jo at Kundalila 2003**

We picnicked on a granite outcrop overlooking the body of the falls. Beyond the faint spray at the falls' edge the mysterious Luangwa Valley beckoned in the distant blue haze. Zanna climbed out on a ledge to get good shots of the falls—one of the most beautiful and least-frequented sites in Zambia. We each wandered off in search of a quiet spot from which to revisit the memories of family outings here. Then we climbed down to the bottom of the falls and braved a plunge in the deep dark pool which had always scared us as children. All that we missed was a billy-can and some real camp-fire tea. It was very difficult to leave Kundalila with its many happy ghosts.

The sun was sinking when we finally tore ourselves away. Zanna had run on ahead and we were to pick her up along the road. Jo and Jasmine were busy making water-lily garlands. By the time we reached Zanna she was distraught at having been out there for so long, in her running shorts, with less than friendly villagers staring at the unusual sight. A subdued atmosphere set in and we wended our way back to Wasa camp at the end of an otherwise perfect day.

# THE TODDS AT CHITAMBO 1952

On 14th November 1952 the Todds were officially welcomed by the Chitambo community. The hospital had been without a doctor since Dr. Mackay left in 1948. Sister Agnes Campbell and Mr. Grant Mkandawire had been holding the fort. In a moving ceremony the Todds' work at Lubwa was acknowledged and their return to Chitambo was greatly appreciated. Their remit was to provide medical services while building a 'proper' hospital. To this end John Todd had been very busy while on furlough in Scotland. His own account of the process explains it best-

### *How to build and equip a modern 70-bed hospital in Central Africa for 6,000 pounds.*

*A Public Works Department (PWD) visitor to the hospital after it was finished, when asked how much a similar hospital would have cost the government if PWD had built it, replied "about 30,000 pounds, but it would have a slightly better finish". The project became possible thanks to the co-operation of many people—government, Indian traders, local people in Africa and many others in Scotland.*

*The project really began in 1951. I had been paying occasional visits to Chitambo, which was served by an old hospital with a sister-in-charge, to see patients and arrange for any surgical cases to travel to my hospital (Lubwa) 240 miles away for treatment. The local people at Chitambo wanted an up-to-date hospital to be built to serve the vast area of many thousands of square miles. The government consented, and also agreed to give some financial help. I was asked to undertake the job of planning and building this hospital. I agreed, provided the local people would give a considerable amount of free labour. It was explained to them that I wanted the hospital to be the best possible for the money available and that I could only buy the necessary equipment in Scotland if money was saved on the building.*

*When building in an outlying district of Central Africa we begin at the beginning. That meant surveying the ground to take levels, the better to calculate foundation depths and also the possibilities of a good water supply. With the measurements I went on furlough to Scotland, drew the plans and arranged some financial help from the Church of Scotland. Then it was a case of calculating numbers of bricks, tiles, sizes and numbers of planks of sawn timber. I sent out to the Missionary-In-Charge, Rev. W. Bonomy, a request for 400,000 bricks and 20,000 tiles and 3,000 planks and beams of various sizes. He was very good at labour relations and got the people going. They dug anthill clay (white for white bricks and red for red bricks) and hand-moulded and burned nearly half a million bricks and 80,000 tiles. The sawyers went into the forest and cut some 400 large trees and cut them into beams and planks of the required sizes. I also ordered 2000 feet of piping of sizes from 2" to ½" with bends, couplings, taps and tools. These things were all ready for me when I returned to Central Africa in October 1952.*

*Meantime in Scotland I was busy getting help from many friends. A coppersmith made high pressure water sterilizers to my design and would take no payment. An electrician drew out a wiring diagram for the hospital in detail. An operating theatre light was made in Glasgow to my own design and only 6.15 pounds was charged for it. It was a similar matter with the operating table, electric lighting plant and small x-ray plant. Other things had to be purchased—window glass, 400 sheets, 2cwt putty, several assorted bags of screw nails and ordinary nails, hinges, locks and door handles, electric light fittings, junction boxes, ceiling roses, bulbs, cables (all sizes) and switches. In addition 3,000 feet of hardboard was ordered from Finland-to be shipped out direct.*

*In October 1952 work began. The first task was putting in the water supply pipes and building sedimentation tanks near the small stream chosen. All pipes have to have their openings protected by fine gauze to keep frogs, mosquito larvae and tadpoles out. The 2" pipes entered a storage tank near the hospital. This brick and cement tank had to be built on an 8 feet high base to give adequate water pressure. It could hold 400 gallons and was continually filling night and day. The bricklayer engaged on the job was not careful enough with the joints and when the tank was first filled water seeped between the bricks and during the night the tank broke up. The job had to be done again and this time I watched every joint and finished the tank myself (with waterglass). It was still good after 16 years. When some of my African friends saw the pipes come up out of the ground and enter the middle of the tank (about 12 feet up) they were very sceptical and said "water does not climb hills". They were agreeably surprised to see that it did. After this schoolboys dug out the foundation trenches, and the Missionary-In-Charge and I had conferences with the bricklayers. We bargained with them for the amount to be paid for each building. We did this building by building so as not to discourage or frighten them by asking too much all at once. I made one condition—that in the evening when I inspected the day's work, if a wall was not vertical I would kick it down before the mortar set and it would have to be rebuilt the next day. This only had to be done on two occasions.*

**John Todd and the water tank 1953**

*During the building work I was carrying on medical and surgical work in the old hospital. During a surgical operation a message would come from the bricklayers asking where the ant-course should go at a certain place, or from the carpenters for more nails or screw nails. The carpenters were excellent. The chief carpenter, Amon, was also a cabinet maker and required no supervision. He could be trusted absolutely. Reinforced slabs for such things as drainage tanks were made by ourselves. The moulds were cut out of the dry ground and concrete poured in, and reinforcing scrap iron laid in. When set, the slabs were dug up and placed in position.*

*By 1ˢᵗ May 1953 the hospital was partly built and ready for the ceremony of laying the foundation stones—carved by me:*

NDI IBWE LYABIKIKWA
MU KUTOTELA BONSE
ABAPYUNGILE MU
KWIMAKA INANDA NJI 1953

NDI IBWE LYABIKIKWA
NO WALUPWA LWA
KWA CHITAMBO
UWAPOKELA DR.
LIVINGSTONE 1873

*This stone has been laid to thank all those who have given their services in the erection of this building in 1953*

*This stone has been laid by the descendent of Chief Chitambo who welcomed Dr. Livingstone in 1873*

*A few months later there was a final scramble to get it finished in time for the opening by the Governor—Sir Gilbert Rennie, in October 1953. All available missionaries were engaged in painting the walls of the operating theatre, sterilizing and labour rooms with enamel paint. They were so energetic that too much paint went on and during the night it ran down the walls and over the cement floor. On the morning of the Governor's visit valuable time was spent scraping it off.*

**Roof tiles drying. Anna Mary's cottage/ guest house in background.**

**Chief Chitambo's grandson laying the second foundation stone**

**Sister Agnes Campbell at the opening of the 'new' Chitambo hospital**

**Dr. John Todd at the opening of the 'new' Chitambo hospital**

*For the first two years after the building 2,500 patients were admitted and almost 800 surgical operations were performed. The hospital has now been taken over by the government and is a training hospital for nurses. Teaching equipment was presented by the World Health Organization.*

*I was working in a new septic tank when a government Messenger arrived from the Boma (50 miles away) with a very official-looking envelope. Inside was word of the award of M.B.E. The hospital became a showpiece. The District Commissioners brought chiefs to see what could be done by co-operation between the races. They were interested in the x-ray but more interested in the flushing cisterns of the W.Cs. It amazed them that water could come out and the cistern fill up and stop of its own accord."*

By 1954, Nancy (nee Todd) and Milton Currie were at Mwenzo, in the far north of Zambia, up the Great North Road. They were within visiting distance, and the Todds could see their four grandchildren, I being the youngest, born at Mwenzo in 1954.

In October 1955 the Todds reached the end of their tour of duty, and prepared to go home. There was another agonizing farewell ceremony at which they were addressed by the local chief—Chief Muchinda:

*Sir, on behalf of the Lala Council and all the people of Serenje District, I, Chief Muchinda stand to thank you for what you have done for us during your period of service in this district. As a Dr. you have not time even to think of putting on a suit, always at Chitambo, Serenje Boma and other places in the district, you could only be seen in khaki short trousers and always busy hunting for sick people and to give them treatment. You have dealt with many kinds of sickness, some of which required operations. Your patience and methods of treatment to both Europeans and Africans have made many, both big and small, to like hospital treatment.*

*You have also put up for us at Chitambo a fine hospital big enough to serve good numbers of both inpatients and outpatients. And when building it, you have had some difficulties and problems to solve, but as a wise doctor you made the Provincial Administrator, the Mission body, the Native Authority and all the villagers to give their assistance towards the work at this hospital. In this, Sir, you have taught us practically that unity is strength. The spirit in which you have worked is an inspiration to all who are working for the harmony of all the people of this country.*

*Sir, you and your work in Serenje and the whole of Africa will not be forgotten by both white and black, you have left in us a memory that cannot be forgotten. Now, Sir I give you this African knife as a remembrance for our thankfulness for what you have done for us. I wish you and Mama Todd a safe and happy journey to Scotland. May God bless Dr. and Mrs. Todd.*

*Yendelenipo umutende.*

*Yours faithfully,*
*Chief Muchinda.*

John and Jean Todd settled in Renfrew where John established a General Practice, and Jean assisted as practice receptionist and, at times, nurse. It must have been a far cry from John's pioneering days in Africa and a great wrench from Nancy and the young family, But the Todds felt that it was time to hand the baton on to younger missionaries.

**The finished hospital.**

# REV. GIBSON CHILONGO CALLING, KASANKA 2003

Back at Wasa Camp we were idling over breakfast on the verandah of the lodge, one morning, listening to the lazy snorts of wallowing hippos. There was a light, fresh breeze and we were tucking into hearty plates of Scottish-style oat porridge, when we were summoned to the camp telephone. Rev. Gibson Chilongo was at the camp gate waiting to see us. He had travelled the 150 Km from Chitambo on his scooter, and was waiting to be collected and brought into the camp.

Jo and I hurried into our smartest clothes, spruced ourselves up, and jumped into the Delica van for the 14 Km journey to the gate. We had no idea what form this meeting would take but we felt that it would be positive. The Rev. was standing amongst a small group of banana—vendors, and he was talking animatedly with the gate-keeper. We climbed out of the van and greeted him with hugs and our limited Chi-Bemba. The onlookers grinned at such a strange sight.

There was no doubt that the Reverend was planning to be entertained at the camp, so we whisked him away and installed him on the verandah while the camp cooks brought refreshments. He regaled us for some time with his good humoured account of how he had become a minister after having worked in the copper mines and as a policeman. He described his work at Chitambo, and the difficulties of ministering with very meagre resources. He had been at Chitambo for two years and he seemed to be well accepted by the people.

Over coffee and biscuits he asked us about ourselves and our families. Then, after a polite pause he looked around and said *"Now where is the big Marion man?"* Puzzled, we asked for clarification. He was looking for the man called Marion who had been corresponding with him from New Zealand. Sheepishly I had to admit that I was Marion, and the man in the photo was my husband Guy, who had stayed home. Hardly batting an eyelid, The Rev. seemed to take all this in his stride, but I wondered how much frantic re-framing was going on in his mind. How would he explain this to the church committee? A delegation of mere women might be less well received. What a blow!

Meanwhile Zanna and Jasmine had wrestled a bulky package onto the veranda and handed it over to the Reverend while we all stood around watching the unwrapping ceremony. With exclamations of joy he peeled back the paper and plastic to reveal the electronic key-board. He then burst into spontaneous sing-song prayer of thanks to God for safely delivering the key-board. This was followed by a long and entertaining session of familiarizing ourselves with the workings of the instrument, and some singing along to the pre-synthesized tunes. Rev. Chilongo's face lit up at Amazing Grace and he sang the tenor part, while conducting an imaginary choir and perhaps an orchestra.

In the early afternoon he announced his departure, and we drove him back to the gate. He chatted good-naturedly all the way and we parted like old friends, promising to meet again on Sunday 17th August at Chitambo.

## DOCTORS MCCULLOCH: 1955-1959

The Todds' departure left a vacancy which the Foreign Mission Committee of the Church of Scotland had difficulty filling. A young couple who were both doctors, with a year's hospital experience under their belts, were persuaded by John Todd's letters that they would be able to '*learn on the job*' at Chitambo. So it was that Joan and George McCulloch were 'rushed out' as quickly as anyone could rush in those days. They sailed from Southampton to Cape Town, and then took the train to Broken Hill, where they were met by John Todd and driven the last 150 miles on the dirt road to Chitambo.

Nothing could have prepared them for the challenges they faced. There was none of the usual gentle induction, with a period of language study. That too had to be learned on the job. George quickly learned enough medical Bemba to get by and Joan learned to communicate both with patients and with domestic helpers. Their two eldest sons were born at Chitambo, and so it was a memorable family time.

The working situation was complicated by many changes of staff, and the hospital was without a nursing sister for a while after Sister Agnes Campbell was invalided home. Rev. and Mrs. Bill Bonomy left at the end of 1955 and were replaced in 1956 by Bob and Pat Blaikie from Lubwa. Sarah Miller who was in charge of the educational work left in 1956 and was replaced by Margaret Malloch. In 1957 Fred and Jean Anderson from the United Church of Canada arrived for a year. The Blaikies and the Andersons left in 1958 and were replaced by Bill and Eileen McLees. 1958 saw the arrival of Sister Jean McKinley for a year, and the departure of teacher Margaret to get married. Margaret was replaced by Lorna McLeish from Lubwa. So, by 1959 the McCullochs were the longest serving European staff members.

The hospital ran a training programme for medical orderlies who, when successful, were awarded a certificate after three years. This certificate was highly prized when they looked for employment with the government or mine hospitals. The McCullochs designed a badge for the orderlies, and together with Miss McKinley, and the students, came up with the motto "To Serve".

The main difficulty with the hospital during this period was financial. The hospital was run entirely on a grant from the government. The mission only paid the salaries of the doctor and sister in charge. In the first quarter of the McCullochs' stay at Chitambo the government cut the grant, and this made it very difficult to make ends meet. Initially Joan worked full time in the hospital, although categorized a 'missionary wife' by the Church of Scotland and therefore unsalaried. The government awarded extra funding on account of having two doctors but the mission insisted that the extra funding be put into a capital project—namely replacing the generator and building a class-room and storage room. It was very difficult to keep a 70 bed hospital going on 2000 pounds a year. The Church of Scotland could not afford to increase its support and there was no other source of income. Two proposals arose out of this situation. The first was to cut the number of beds from 70 to 50. At the time this was suggested there were 70 patients in beds and 29 on mats on the floor.

The second suggestion was to introduce fees. This caused a great furore as John Todd had reached an understanding with the local chiefs that the people of Chitambo would receive free health-care in return for their labour in the building of the hospital. The McCullochs left Chitambo in June 1959 with some sadness and frustration. They felt that there was so much more that could have been done, with better resources.

## MWENZO 1959

Meanwhile events were unfolding at Mwenzo Mission in the far north of Northern Rhodesia, which would have a significant impact on Chitambo. Dr. Hamilton ('Milton') Currie and Nancy Todd were expecting their fifth baby. Things had gone well with the births of the other four—two in South Africa, one in Scotland and one in Mwenzo. There was no reason to suspect that this one would be any different. Nancy had been tireder than usual during the pregnancy and had often suffered from headaches. It was January 1959. The two older boys were at boarding school at Fort Jameson, across the other side of the Luangwa Valley. David had been flying off to school in a tiny chartered plane for the previous 2 years. Douglas, aged 8, had joined him for the first time in 1959. Joan was having correspondence lessons at home and I, the youngest of the four, elbowed my way into the lessons whenever I could.

Milton's own words best describe the tragic events that took place on *January* 23rd 1959-

He wrote home to the Todds:

*Dear Dad and Mum,*

*You will have received my wire, and you are stricken with grief and shock as I am. I still can't realise that it has happened. I am in a daze, and I am now sitting down to write to you and unburden myself of my grief.*

*Nancy began in labour yesterday and we expected the baby last night. All seemed normal. The baby had been lying as a breech some six weeks ago but I turned it and yesterday I checked by PV that it was lying as a vertex. I called (Sister) Margaret Moore down last night, about 5 pm and she had supper with me. She stayed all night and Nancy did not make the progress we had expected. This morning I did a PV again and found an occipito-posterior. So I took her up to the theatre where I proceeded with a pudendal nerve block to do a forceps delivery. In the midst of the delivery Nancy, who was also using Trilene, went into a convulsion. I succeeded in extracting the baby alive and well with very little trouble but Nancy went on having convulsion after convulsion. I gave Pentothal about ¼ gram altogether, which had some beneficial effect, but very transitory. Then I gave phenobarbitone by injection. There seemed to be some improvement but the fits were coming about once every five minutes. This went on for about one and a half hours—severe convulsions which stopped the breathing for half a minute at a time. And then suddenly the breathing began to fail. I had to use coramine in spite of the convulsions and I gave artificial respiration by endotracheal tube. Even this failed and I as a last resort began cardiac massage through an abdominal incision. I got the heart started again and beating strongly with injections of adrenaline but it was only for a little while, and it stopped again and I could do no more.*

*The baby seems to be quite alright—a little girl. Nancy had wanted her to be called Catherine and I had agreed. I have no other names to add. Let the one which Nancy wanted be the only one. She never saw the wee one.*

*Oh Dad you must know what it's like. I am stunned, and I can't fully grasp yet what has happened. The two little girls, Joan and Marion are with Eddie and Betty (Weir) and I have been up and broken the news to them. Marion hardly comprehends it yet, but Joan does, and has been weeping, but is very brave none the less, and has been a great comfort to me already. The baby is even now being taken up to the Weirs by Eddie and Margaret and Evelyn, who, like everyone else, are rallying around me. (Revds.) Simwanza and Mugara have been a great comfort and a tower of strength. I met Dinah (the house-girl) weeping on the avenue as I came to write this.*

*I have sent a wire to Kochira, and Gordon (Milton's brother) will have to break the news to the boys. I am most pained for their sakes. They went off on Tuesday (20th) with Eddie and got on the plane the next day. He saw them off. Douglas was full of the thrill of it, but David was much more sensitive to the parting from his mother. He is a sensitive wee chap, and I stune with anguish to think what a blow the news will be to him. If only I could be with him now!*

But Gordon and Morag and Granny are near. Douglas will feel it terribly too, just newly at school for the first time.

I have no words to express what I feel. The words keep running through my head "Where thy treasure is, there will thy heart be also". My greatest treasure of all is there now, and I could wish I were there too, only that I have the children to live for and bring up.

I am blaming myself bitterly, and thinking of all that I might have done, or done otherwise, that this should not have happened. Nancy seemed well enough. She walked to the car and into theatre. We were alone together just before I scrubbed up and I gave her a kiss, and told her I didn't do that for all my maternity cases. These were nearly our last words. She had had a bad night of pain, not so much contractions as an almost continuous pain at the end. Margaret and I kept watch and slept at times, Margaret in the downstairs bedroom where the confinement was to have been, and I in the sitting-room. Looking back it all seems like a night-mare. Looking forward it is very hard to see the way god is leading us, and I just pray he will make the way clear.

We shall be feeding the baby on Lactogen which Nancy and I had bought for an orphan at the hospital, never thinking our own baby would be an orphan too.

**Currie family at Mwenzo 20/1/59**

*I am enclosing a photo. It was taken by Evelyn, of the family on the morning the boys left for school. It is a precious one now. There are also a few other pictures in the coloured spool which is still in the camera. We shall get them in due course, and you shall see them.*

*There are no more words I can write today. Most likely there will be a letter from you in tomorrow's post. It will be like salt in the wound. I have no heart to receive or write letters. This is, I think, the hardest blow that life can deal any one. May god give us all the strength to bear it, and the faith to triumph over it.*

*Love from Milton.*

## MWENZO 2003

In 2001 the child I was sponsoring in Rwanda came of age and moved out of her village. World Vision asked me if I could sponsor another child and I requested one in Zambia, as I knew they had projects there. A package duly arrived from World Vision bearing the details of a little girl born at Mwenzo—in the Nakonde district. Immediately Suwilanje and I had something in common. We were born in the same remote corner of Zambia. Her village was about half a kilometre from our old house. I knew that I would one day visit her.

While World Vision are not over-enthusiastic about sponsors visiting 'their' children, they did the necessary police check and wrote letters to their counterparts at Nakonde. I had already asked Edmund if he could fly us from Kasanka and he had agreed in principle. He would check out the nearest airstrip to Nakonde. When he e-mailed back that it was at Isoka, about a hundred kms from Nakonde, I contacted the World Vision team on the ground to see if they could meet us, and we arranged a day and time.

And here we were—Jo and I, Zanna and Jasmine, about to board Edmund's tiny plane for another uncertain adventure. The morning was cool and clear. We drove out from Wasa Camp to the airstrip, which was on the other side of the game park. This involved driving through a river, the advice being to do a 'banana'—to point upstream first and then allow the current to direct the front of the van downstream at the other side. Breathing a sigh of relief when we reached the other side, we followed the signs to the airstrip and then drove down it to where the plane was

117

waiting at the other end. We had each brought small overnight bags, and had given Edmund our combined weights in advance, so that he could be sure the plane would not be overloaded.

Once airborne Edmund confessed that he had not checked out the airstrip at Isoka, and was unsure if anyone had landed there in the last year or so. We flew over the edge of the Bangweulu swamps and Lake Shiwa, crossing the hills of Shiwa Ngandu, site of the "Africa House". After flying for about two hours Edmund started searching for Isoka airstrip. For a while it looked as though our journey was in vain, and then he spotted it—a simple strip in the midst of bush, and edged with white-painted stones. A vehicle glittered at the far end. Edmund circled and landed neatly on the bumpy runway.

We were greeted by Mr. Chitaze Kawilila, the Nakonde World Vision programme manager and driver Edwin Nkhoma. They whisked us away in their air-conditioned Toyota land-cruiser and we sat back to enjoy the drive to Mwenzo, along a tar road in reasonable condition. Deforestation was striking, and people obviously had to travel long distances in search of firewood for cooking. As we travelled they told us about their work and the many challenges they had faced in their 13 years' project. They were proud of their mission statement:

*"Nakonde Area Development Project (ADP) is a team of Christians whose mission is to follow the Saviour, Jesus Christ, in working with the Community to promote sustainable human transformation in child rights, gender, health, education, agriculture and conservation and proclaim that Jesus Christ lived, died and rose again victoriously from the dead."*

Our first priority on arriving at Nakonde was to visit Suwilanji and her family. The little girl would have been told that she was having special visitors from far away. How would she be feeling? Although we were well aware that the World Vision project was about communities and not about individual children, I felt a great surge of warmth towards the tiny, shy six year old with the big eyes and thin arms. Her family invited us into their home—a rectangular thatched mud hut, with a shady veranda. Her mother was solemn and silent. She and Suwilanji's father, Bonomy, had eight children and he was unemployed. He made a short and very moving speech of thanks to World Vision for their support and to us for ours. I fought back my tears in order to make a dignified reply. Then we all sat down to lunch together—chicken, rice and cold Fanta. It was one of the most memorable meals I've ever had.

After lunch, while we were taking photos, Suwilanji appeared with a bouquet of red bougainvillea and she posed solemnly to have her photo taken with me. I think we both felt quite overwhelmed for different reasons—Suwilanji at the strangeness of the occasion, and I at having come full circle in returning to the place of my birth. There was also the constant anxiety about being a well-fed westerner in a poverty-stricken developing country and the uncertainty about the effects of overseas aid.

In the afternoon we were taken on a tour of the hospital, now a fully-functional outpatient clinic, overseen by World Vision. I lingered in front of the building that had been the 'theatre block' for it was here that our Mum had died. As was customary at the time we did not see her again. Nor did we attend her funeral or see her grave. Here we were forty-four years later, walking past the big old Scottish-style church to the graveyard behind it. Someone had gone on ahead and pointed out Mum's grave—neatly kept *"Nancy Helen Currie born at Livingstonia 8*th *June 1926, died at Mwenzo 23*rd *Jan 1959"*.

Jo and I stood in silence for a while, lost in our own thoughts, then a voice near my elbow burst out *"Why did you die and leave us?"* as Jo moved past me with wildflowers to place on the grave. I have to admit that my heart had almost stopped and I felt rooted to the spot, frozen in time, like the 4 year old that I was when we left Mwenzo. That lonely grave in the quiet glade behind Mwenzo church had swallowed up our hearts, just as surely as Livingstone's lay beneath the mpundu tree at Old Chitambo's.

And then it was over, and we were being shepherded back to the vehicle. Children from the local primary school ran up to us, eager to show us their homework books. The girls were clad in the familiar standard primary school uniform: green short-sleeved dresses with white cuffs. In our Lusaka Girls' School days there had been 'knickers-to-match' and a regulation green felt hat to complete the outfit.

The World Vision team were keen to show us their projects, and for us to meet the Chieftainess of the Winamwanga, Chieftainess Waitwika, who shared the chieftainship with her brother, Mukoma, who lived over the border in Tanzania. We visited WV headquarters and one of the people they had helped to set up a small business. Then our hosts needed petrol and the nearest filling station was across the border at Tunduma. Obviously the WV vehicle was well known to the customs officials who waved us past the queues of traffic on either side of the border. We wandered round a dusty market, and sympathised with the truck drivers who waited days for their vehicles to be cleared by customs. The long delays meant good business for the purveyors of food, drink and prostitution.

Sadly there was no time to visit the Chiefteness, as it was now late afternoon, and Edmund was camped, all this time, by the plane at Isoka airstrip. Our hosts drove us back to Isoka and we sank into silent reverie, each lost in their own thoughts about the day and the memories it had stirred up.

Back at the plane, Edmund was pleased to see us and we took off for the shorter journey to Shiwa Ngandu and the Kapishya Hot Springs. We enjoyed an eagle's eye view of Lake Shiwa, one of Livingstone's favourite stopping places. At Shiwa we were met by the owners of the Kapishya Lodge and taken in their Land Rover to this most comfortable and relaxing of watering-holes.

Jo and I shared the Chipembere lodge—so named in memory of Sir Stewart Gore-Brown, owner of the 'Africa House' at Shiwa Ngandu. The rondavels faced across beautifully kept gardens to the Mansha River. Upstream from the lodge was a natural thermal pool. Following a lodge tradition we ordered drinks from the bar and sat in the hot spring with our drinks floating along-side. It was a most luxurious way to unwind after the travel and emotion of the day.

In the morning after a hearty breakfast in the open-sided lodge dining-room, Edmund accompanied us on a trip to Shiwa House. Our guide regaled us with the history of the house and some of the many tales told about it. The name—Shiwa Ngandu, for example, means Lake of the Royal Crocodile. One of the legends has it that during the great migrations from the Luba country in the north, one of the first Bemba chiefs named Chiti, met a woman whom he did not recognize as his own sister, and took her as his wife. She conceived a son, Nkandu. The man denied responsibility for the child, saying that a crocodile had fathered the child, while the couple bathed in Lake Shiwa. This resulted in a bitter split between the Bemba and Bisa people. To this day the crocodile is the totem of the Bisa.

The grand old house was built in 1921 by the eccentric Englishman, Sir Stewart Gore-Browne. He later married the daughter of his first true love and spirited her away to his African mansion where they raised their two daughters and became enmeshed in the life of colony of Northern

Rhodesia and its struggle towards independence. Renowned for his hot temper and his tendency to beat his workers, Gore-Browne gained the nick-name "Chipembere" which means "charging rhinoceros". In spite of this, he supported the young Kenneth Kaunda in his ascent to the presidency of Zambia in 1964. For this he was knighted, and when he died in 1967 he was the only white man in Zambia ever to have had the President attend his funeral. My brothers remember the Independence service in Lusaka cathedral, and there was Sir Stewart, with his African butler, Henry, alongside, decked out in three piece suits for the occasion.

The house at Shiwa has recently been renovated by some of Sir Stewart's grand-children, the Harveys, who now run it as an exclusive guest house. The décor has remained virtually unchanged, and meals are eaten at the vast mahogany table in the great dining-hall. There is an exquisite tiny chapel, resplendent with the Gore-Brown crest and family tree. My grandparents, the Todds were invited to the wedding of Sir Stewart's daughter, Laura, in the chapel and they recalled a beautiful African choir singing unusual renditions of well-known hymns. My favourite room was the library on the first floor. The walls were lined with book-cases, bearing intriguing titles. There was a whole wall devoted to African history and politics—ancient and modern. Sadly some of the older books had suffered at the mandibles of white ants, while the house was unoccupied for five years.

In the main living-room Edmund sat at the grand piano and played Chopin nocturnes. Time seemed to stand still, and the magic was only broken by the whistling and cat-calls of the parrot on the upstairs balcony. Shiwa was renowned for its large herds of cattle, and in our time at Chitambo, our parents had sometimes ordered meat from Shiwa. While we were still looking round Edmund did a deal with the farm manager and a large package of fresh meat was loaded onto our plane for the return trip to Kasanka.

**Shiwa Ngandu: "The Africa House"**

# THE MUSKS AT CHITAMBO 1959

In 1959 there were problems at Chitambo. The Foreign Mission Committee (FMC) of the Church of Scotland was finding the running costs of the hospital unsustainable. The Drs. McCulloch were leaving after their turbulent four-year term. The United Church of Canada had withdrawn its offer of support for Chitambo. One possible solution was to continue to run a training school for nurses and medical orderlies, without the need to pay salaries to the trainees. The government, however, stipulated that a training hospital of 70-80 beds required at least one doctor and three nursing sisters. Each of the three mission hospitals in the northern region had only one sister. It was looking as though two hospitals would need to close. And so the government took over Mwenzo Hospital, which continued to operate under a Medical Assistant with occasional input from lady doctor Hope Trant. Lubwa hospital would continue for two years under Dr. Malcolm Moffat.

On 16th May 1959 Scottish doctor Chad and his wife Lily Musk arrived from Nyasaland, having worked first in Blantyre and then Livingstonia, so that Chad Musk could take over as Medical Officer in charge of Chitambo while the McCullochs were on furlough. The Musks spent five weeks with the McCullochs while making this transition. The expatriate staff at the time were Rev. Bill and Mrs. Eileen McLees, Lorna McLeish who taught at the school until it closed, and two nurses—Isobel Ross who was due to retire, and Margaret Moore who had been transferred from Mwenzo. Lorna, the last expatriate teacher, was married at Chitambo and left in 1959. Senior Medical Assistants Grant Mkandawire and Welton Chavula, both Nyasalanders, trained at Livingstonia, had responded to a plea from Sister Agnes Campbell to help at Chitambo. These were gifted and dedicated men who gave years of their working lives to Chitambo Hospital.

**The Mkandawire family, Chitambo 1959**

The Musks occupied the big, old, doctors' house, first on the left on entering the station. Unbeknown to Chad and Lily Musk, they were arriving at Chitambo at a critical time. The FMC had decided to go with the fee-charging option, in order to keep the hospital open. The local people had not been consulted. Nor had the government. The Northern

Rhodesia government was already off-side with the Church of Scotland's political line-(against Federation and in support of African Nationalism.) In addition they were aggrieved that decisions to close schools and hospitals had been made without consulting them. The Musks were in for a storm.

In August the people began to boycott the hospital. Very few outpatients attended and the in-patients left as soon as they could. It was therefore decided to hold an Open Day to which the Chiefs or their representatives were sent. The District Commissioner came too, and he sided with the people against the mission. The community voiced their grievances—that they had given their labour to Dr. John Todd for 3 years in return for free medical treatment. There was great bitterness that things had not been discussed fully with the chiefs. Chad sent an urgent letter to Eddy Weir (Secretary of Church and Mission Council) asking him to delay a decision until after the Lala Council (the meeting of all the Lala chiefs) in November. At that meeting, the Lala Chiefs offered to pay the sum required to balance the budget. Meanwhile Lubwa hospital was struggling with the same issue, and the Church of Scotland Foreign Mission Committee in Edinburgh was forced to reconsider its policy of charging fees. The situation slowly resolved itself, but not without a great many letters from Chad, in an attempt to negotiate a peaceful solution.

Dr. Malcolm Moffat, son of Unwin, and grandson of Chitambo's founder, called in to visit the Musks, on his way to Lubwa. Malcolm, like Chad was an Edinburgh graduate, who had qualified a year after Chad. He had spent a student 'elective' at Chitambo with John Todd during the rebuilding of the hospital. In October 1959 Rev. Yafet Mugara of Mwenzo was instated as the new minister at Chitambo. According to Chad Musk *"This was a mighty occasion and the hymns filled the station."* There was a commitment from hospital staff to support the work of the church.

At the end of September 1959 George McCulloch wrote from his furlough in Scotland to say that he was resigning from the mission field. The Musks were due to go on leave but had to delay leaving. Again the future of Chitambo Hospital hung in the balance. Again the FMC was begged to improve the financial backing of the hospital. If the staffing levels fell, the government grant for the training school would be withdrawn.

The Director of Medical Services agreed to continue to recognise the training school provided a third sister could be recruited. He also approved of the plans to extend the hospital and offered to pay half the costs. An application would be made to the Beit Trust for the other half. The Provincial Medical Officer approached Chad and asked if he could visit Serenje government hospital on a regular basis. This would bring in some extra income for Chitambo and serve as a link with the outside world.

Meanwhile the political tension in the region was rising. The District Commissioner (DC) at Serenje informed Chitambo that there was to be a visit to Serenje by the Monckton Commission, regarding the future of the *Central African Federation of the Rhodesias and Nyasaland.* The African people of Northern Rhodesia were deeply mistrustful of the Federation, which they regarded as the consolidation of white power, based in Southern Rhodesia. People were invited to make submissions to the DC. It was not entirely clear how this information was to be used, and whether it might be passed on to the Security Police. The missionaries were already regarded unfavourably for their pro-African stance. Not quite trusting the DC, Chad sent his submission directly to the Monckton Commission.

The Commission of 26 people had been set up by the British government to recommend constitutional changes with a view to salvaging the Federation—a 7 year old amalgam of the two Rhodesias and Nyasaland, so widely detested by the indigenous peoples. It quickly became apparent to the Commission that the only way ahead was to sweep away the Federation's central structure and replace it with three semi-autonomous territories, Southern Rhodesia, Northern Rhodesia and Nyasaland. The central government would only retain control of foreign policy, defence and broad economic matters. The new territories could raise their own taxes. There would be voting parity, and an end to racial discrimination. At the end of a 5 to 7 year trial period each of the territories would be allowed to secede. Sir Roy Welensky, the Prime Minister of the Federation, was outraged and accurately described the report as "the death knell of Federation". Most white Rhodesians agreed, while the young Kenneth Kaunda said *"Away with Federation now!"*

On the home front Lily Musk had to contend with several carloads of tourists from the Copperbelt, who arrived un-announced to see what 'real live missionaries' looked like. Refreshments were served and they toured the hospital, which they found 'primitive 'and 'worse than the army'. However they did make a donation of 3 pounds!

In early 1960 Chad saw a lot of TB patients and some with sleeping sickness. Amoebic dysentery and trachoma eye infections were prevalent too. One day Mr. Nawa Namukolo, the Medical Assistant at Serenje, brought a very sick patient. Mr. Namukolo had lunch with the Musks, but it was interrupted by a man shouting "Nkalamu"—which means "Lion". Mr. Namukolo said that it wasn't necessarily a lion, but also meant danger. The 'lion' turned out to be a ten foot long python stuck in the mesh covering of the Musks' water tank, about 300 yards from the house. Ba-Alifeyo, the store-keeper, arrived at full speed on his bike with his rifle over his shoulder, pursued by an excited band of youngsters. Two shots killed the python which was about the thickness of Chad's leg. The Musks were really impressed, but Mr. Mugara, the Minister said "That's just a young one. Wait til you see one as thick as a tree trunk, especially after it has swallowed a duiker!"

Chad discussed plans with parents of schoolchildren to use Chitambo mission buildings for a Standard 5 classroom. By the beginning of May 1960 morale was improving and better resources for the mission were promised. Chad drew up plans for a new office block for the hospital and Lily typed budgets, stock sheets and accounts. Her little typewriter could take a dozen sheets of thin paper, so that copies could be made, if she bashed the keys hard enough. The Mission Council accepted Chad's plans for the office and work began as soon as the Council was over. They also agreed in principle to having a herd of cows at Chitambo, once more, and Mission Headquarters in 121 George Street, Edinburgh was approached for funding. News came of the possible posting of a Rev. Charlie Catto and his wife to Chitambo by the United Church of Canada.

Chad then found himself landed with major repairs to the houses of the nursing sisters, as well as organizing housing for three nurses and burning bricks for the hospital expansion. The Beit Trust came up with 4,000 pounds for the new buildings, including 1,000 pounds for a new Maternity wing and sanitation block. Joey Smith (from Shetland) was to come from Lubwa in August. She would be Matron/Tutor, and Isobel would leave in September. A new builder, Ron Swanson, would arrive in August with his wife and three children. Milton Currie would come from Ekwendeni, and would take over the running of the hospital from Chad. The Musks now busied themselves with preparing for the new arrivals, and making plans to go on furlough.

In the old style, Chad negotiated with those who would make the bricks. Some of the original hospital buildings had been demolished and the bricks carefully saved for re-use. The brick fields were a hive of activity—a large area, carved out of the bush, boys and girls scuttling from ant-hill to field with their mould full of wet clay, dumping it on the field to dry and scurrying back for more, with the foreman yelling instructions and hurrying them on all the while. On the field the bricks were laid in rows and covered with dry grass, so that they dried slowly and did not crack. They were then put in home-made kilns and heated with charcoal for several days. The fire had to be watched day and night.

Repairs on the nursing sisters' houses were more problematic. A wall in mud mortar had to be rebuilt, roof timbers were rotten and many tiles were broken. Old Andrea the tiler felt the cold terribly and never managed to get to work until the sun was getting warm. Even then he spent time crouched over a fire, or perched on a roof paralysed with numb and cold. Meanwhile the medical work had to go on, and there were always more patients than beds.

There was political unrest in the Belgian Congo, which was not far from Chitambo as the crow flies. News came that the Katanga Province of the Congo (rich in diamonds and minerals) wished to secede. Would Southern Rhodesia want to link up with the Congo? Jonathan Chileshe, the new school-master of Mabonde Upper Primary (in Chitambo buildings) stayed with the Musks while his house was being built. This was the beginning of a lifelong friendship between the Musks and Chileshes. Jonathan, whose orphaned father narrowly missed being onsold to Arab slavers, (according to Jonathan's own writings) went on to have a distinguished career as an economist with the United Nations

At the beginning of August the Musks realized that before their return trip to Scotland, the children-David and Elspeth, would need Yellow-Fever vaccinations. These had to be done in Broken Hill. The Dodge, their only transport, had broken down on Chad's medical visit to Serenje. Chad had come home late that night in Fred Anderson's Land Rover. The mission driver took Lily and the children to Serenje, and returned Fred's Land Rover. Lily picked up the patched-up Dodge for the trip to Broken Hill where they were looked after by the Methodist minister and his wife. The Dodge was repaired and the children were soon vaccinated, and on the road home bearing sausages and boiled ham. Chad went down with flu, but could not rest at night as there was a bat in the bedroom. Unable to get rid of it, they moved into the guest room. While Chad languished the next day, Lily supervised building, painting, ditch-digging and the cleaning of the house for nursing sister Joey Smith who was due to arrive that week.

That same day, in the afternoon the Canadian Rev. Charlie Catto, his beautiful wife Barbara, and children Dan and Linda arrived, from Mombasa, tanned and fresh from their holiday in Kenya. Charlie, bouncing with enthusiasm, 'machine-gunned' the Musks with questions and propounded mighty schemes for laying electricity for the whole station. At the time there was a small generator for night surgery. He also proposed buying a tractor and setting up a demonstration farm, organizing classes in sociology and anthropology for the older people in the villages. Chad, who had dragged himself from his sick bed, *"smiled on our guests like cold milk pudding"*. Every now and then he bleated *"Where will you get the money Charlie?"* The Cattos stayed for two days and nights, and the pace never slackened. Chad did his best to keep Charlie from "going into outer space". Lily showed Barbara round the station in the morning, and she became very quiet. In the evening there was a big gathering to meet them. Lily played the piano and sang. Charlie got out his guitar, sang songs of old Canada, did some comedy stunts and showed the assembled gathering how to play the Indian game of slummie-sticks. They left the next morning after prayers for a safe journey. They had no spare tyre, having ripped up two travelling at speed on bad roads. The Musks looked forward to the "Catto magic" at Chitambo but alas, Barbara became ill soon afterwards and was advised that she shouldn't live 'up-country'.

Two days later Joey Smith arrived from Lubwa. Quiet and good-humoured, she settled in well. Shortly after her arrival came Ron and Mary Swanson, their three children and nursing sister Jean Gilligan, just out from Scotland. Chad was very busy at the hospital, so Lily welcomed the newcomers and also coped with many minor calamities. By the end of August the Musks were packed and ready for home. Milton Currie was due to arrive on 30th.

# CHAPTER 4

# THE COMING OF AGE

## REACHING CHITAMBO 2003

On the 17th August the sun came up as reliably as on any of the previous days. The morning was crisp and clear. We were expected at Chitambo at about 10 am, so we had to be up early. There was an unmistakable tension in the air. This was the day we had all been waiting for, and now, suddenly, we weren't so sure. What kind of reception would we get? How should we respond? Would we be expected to make speeches? What should we wear? Would it be overwhelmingly sad?

Breakfast was hurried and subdued. We dressed as smartly as we could. Jasmine's hair was neatly plaited, Zambian style, by Bethsheba. We put together a small picnic which we planned to have at a special childhood picnic place known as 'the Rocks', on the road into Chitambo. The camp staff turned out to see us off. Jo and I had gathered a small bouquet of wildflowers—including proteas and 'everlasting daisies', which we planned to place on Dad's grave.

Soon we were off, bumping down the dusty track in the black Delica van away from Wasa camp, towards the main road. At the camp gate there was a group of ladies with bunches of tiny plantain bananas. We bought some for the journey amidst a cheerful banter and much giggling at our halting attempts at Chi-Bemba. We probably had enough petrol for the return journey to Kasanka but what would we do after that? It was too late now to get to the Serenje filling station. We just hoped for the best.

The main road was wide and quiet, and remarkably good apart from the occasional unannounced pot-hole in the tarmac. Sometimes they could be spotted in advanced and neatly avoided. Every now and then there were roadside stalls, often guarded by children, with small piles of sweet potatoes, pumpkins, and tomatoes. Others sold wild honey in a great variety of containers.

At Kanona we noticed that the Post Office door was open, and in spite of the fact that it was Sunday, the postal worker welcomed us and agreed to sell us some stamps. Nearby an open-air church was in full swing, the congregation singing heartily and all apparently dressed in white. It never ceased to amaze us how village people turned themselves out immaculately for special occasions in the absence of most 'mod cons'.

At the Chitambo road end we met a group of smartly dressed young men heading for Chitambo. Lake Lusiwasi, previously visible opposite the Chitambo road end, was now hidden behind the high railway embankment. We turned off past Chansa village and bumped down the 'Chansa' road until we came upon the familiar rocky outcrop where we had stopped for many a childhood picnic. Climbing up to the top of 'the Rocks' we found a shady spot with a fine view across the surrounding countryside. Unsure quite what to do with ourselves we sang some of our favourite old hymns and shed a few tears of apprehension and nostalgia.

## CHITAMBO 1960-1961

Milton Currie arrived at Chitambo on 30th August 1960, having driven south from Ekwendeni via Lubwa. Milton was welcomed by the Musks, Matron Joey Smith, Sister Jean Gilligan and the Swansons. Over the next few days he took over the medical work and the hospital administration from Chad. There were welcome tea parties and a concert was put on by the hospital orderlies. He was housed in Anna Mary Livingstone Wilson's cottage. "The cottage", as we came to know it, had also been the Todds' house and John Todd had done some refurbishing, including building a rough cement bath which was to become a source of amusement and consternation to us children. Tadpoles came through the taps, and frogs would sometimes be seen sitting in the plug-hole. The rough cement surface of the bath certainly prohibited any childish sliding around.

The student examinations were in full swing and there were drugs to be ordered. The medical work was not too demanding initially—fractures, skin grafting, and teeth to be pulled. There were second-hand spectacles to be sorted and language study. The doctor still had to turn his hand to many non-medical tasks such as servicing vehicles, repairing instruments and preparing the occasional sermon. There were less pleasant tasks such as performing post-mortems on long-dead bodies brought in by the police or sorting out hospital staff disputes.

The other missionaries were friendly and hospitable, but it must have been a lonely life for Milton. Baby Catherine, who was with Milton's brother Gordon and his wife Morag, in Nyasaland, had died of malaria or meningitis in January 1960, a day before her first birthday. The other two girls were in Scotland with the Todds, and the boys were at boarding school in Fort Jameson, to the south-east, close to the Nyasaland border. Milton's luggage came from Ekwendeni on a lorry. In it were some of the children's toys including the girls' wig-wam, which he gave to the Swansons. In his time off Milton visited Lake Lusiwasi and thought about building a boat. Kundalila Falls became a favourite picnic spot. He listened to the BBC world service at night, and enjoyed reading the Guardian newspaper, which was passed round the station.

There were occasional trips to Serenje on medical business, or to stock up with supplies. It was on such a visit that Milton had a tour of the new Malcolm Moffat Teacher Training College, (which was officially opened on 19/11/60,) and met Australian teacher Elizabeth Luker. Milton mentions Elizabeth (Libby) several times in his diary. It was his habit to record names of people with whom he had significant interactions, on a daily basis. Hospital staff, other missionaries, and visitors featured regularly. Generally he did not record his feelings, with the exception of the day that Nancy died—*the saddest day of my life* and the day that baby Catherine died—*another of the saddest days of my life*. Little did Milton know that the meetings with Libby were carefully orchestrated by Serenje staff, so that she could get to know this eligible widower.

There were visits by David Moffat, Unwin's son who now farmed with his father and Sir John Moffat at Mkushi. David brought welcome news about a herd of cows for Chitambo. He and Milton *tramped the paddocks* to make sure the land was suitable. Malcolm Moffat, (David's brother) while running the hospital at Lubwa, was also a visitor. He and Milton acted as doctors for each other, examining each other and offering advice.

Friday was Milton's day off, but he would have to attend urgent cases if called. He generally spent most Fridays catching up with office work and balancing the books, as well as doing any repairs on hospital equipment or his car. Meat from Shiwa Ngandu was bought regularly for the mission staff, and had to be fetched from the store at Chansa. There was language study most days, and there were prayer meetings, bible study and Sunday services to prepare as well as lectures for the nursing students. He fostered his interest in photography, and developed his own films in the x-ray dark room. There was precious little time for relaxation.

Milton developed a blood transfusion service. In the absence of compatible volunteers, he often donated his own blood, sometimes to no avail. There were some desperate cases—babies who died of malaria or malnutrition, mothers who died of post-partum haemorrhage, difficult deliveries. They are all recorded matter-of-factly in his diary, but each one must have tugged at his heart. He stitched up a man with a buffalo wound, and another who had been mauled by a leopard. He enucleated an eye. He was often up in the night for emergencies, and back on duty in the morning again. He gave and gave. He developed the habit of having a short sleep in the middle of the day, which revived him.

On 12th April 1961 he recorded "*MAN INTO SPACE*" in his diary, and continued pulling teeth while organizing the repainting of the theatre, arranging the installation of an x-ray development tank, and sorting out *milandus* (disputes) of one kind or another. For several nights that April a satellite was visible in the evening sky. On 29th April, there was a joint picnic with Milton's visiting brother Gordon, his wife Morag, their children—Alasdair and Sheila, Milton's boys—David and Douglas, and some Serenje staff, including Elizabeth Luker. The boys enjoyed a trip to the nearby hydroelectric station on the edge of the Luangwa Valley—from where they could see elephants. In his years as a solo parent Milton had invented some story characters with which he entertained the boys. Noteworthy were *Buffalo Bill* and *Big Dog*. Word of his story-telling leaked out, and in May 1961 a Mr. Blackall came to record some Buffalo Bill stories for the national radio. On 28th May there was a visit from young Kenneth Kaunda, son of David Kaunda of Livingstonia.

By early July 1961 Milton's year-long stint at Chitambo was over, and the Musks were due to return from their furlough. Milton busied himself with packing and preparing to leave. The Church of Scotland organized 'digs' for him and the boys in Glasgow. He visited Serenje to bid farewell to staff there. In his diary he recorded *Lunch with Elizabeth Luker?* He did not explain what the question mark represented, but when they met again on the eve of his departure from Chitambo he proposed to her. When he and the boys embarked on their ship at Cape Town on 4th August there was a letter from Libby saying "*Yes*". They set sail in rough weather at 4 pm but had to turn back to put off a stowaway.

## CHITAMBO CHURCH 2003

Pulling ourselves together we climbed back into the Delica van and drove slowly down the bumpy Chansa road. A Yugoslav road company had done a superb job of tarring the main TanZam road during our time at Chitambo, but the Chansa road remained corrugated and rocky, unchanged since John Howie's time, as though to permanently dissuade the faint-hearted from what might await them at Chitambo.

The forest on either side of the road was thinner than we remembered, cut down, no doubt for firewood and building material. We passed no other vehicles, and soon the forest started giving way to cleared land. A whoop went up from Jo who spotted 'the furrow'—that life-giving water supply for the homes and the hospital, as well as source of hours of childhood entertainment—racing stick boats, or skinny-dipping when no-one was looking. Jo begged to be let out and she walked the last hundred yards into Chitambo ahead of the van. On the left were the ruins of the original doctors' house, and to our right, the dilapidated but still apparently inhabited Moffat house, with its sentinel jacaranda tree. As we came alongside the jacaranda, we looked down towards the end of the station where there was a large crowd outside the church. What was happening here today, we wondered?

We had not gone much further when members of the crowd appeared to turn and see us. Suddenly there was shouting, whooping and then clapping and singing as they began to run towards the van. We were utterly shocked as the van doors were prised open and people piled in shouting greetings and dragging us one by one out of the van, and bearing us along towards the church. Still in a state of shock, and with tears pouring down our cheeks we arrived at the church, where we ground to a halt amidst a sea of people, all clamouring welcome greetings, singing, dancing and drumming. Rev. Gibson Chilongo was there and we were ushered into the vestry and solemnly introduced to the church elders. Meanwhile the keyboard, in its brown card-board box was borne aloft like some strange mini-coffin, by a group of men who now started a slow, heart-wrenching song as they shuffled rhythmically in single file towards the church. All we could do was follow.

Once inside the body of the church, the singing changed—to more of a hymn tune. The walls were brightly painted—blue and green. We looked up at the arched ceiling where bats sometimes lurked. There were none visible, but the same faint smell of bat hung in the air. There was barely standing room. Rev. Chilongo presided from behind the altar. He spoke in English and a young minister-in-training took the pulpit and translated everything into Chi-Bemba. We were ushered forwards to the front seats—the same old wooden benches where we had sat out some long sermons on Sundays past and as we stood to sing the first hymn we were all in tears again. Like Maria Jackson arriving in Bandawe, we had never experienced such a warm welcome.

The Reverend, rising to the occasion, talked of love and international relations. The choir stood and sang "Twa Wa Bona" (We Have Seen Him), which I had first heard in Wanganui, New Zealand, learned by my choir conductor, Teiron Jones, when he had lived in Zambia. When the drumming got going people started dancing in jubilation, and a roar went up when Jo joined in. The Rev. had to raise his voice to restore order.

Then there was the ceremonial unwrapping of the keyboard, whose music seemed to us a little puny in the face of the singing we had just heard. Electronic Amazing Grace was played for all to hear, and, in a haze of unreality, we each spoke a few words to the congregation. Then we were out in the sun again, walking past the giant blue gums, with their cawing crows, down the road towards the mission graves, and somewhere in the background we heard boys' voices calling to each other, and the thud of a football being kicked across a dusty pitch.

## CHITAMBO 1961-1962

The Musks arrived back at Chitambo in mid July 1961, just before Milton's departure. Chad had spent part of his furlough studying for the Diploma in Tropical Medicine and Hygiene, in Edinburgh, and their son, Stewart was born six weeks before their return journey to Chitambo. Meanwhile Ron Swanson had received estimates for the wiring of the whole station—for 1700 pounds. Ron was concerned about the state of some of the mission buildings. The Musks' house,(the original doctor's house), for example, was badly in need of repair.

Politically Chitambo remained quiet, in spite of increasing opposition to Federation in other parts of the country. Police road blocks sometimes interfered with the weekly meat delivery from Shiwa Ngandu. Occasionally the police broke down villagers' doors and took away their hoes and axes in case of trouble. Chad was asked to write to the DC about this. The young Jonathan Chileshe, who had been teaching at Mabonde Upper Primary since August 1959, was granted a scholarship to Keele University in Staffordshire.

Nursing sister Margaret Moore left Chitambo in August 1961 for Scotland, and to marry Tony Ball. My sister Jo and I, who were in Scotland, living with the Todds, were bridesmaids at her wedding. The scent of the freesias in the bridesmaids' bouquets still invokes that day. Jean Gilligan missed Margaret a great deal and decided not to renew her contract when it was up.

In September 1961, on completion of two years at Lubwa Hospital, Dr. Malcolm Moffat called in at Chitambo on his way south. Chitambo was now the only Church of Scotland hospital in Northern Rhodesia. All the same, the church at Lubwa continued to thrive, and Alex Slorach from Scotland continued to work there as church accountant. Later in September Nursing Sister Janet Jack and Women's Worker and part-time accountant Lesley McNair joined the Chitambo staff. Both were very keen to start work but were instructed by the Church to spend several months in language study.

In September 1961 the Secretary General of the United Nations Dag Hammarskjöld was killed in a plane crash in Northern Zambia. He had been on a secret mission to negotiate a cease-fire between rebel Katanga troops and the UN peace-keeping forces in the now independent Congo. The USSR had strongly opposed his previous efforts at resolving the conflict in the Congo. The sensitivity of his mission was such that the flight plan for his plane had not been filed, and a decoy plane had gone ahead by a different route. No evidence of bomb, missile or foul play was found at the crash site, but conspiracy theories were rife. His funeral was held in the Copperbelt and apart from the world's press, it was very poorly attended. Missionaries who managed to get there had to return to the Northern Province via the Great North Road instead of across the Congo Pedicle, because of continuing political unrest in the Congo. Some of the returning missionaries brought a first-hand account of the funeral to Chitambo. Dag Hammarskjold's remarkable life as a peace-maker was acknowledged with the posthumous award of the Nobel Peace Prize. He is the only UN Secretary General to have died in office. His book *"Markings"* found its way into the Currie house and became a source of inspiration to Milton and later to others in the family.

In October 1961 a church conference was held at Chitambo. At the same time, Ron Swanson, the builder, became ill and was transferred to Broken Hill for an appendicectomy. This frustrated his building plans as the rains then set in. A piece of plaster, weighing 5 pounds, fell from the ceiling onto the pillow between Chad and Lily Musk. Due to the heavy building programme, (a new house for the nursing sisters), the ceiling was not fixed until well into 1962! A Rev. Ronald Ndawa stayed with the Musks for 3 weeks, so that Lily could help him write down hymns that he had composed in his head. *Music bubbled from him, his powerful voice and joyful hymns filling the house—quite a tonic,* wrote Lily.

The mission driver of twenty five years had a dispute with Ron and left of his own accord. Chad had to take on the task of driving for the mission—to collect heavy packages, from Chansa at the road-end, to pick up Rev. Mugara who had been out taking services over the weekend, and to collect firewood for the mission—on top of his clinical duties. The paperwork was neglected until Lesley McNair was able to take some time off language study to type up lectures and pay the labourers' wages. On occasion Janet Jack also took time off to help out with emergencies in the hospital. Elizabeth Luker called in to say goodbye before setting off to meet and marry Milton Currie.

1961 ended dramatically with the suspension of the mission foreman, who had worked at Chitambo since 1915 and had been a church elder since the 1930s, for confessing that he had killed a woman elder of the church by witchcraft. Everyone was shocked. The woman, wife of a much respected man, was brought into hospital in a coma following a stroke. The mission session *'did not believe he actually killed her by witchcraft but the wrong is he had it in his heart to do so.'*

In his annual report for 1961 Chad wrote *Contrasting with these beliefs from the past, there is the present day cry of 'One Man One Vote'. Most church members are also members of UNIP, Kenneth Kaunda's political party. In this area the Church is not numerically strong and therefore Christians make up only a minority on UNIP Committees. However a UNIP official, who was one of our study group, had no doubt that the voice of this Christian minority had often restrained others from acts of violence and had kept bitterness and racial hatred out of the politics in this area. In the disturbances of last August, this area kept calm and there were very few acts of violence by the people.*

*Retaliation by government forces was indiscriminate and unjust, and the Chitambo station committee lodged a protest with the District Commissioner condemning the violence of both sides. Since then the government has made a real effort to improve relationships and to compensate innocent sufferers. We feel that these episodes are now better forgotten.*

In early January there was great jubilation when Chad Musk arrived back from the Moffats' farm at Mkushi with four Jersey cows. The Church of Scotland had allowed Chad to make a special appeal and people all over Scotland gave generous donations. A sum of 600 pounds was raised to cover the cost of the cows, a cowshed, a dairy and the salary of the cow-herd. The man appointed was of the Winamwanga tribe of the Mwenzo district who were used to rearing cattle, unlike the Lala.

It was a long, bumpy ride for the cows over muddy, corrugated roads, but they arrived safely. Two of them produced three gallons of milk per day and the other two were in calf. The milk was greatly appreciated by the hospital patients. Janet and Lesley held a mission party by way of celebration.

The Beit Trust gave a grant of 3000 pounds for a house for Milton and Libby. The Church of Scotland FMC gave additional grants—2,300 pounds for houses for African staff, 250 pounds for upgrading the water scheme, 200 pounds for furnishing the new sisters' houses and 250 pounds for an ablution block for hospital workers. A further 650 pounds was made available to extend 'the cottage' so that a missionary family could live there. Rev. Alan Roy, based at Serenje, brought and planted 36 fruit trees and 20 flowering shrubs, with donations from a Sunday school in Scotland. A hospital orchard was begun—with orange and paw-paw trees. The hospital vehicle gave up the ghost when its gearbox finally went.

There was disappointment in March when a letter from the Provincial Medical Officer came with news that there would be no grant for a second doctor. This directive came from Salisbury, the Federation capital. The agenda, put forward by Roy Welensky, was to reduce the health budget in order to meet defence costs, to keep the Federation together at any cost. Milton was due back from leave, and one of the doctors would transfer to the London Missionary Society mission of Mbereshi in the north, while Dr. John Parry went on leave.

Meanwhile the Chitambo nursing students lived in sub-standard accommodation. Their food was cooked over an open fire in a thatched, fly-ridden kitchen. A new student hostel would cost 6500 pounds. A donation of 100 pounds from an Indian patient at Serenje and 200 pounds from the medical visits to Serenje enabled a bathroom to be built onto the children's ward, and showers in the other wards. The hospital woodwork was painted for the first time ever, and the paths marked out with bricks. There were plans for new oil-burning stoves which would provide hot water for the kitchen, laundry and maternity wing. The possibility of solar water-heating was raised by Alan Roy, who had seen solar panels on houses in Israel.

In March Chad attended an 'integration' meeting in the Copperbelt. The integration movement was an effort by the London Missionary Society, Church of Scotland and United Church of Canada towards forming the United Church of Central Africa. It was hoped that the Methodists would join later. How Livingstone would have rejoiced!

Chad expressed concern about the stresses and strains of mission life on the women missionaries. He acknowledged that life was tough for all mission staff but that the single women could not get away easily. While climate and altitude were blamed for some of the stress, Chad felt that the missionaries were not entirely at home in an African setting, and that the gap in the levels of education between the racial groups was significant. Asked what makes a "good missionary" Rev. Mugara replied "*They have to suffer. Those who were not happy did not give themselves fully.*"

Another area of concern was the lack of transport for the sick to hospital. Unless people could afford to hire the mission vehicle, they had no chance of getting to hospital other than by bike or on foot. Chad and Lily decided to spend their last 150 pounds on a car. Chad accompanied patients to Broken Hill in the hospital Land Rover and then hitch-hiked to Ndola, where he collected the car and loaded it with shopping for the return journey. Now that there was the possibility of getting away at times, the stresses and strains did not seem so bad. Another vehicle at the mission would be very handy. In time an all-terrain ambulance would become a necessity.

One of the cows was bitten by a snake and died. Chad went down in the lorry to Kapiri Mposhi to collect four new cows. Ron Swanson had fitted the lorry with a tarpaulin on a wooden frame to give the cows some protection. Since the return journey took eight hours, Chad spent a night at Mkushi with Unwin and Sheila Moffat where he was revived by their warm welcome, delicious food and peaceful garden.

In May the District Commissioner warned that Chitambo would be visited by the Governor-General of the Federation, Lord Dalhousie. The DC advised Chad that Lord and Lady Dalhousie were to be addressed as "Your Excellency", but every third or fourth time would be acceptable. The DC's wife offered to teach staff how to curtsy. Problems with the hospital sanitation threatened to spoil the day, and the Musks' own W.C. sprang a leak which was repaired a few hours before the visit. This was fortunate as the Dalhousies were coming to tea.

Last-minute painting and repairing of broken window-panes was still going on when the entourage rolled in. The grounds were tidy and the hospital had been painted and whitewashed 2 months previously. They arrived at the Musks' house first and were introduced to the rest of the staff. Then there was a tour of the hospital, where all the patients were neatly tucked into new, clean sheets.

Ron Swanson showed them the doctors' and sisters' houses, which had been built with grants from the Beit Trust, of which His Excellency was on the advisory committee. The plans for the nurses' home were mentioned. A word from H.E. might do the trick! Chad had a "little moan" to H.E. about the Federal government's hard dealing with the hospital. Their Excellences swept away with their retinue of police Land Rovers. Unlike their counterparts at Livingstonia on a similar occasion, the Chitambo people did not stage a demonstration against Federation, the general feeling being that it was dying a natural death.

In June Minister Mugara asked to be transferred back to his home at Mwenzo, on grounds of feeling unwell at Chitambo. Perhaps he felt discouraged at the apathy in the local church after so many years' work. It seemed that Chitambo was a tough place for people far from home.

By July the sisters' semi-detached house was ready for occupation by Janet Jack and Joey Smith. No sooner had they moved in than the water system failed. The stoves could not be lit and the pipes leaked, flooding the house. Ron Swanson had gone on holiday. No sooner was the problem solved than the hospital water system failed. Chad had to devote a great deal of time to this, as 80-90 people were relying on water-borne sanitation. The cause of the problem was a fish blocking one of the pipes.

The Foreign Mission Committee left it up to the doctors to decide who would stay at Chitambo and who would go to Mbereshi. Presbytery required Chad to sit a Chi-Lala exam and to start studying Bemba, his fourth African language since coming to Africa in 1957 (after Chi-Cewa and Chi-Tumbuka). Chad and Lily, expecting their fourth child now set their minds to the possibility of transfer to Mbereshi, while Milton Currie and his new wife, Libby, along with Milton's four reunited children made their way to Chitambo.

## CHITAMBO 1962-1964

Milton's return to Chitambo with Libby and the children in August 1962 was the start of a new and turbulent era both in the history of Northern Rhodesia and for Chitambo Hospital. Chad and Lily transferred to Mbereshi in August 1962, returning in February 1963, with 3 month old Jennifer. On their return their house was not habitable. Ron Swanson had started work on the kitchen but had been unable to finish it before moving to Lubwa. The Musks, therefore, moved into the house just vacated by the Swansons. This was the original Moffat house. Libby and Milton were initially housed in 'the cottage' before moving to the new bungalow, where Libby immediately set about creating a magnificent fruit and vegetable garden. This modern house, built with a grant from the Beit Trust, remains 'the doctor's house' to this day

Chitambo was now officially a two-doctor hospital but during the year Milton and Chad each had two months off for language study. Chad, as Medical Secretary of Presbytery as well as a member of the Finance and Executive committees, was away at meetings for almost a month during the year. Taking account of holidays for each there was in fact only one doctor available for 8 months of 1963. On June 16th 1963 Chad reported a real day off for the first time since he came in 1959. It is not surprising that Milton and Chad were quick to respond to a letter in November from the United Church of Canada asking whether there was a vacancy for a doctor at Chitambo. It was to take another three years for the new recruit to arrive.

In September 1963 Sister Joey Smith left and was replaced by Eileen Taylor from Mbereshi. It had been agreed that Chitambo could "borrow" Eileen for a few months until the new Scottish nurse Jenny Dyer had completed language study at Mbereshi. It was felt that Eileen's experience would help the two much younger nurses. In fact her energy and enthusiasm were enjoyed by everyone. In October came a request from the Roman Catholic Bishop that one of the doctors might visit Chilonga Hospital regularly to help them keep up their training requirements. Chilonga was ninety kilometres north of Chitambo. Soon Milton had taken on the job, and this was the beginning of a special friendship between the staffs of the two hospitals.

St. Andrew's church in Lochgelly, Scotland had been very supportive throughout the Musks' time at Chitambo. They responded generously to yet another appeal sent on 1st October—this time to help George Kansembe. Lily Musk wrote "*George has epilepsy. He passed his exams for secondary school and was about to leave home for the first time when he had his first fit. His father took him, as is the custom, to a village Medicine Man; for few people have realized that modern medicine can help this illness. They believe that George had been bewitched. Eventually his father brought him to Chad, and in the last two months he has been on a dosage that has controlled the fits. He could not be passed as fit for the Nursing course, but knowing that he will find no job elsewhere without further education Chad is very keen to give him a job in the hospital laboratory. He would be willing to work there for 3 pounds a month plus accommodation and food. At the same time he hopes to do a correspondence course towards sitting his Form 2 exam. He has a pretty good knowledge of English, is bright and willing, and was overjoyed when Chad suggested this to him, but I wondered if you had any ideas for making a little extra to help out?*

*The other person is Glory, daughter of Grant Mkandawire, the Senior Hospital Assistant. She had polio when she was about four years old; it has left one leg very weak and now it is twisted, and she can walk only very awkwardly with a stick. She is eight years old now—a very nice bright wee lass. I felt for long enough now that we must do something to help. Ours are all so healthy and here she is with such a handicap. On 27 pounds a month they managed to scrimp and save to buy her a caliper earlier on. Now she has outgrown it and there is no money for more. A new caliper would cost about 15 pounds.*"

On 21st October 1963 the Musks wrote to Lochgelly "*Wonderful news that St. Andrew's church will foot the bill! Chad informed Grant on Saturday, and Grant brought little Glory along to be measured on Sunday. The order will go off to the firm in Bulawayo tomorrow. Needless to say they are delighted.*

*George Kansembe has started work and is proving most helpful and willing, and keen to learn. It is wonderful to see him getting this chance. Jobs are so very scarce in this country that with his disability he would have little chance elsewhere. It is wonderful to see him learning something worthwhile instead of being forced to hang around in his village—a 'baloafa' (loafer) like so many thousands of others. Lesley McNair has promised to help him with book-keeping studies too.*

*30ᵗʰ November 1963—George Kansembe is doing a good job in the lab and Lesley is tutoring him in book-keeping and typing so that he can get ahead in his commercial correspondence course to train him for the kind of job that will suit him. Little Glory's caliper is on order. She still struggles the two miles to Mabonde and back each day to attend school. According to her father she is progressing well. The caliper should be a great help.*

*Earlier this year the Federal government said there would be no grants made for equipment this year but for drugs only, so the Small Donations Account, which helps for Christmas treats etc., had to be used with every available penny just to keep the patients covered with sheets and blankets (sheets being a recent luxury). So the money I have collected through sales of clothing etc. will go towards Christmas gifts for patients and staff. Sister Janet Jack has left to be married. She has made a tremendous contribution during her time here."*

Chad's letter home in November 1963 summed the year up-:

*Dear Friends, the rains have come bringing a welcome coolness and refreshment. As we write this, flying beetles are circling the Tilley lamp and giant spiders are coursing round the ant-proofing at the base of our sitting-room wall. Dozens of frogs are serenading in the irrigation furrow which passes near the site of the house. Sometimes there is a lull and then we can hear the high song of the tree crickets or the mournful flute of a night bird. Outside it's pitch dark but there is a good smell of growing things, not quite like spring in Scotland but almost. It is certainly turning our thoughts homewards to the many friends we so often think about but seldom write to. Perhaps it is some excuse to say that it has been difficult to know what to write. This time last year we were in the middle of a six month spell at Mbereshi, formerly a London Missionary Society station, now along with Chitambo, under the authority of the church in Northern Rhodesia. Dr. Currie had returned from leave but we had only a few days together and had no chance to get the feel of Chitambo as a two-doctor hospital. Our time at Mbereshi was stimulating and enjoyable, memorable, not least because our little red-head, Jennifer Ruth was born there a year ago. The hospital is newer, better equipped and more adequately staffed than ours and is blessed with a doctor and sisters who have been there for a number of years and so have been able to get the hospital running smoothly and themselves fluent in the local language (Bemba).*

*At Chitambo we are losing Sister Janet Jack who gets married next month. She has done an enormous amount to improve the efficiency of the hospital in a brief two years. There is a big question mark over the return of our Matron and Tutor Joey Smith, who is at present home on leave; she would be a great loss. Sister Irene Sneddon has only a year left with us. We look forward to the arrival of Sister Jenny Dyer towards the end of this month. Like Sister Sneddon, she has been sent out in response to an urgent need, without missionary training and for a short tour of service. Sister Eileen Taylor, with fifteen years of experience at Mbereshi behind her, has come over to help us but she is needed there and must soon return. One hears now about many doctors and sisters leaving government service and going back home because of anxieties about the political future of the country.*

*In the church we have grown accustomed to the idea of African government and we are thrilled of the opportunities that may well be ahead of us—without having any illusions about the problems. A training hospital like Chitambo has a significant part to play, so we believe, if only nursing staff from Scotland will come and help us. It's no easy job; everyone acknowledges the need for more trained African women, yet we have lost several of our student nurses in sad circumstances; we must accept much of the blame because of our failure to provide, until now, a house-mother for the girls and perhaps also because we have not done enough about organizing recreational activities for the students.*

*In the wards, work is always a full pressure. As a training hospital we are constantly asking higher standards of ourselves. Yet the beds are too close together and there are often patients on the floor in the small spaces between them. There are always occupied beds in the corridor. One of our biggest problems recently has been babies with pneumonia. Malnourished babies without much hold on life. Milk from our own cows—as much as we can use—is working miracles. This year the dry season has brought even more folk than usual suffering from extensive burns. Several are epileptics. Some were in hospital last year. After much labour dressing and skin-grafting they were healed and able to go home. Some made an effort to return to hospital every month to receive supplies of drugs to control their fits. But in most cases the effort, if made at all, was soon abandoned. The patients lived far away, they were of low intelligence or unstable temperament and, anyway, no-one in the village really believed that there was any cause of epilepsy other than spirit possession, so what was the point of taking hospital medicines at all?*

*It's not always like this of course. There's George Kansembe, a highly intelligent young man now working in the hospital laboratory whose fits are completely controlled and who has nothing but a few scars to show for the wasted years when his father took him from witch-doctor to witch-doctor until at last someone told him the hospital could help. Six year-old Changwe relieves the labour of a ward round with his un-self-conscious singing, sweet and tuneful, and twinkling eyes that make you laugh at him. He is an epileptic with a deep burn of his hand and arm. He is going to lose some of his fingers. One wonders what his future will be.*

*We had visitors with us last week-end, when late one evening a student reported "Doctor, I have just admitted a child to isolation. I think he may need a tracheotomy through the night." Our visitors were an anthropologist and his wife who were studying the lives of villagers very near the home of this student. They were astonished at his (the student's) obvious grasp of the job.*

*Earlier this year we had a spell off hospital duties for language study. The period was short and the language is hard but we made some progress and Chad has been able since to take his first full service in the vernacular. We have made new friendships because we had time to sit and talk. There is not much chance for this sort of thing for either of us at the moment. Dr. Currie is having his turn of language study and the hospital is more than enough for one doctor. Lily has been teaching David and he is now coming to the end of his first year "at school". His supervisor in Salisbury seems pleased with his progress. We hope Elspeth will be able to begin school by correspondence in January, although she is not five until March; she plays at school just now while David is doing his lessons. Two-year-old Stewart is reveling in this season of creepie-crawlies and he regularly comes in in high triumph with a new caterpillar or beetle he has tracked down and captured.*

*We seem to have gone full circle now-so perhaps this is the time to stop. With very best wishes to you all at Christmas time.*

*Love Chad and Lily.*

Milton's letter of January 1964 gave some of the political back-ground for that year.

*The beginning of a New Year seems a good time to write a newsletter about the stirring changes taking place in this country, particularly as they affect the life and work of the United Church of Central Africa here at Chitambo. Federation, which was so resented by the peoples on whom it was imposed, is ended. More than a million voters have gone to the polls to elect Northern Rhodesia's first African government under a new constitution, and the elections have gone far more smoothly and peacefully than most of us expected. Dr.*

*Kaunda has won a resounding victory and is our first Prime Minister. The United National Independence Party (UNIP) candidate (Mateyo Kakumbi) for this district was returned un-opposed. Tragically he was stricken with a very serious illness and was admitted to Chitambo hospital.*

*Sadly Mr. Kakumbi has died, of myeloid leukaemia, which we knew would prove fatal. We had the heartbreaking duty of breaking this news to his relatives a few days before he died. One of these was his son who is one of our students at the hospital. Our African Minister Rev. Yaphet Mugara was a tower of strength to the family in those last few days. He knew how quick many people would be to ascribe the death of this man to witchcraft, especially because of the sudden nature of the illness in an otherwise healthy and strong man, and because of the importance of his position. In fact he had no sooner died than one of his brothers began to make such accusations. "All Africa" was at the funeral and one of the local chiefs, Chief Mailo, launched into a bitter attack on Europeans in general and the District Commissioner in particular, for preventing the people from carrying out their usual custom of finding out by means of omens who it was who had killed Mr. Kakumbi. He made no secret of his opinion that such a person should be sought out and killed. In this he was applauded by quite a large section of the crowd.*

*Earlier this week I conveyed a message from my patient (Mr. Kakumbi) to the Prime Minister in Lusaka where I had gone to take my children back to school. It was interesting to see the new Ministers arriving at the Secretariat in their luxurious cars, carrying bulky brief cases and looking tremendously important.*

*Many changes are apparent already. In the schools to which our children go, a number of African and Indian children have been enrolled—not a very large number yet because these are fee-paying schools, but nevertheless a very important and desirable change. We are most heartened to find that there is no shortage of teachers after all. Many have left, but others have come to take their places. The Europeans who remain in this country are those who are prepared to accept an African government, and to work for the good of the country.*

*It is too early yet to know what the policy of the new government will be towards the church hospitals but we hope and pray that it will be more sympathetic than was the Federal government which seemed to regard such hospitals as un-necessary extras, and not part of the essential medical services of the country. Many doctors and nurses have left the country. There is all the more need for those who remain.*

*It would be impossible in a short news-letter to give anything like a survey of the medical work of Chitambo Hospital. I can only pick out some of the more outstanding features of the work, of the thousands of ordinary illnesses and injuries treated. Chitambo itself is in a healthy situation, thanks to the wisdom of its founder, Malcolm Moffat, but in some of the low-lying areas around us the dreaded tsetse fly still spreads sleeping sickness, a disease peculiar to tropical Africa. Many of these cases come to us, some of them already in the sleepy stuperose stage which gives the disease its name, and which marks the beginning of the end. Sometimes they come too late to be saved, but in the majority of cases we are able to save them with injections of a drug called Mel B (Melarsoprol). It is most thrilling to see these dull-witted apathetic people coming back to normal, and going out of hospital full of the joy of life again. The treatment is not without its risk because Mel B is a most powerful and dangerous drug, and has to be used with the greatest of care.*

*Another feature of the work at Chitambo is the number of very bad burns we are called upon to treat. Many of these are due to falling into the fire during epileptic fits. Many need months of hospital treatment and repeated skin grafting operations. Some, like Milika Mvula are so badly burned that they have to have a leg amputated. After her amputation, and the refusal of the Federal ministry of health to fund a prosthesis, the makers of surgical prostheses in the Copperbelt appealed to a charitable organization in the Copperbelt, who paid for the leg in full. I had the pleasure of taking Milika back to her home by car and seeing the rousing welcome she received*

*Gunshot wounds are common in this part of Africa. Sometimes they result from shooting accidents. A man was riding his bicycle a few months ago, followed by his friend on another bicycle, carrying a loaded gun. The gun fell and went off, shooting the front man in the foot. I had to extract the bullet, an old piece of 3/8" iron rod from his sole. More often the injuries result from the explosion of ancient muzzle-loading guns which have been charged with more powder than they can stand, and this result in horrible mutilations of hands. Sometimes the whole hand is blown off. These guns are family heirlooms, handed down from generation to generation, and some of them are more dangerous to the hunter than to the quarry.* (Perhaps some of these guns had been exchanged for slaves?)

*Yet another injury which is common here is the human bite. Of all the animals that can bite a man, there is none more dangerous than homo-sapiens.*

*Many a septic hand or arm we see as a result of a human bite of a finger. One old woman in the hospital was bitten on the finger by her husband. We had to advise her to have the finger amputated. She agreed, on condition that we put one of her husband's in its place!*

On Feb 19th 1964 Chad Musk wrote *Milton returned (from Lusaka) with new mother (Libby) and baby Anne.* (Milton was clearly not going to take responsibility for another obstetric tragedy.) *On the same night the Wilkies arrived from Mwenzo—Jim with hepatitis.*

*We have been realizing how well things have come on in the hospital in the last year or so and how well off we are compared with government hospitals. Our students are developing a real sense of responsibility for patients and it is hard to remember when we had our last disciplinary trouble. The Sisters and students are working well together.*

On March 16th 1964 Chad wrote *Ron Swanson has handed in his resignation on Doctrinal grounds. He came to Chitambo in September 1960. It will leave us without a builder and we have just heard that the Beit Trust and Church of Scotland are each giving us 3,000 pounds to build a nurses' home. Now almost certainly money is to be awarded to us to start our Mobile Clinic work. The new vehicle from Canada will not be here until September.*

On May 3rd 1964 Chad records—*This morning the Hospital took the (church) service. Mr. Grant Mkandawire led Worship. He and Mr. Welton Chavula are often in the pulpit so this was nothing unusual, but the rest of the service was a departure from normal. Milton led the Prayer of Intercession and the students took the offering. At sermon time Mr. Chavula rose (to his full 6 feet) and announced that he was Luke, the Doctor. He talked about Jesus' work of healing and he connected up four playlets and 2 narrations by eye witnesses of Jesus' healing miracles. The son of the widow of Nain was the climax—the party bearing the body came into the church with the most genuine wailing and there was mighty jubilation when the hospital odd-job man leapt up from under his sheet. St Luke ended his narration and the 'Sermon' with a very long prayer. Grant took the opportunity of the Benediction to drive home the point of the service in another long prayer. Later the old stalwarts of the congregation expressed great appreciation of the service.*

**Welton Chavula and family**

Chad continued the outreach work in the old Land Rover with *2 cardboard cartons of medicines, the black bag and the midwifery case. July 19th—First stop Chief Muchinka's village—over 100 patients seen. Moved on 30 miles to Chief Kafinda's—spent the night there and then between 8 am and 2 pm we saw over 100 more patients. Malarial mosquitoes are doing their work in this lower-lying area. Then a 2 hour trip further into the bush to Mpelembe where more patients waited. The last lap was in the dark on a real bush track to the place where Livingstone died. The 3rd day was spent at a government-run dispensary near the Livingstone memorial where the Medical Assistant in charge had set himself out to make the best use of the first visit of a doctor for two years. July 31st-Jenny Dyer (nurse) has come from Harthill (Lanarkshire)—a very nice girl with a great deal of sense. She came out for two years but has decided to stay for four.*

While there was little political unrest at Chitambo itself, in 1964, there were outbreaks of violence in other parts of the country as Northern Rhodesia struggled towards independence. One of these was the Lenshina uprising at Chinsali in August 1964. The tragic story of the Lumpa church revolt is told in John Hudson's book "*A Time To Mourn*". Hudson was District Commissioner of the Isoka district in 1964 and he was personally involved in seeking a peaceful solution.

Milton wrote on 14th August 1964—*Alice Lenshina is a self-styled prophetess who had a very large following, especially in the Chinsali District, where she drew very many members away from the United Church of Central Africa. Within the past three weeks her followers have unleashed a reign of terror against the people of the Chinsali and Lundazi districts, which resulted in the army being called in, and still further bloodshed as the Lenshina followers were driven out of their fortified villages. None of this trouble has touched Chitambo directly, since we are 200 miles from either of the troubled areas, but we did see the army moving north two weeks ago. More recently, leaders of the United Church of Central Africa are on their way to Chinsali to try to mediate in the fighting, and to help in the work of reconciliation and rehabilitation. Now that Alice Lenshina has given herself up, we hope and pray that the bloodshed will cease. We have heard already of a great return of many of her erstwhile followers to the church in Lubwa. The church now has a great opportunity and challenge to witness through the work of reconciliation. Pray that it will be equal to the task.*

Milton continued:

*A week ago Chitambo had a visit from the Parliamentary Secretary to the Minister of Health. We showed him round the hospital and told him of our hopes for the future under the new African government. We got the impression that his government was very much more sympathetic to the work of church hospitals like Chitambo than the Federal government had been, and we have good grounds to hope that this hospital will be much more fully supported by the government as the main hospital for the district.*

Of his own visits round the district Milton wrote—*These visits have been enthusiastically received by the people and there have been large crowds at the various centres visited. I have paid two visits to the village of Chief Muchinda, ninety miles by road from here. This particular village serves largely as an administrative centre for part of the district. Here the chief has his court house, where he hears cases and gives judgement. It was in the courtroom that I spent the night, and also examined my patients. The village consists of about a dozen brick houses roofed with corrugated iron, a small store, and a number of more primitive thatched houses. It has neither a church nor a school.*

*On my last visit there my ordained missionary colleague, Rev. Alan Roy was also visiting in that area and took with him an African theological student, Wallace Mfula, and an evangelist. These two conducted a service with the 98 patients who came to see me that day, emphasizing that this work of medical visitation is an integral part of the work of the Church. It has been a great thrill to me to be able at last to get out into the district and see the homes of the people. This is possible because there are now two doctors at Chitambo, and Dr. Musk shares in the work of medical touring.*

*On one of my tours, I found at a certain school a young man with an acute attack of pleurisy. He had not known that there was a doctor coming, and he was delighted with his good fortune to get medical attention just when he needed it. On the same trip, I was stopped by a man whose little boy had just received a nasty cut on the head a few minutes earlier. He wanted me to take the boy to Serenje dispensary 40 miles away. He considered himself fortunate that a vehicle had arrived just when needed and he was amazed when he found that it contained a doctor. He is an elder of the church, and so we were all the more pleased to meet each other. The little boy is doing well in Serenje Dispensary after getting first aid by the road-side.*

*These medical visits allow the church to make a much greater impact on the district. Many simple ailments could be cured even on a brief visit. Many bad teeth are painlessly extracted. Many of the more seriously ill are given the chance of coming into hospital. The one problem, which I have foreseen all along, is how to cope with all the patients who are now flocking into hospital. Already we are full to overflowing, with a daily average of 118 in-patients.*

*One of the striking changes which one notices while touring this district now is the extent to which people are growing tobacco. The government has been actively encouraging this project, and everywhere there are small plots of Turkish tobacco, with drying sheds and barns. Agricultural demonstrators are scattered through the district to give help and advice to the growers. During the year some 40,000 pounds came into the district to be distributed among about 1,200 growers. Roads are being improved to enable the crops to be transported. Speaking personally and speaking as a doctor, I could wish that the cash crop had been something more beneficial to humanity than tobacco, but at least it is good to see more money coming into the poverty-stricken rural areas, so that the local people can have a home industry and be less dependent on employment in the towns.*

*I would be glad to see more stock farming, to improve the diet of the people, especially the diet of the children, so many of whom still die of malnutrition. Here at Chitambo we have set an example by keeping a herd of dairy cattle, the gift of a large number of friends in Scotland, and these lovely cows provide about 30 pints of milk a day for the many malnourished children and our growing collection of patients with tuberculosis.*

*The hospital has set aside 15 beds for patients with tuberculosis but we now have far more than that number of sufferers. It is one of the major medical problems of this district, indeed of this country. Modern medicine has made it possible to cure this disease and it is one of the most gratifying features of our medical work to see these miserable sufferers, many of whom are small children, returning to full health and strength. But we are very conscious that we are only nibbling at the fringe of the problem, which requires to be tackled on a national scale.*

*Another disease which is prevalent in Northern Rhodesia at this time is smallpox. We have had our share of smallpox cases. The big difficulty in this country is to isolate the cases, and to follow up the contacts. The government is doing all it can in sending out teams of vaccinators to the villages. There is as yet no cure for this terrible disease, so the main reason for admitting cases to hospital is to prevent its spread, but it is very difficult to prevent friends from visiting these cases in hospital, and in fact some friends have been infected in this very way.*

*Two months ago a girl of 12 was brought into hospital extremely ill with sleeping sickness. She had been ill since April, and arrived at hospital in the last stages of the disease. She got gradually worse during the first few days in hospital and her mother implored me "Let me take her home and bury her." I said "She is not dead yet. Don't speak of burying her before she is dead." "Oh yes, she is dead already", wailed the mother. But we persisted with our treatment, though the girl was unconscious and really at death's door. I had prayer with the mother at the bed-side, and told her to go on praying, which I noticed she did. Gradually over the course of many weeks the girl improved, first physically and then mentally, until at last she made a complete recovery. Two weeks ago we had the joy of seeing her go out of hospital completely cured.*

*On the same day we discharged another little girl who had come in with cerebral malaria, and who had lain unconscious for many days. When at last she regained consciousness, she was unable to speak. It took many weeks before she was able to speak again and still longer before she could walk. All along she was a most brave and cheerful patient, and at last she recovered completely.*

*We grew to love her very much while she was with us, and she was in tears as she parted from us, but we were thrilled to see her fully restored to health. Someday we'll see her again when we visit her home village with our new Mobile Dispensary.*

*Next week we hope to welcome back our matron, Sister Joey Smith, who is returning from Scotland, and then we shall be fully up to strength again to carry on the growing work of healing and training and evangelism at Chitambo.*

# THE BIRTH OF ZAMBIA OCTOBER 1964

At the end of 1964 Milton summed up the events of that year in a special newsletter-:

*We have come to the end of a very memorable year, both for Chitambo and for this country. This time last year we were in Northern Rhodesia: today we are in Zambia. 1964 will be remembered as the year of our independence. I was fortunate to be able to be in Lusaka, the capital, at the time of the Independence Celebrations. (24th October 1964). I had a special reason for being there apart from having been invited to the celebrations. A special invitation had been extended by the government of Zambia to a number of former Church of Scotland missionaries to come to Lusaka for the celebrations. These included Dr. and Mrs. Todd, who rebuilt this hospital, sister Margaret Turnbull who once served here, Rev. Kenneth McKenzie who also served at Chitambo, and who has been a great champion of African freedom, and sister Ruth Service, who has the honour of having brought Dr. Kaunda, the President of Zambia, into the world. I went to meet these Very Important People at the airport, and bring some of them to Chitambo, scene of their former labours.*

*It was a great source of joy to the local Christians that the new government had honoured the Church of Scotland in this way. They do not forget how again and again the Church of Scotland spoke out on behalf of the African people during the years of Federation, and often much to the annoyance of the Federal government.*

A special service of thanksgiving for Independence was broadcast from Lusaka Cathedral.

Meanwhile at Chitambo the hospital staff celebrated with an *Independence Ball*. Chad reported—*It was an impromptu affair but a great success. Women brought loads of firewood during the afternoon. After dark a great bonfire was lit in front of the hospital. One of the long-stay patients was soon performing skilfully on his Ilimba—an attractive instrument made from a large gourd. Two of his friends joined in with drums which they held between their knees and beat in fantastic rhythmic duet with their hands. That was enough. Every patient who could walk was out and waiting expectantly round the fire. The drumming became more and more urgent and from every direction came the entire population of Chitambo, grannies helping with toddlers and mothers with babies on their backs. Young and old, doctors and sisters too were soon joining the dance round the drummers in the light of the blazing fire. There was lots of laughing and hand-shaking. The full moon rose high in the sky and we served cocoa to everyone—gallons and gallons of it. And so we celebrated at Chitambo, as one ZBC commentator put it "the birth of the new baby, Zambia, among the nations of the world."*

Milton continued—*Dr. and Mrs. Todd were able to spend three weeks at Chitambo, and got a rousing welcome from the people of this district, who remember so well the work they did here. It was a special pleasure to be able to show them the developments and improvements in the hospital that have taken place in the nine years since they left.*

*There have been some exciting improvements to the hospital during the past year. One was the installation of gas stoves in the sterilizing room of the operating theatre, for sterilizing instruments and dressings. Formerly we used primus stoves, which blackened the walls and ceilings when they smoked. This great improvement was made possible by a gift from a member of Battlefield West Church, Glasgow. We took the opportunity to get the theatre and sterilizing room painted. A group of young Christians, all Europeans from congregations on the Copperbelt camped at Chitambo for a long week-end, and did some of the painting as a piece of voluntary service to the hospital.*

*Another most valuable gift to the hospital came from Canada. The father-in-law of one of our Canadian ministers had died, and the family suggested that their friends, instead of sending wreaths, might make donations to the United Church of Central Africa. With these gifts, Chitambo Hospital was able to buy loudspeakers for all its wards, and a radio, tape-recorder and microphone. We are now able to broadcast to the wards, and we conduct our daily service of worship in the dispensary, which serves as our broadcast room. The patients stay in their wards, instead of all trying to crowd into the one ward in which the service was being conducted. We find that people now hear much better, and pay better attention, and even those who are completely confined to bed are still able to take part in the services. In addition the radio can be played to all wards, and I have often seen patients dancing in the wards to popular African music. At Christmas time we gathered a choir of nurses and tape-recorded our favourite Christmas hymns, which were then relayed to all the wards on Christmas Day. Two days ago we had a visit from a wandering blind African minstrel with his 'harp' if you can call it that. The instrument is called a 'chilimba' and consists of a number of metal keys on a wooden board, which are plucked with the fingers. The man wanted lodging for the night, and in return, gave us a recital, which I broadcast through the hospital, and at the same time recorded to be used again. It was immensely popular—much more so than any European music would have been!*

*Still another valuable gift from the Knox Memorial Church, Winnipeg, Manitoba, made it possible for us to buy a modern anaesthetic machine, a thing we have been wanting for years. Now it is in use, and Dr. Musk and I are thrilled to be able to give anaesthetics the modern way, instead of dropping ether onto a face mask in the manner of last century.*

*At present the children are on holiday with us at Chitambo, and are as usual enjoying very much being at home. They are especially enjoying their baby sister, Anne (Zanna), who is now nearly at the walking stage, and who, in turn, enjoys their company very much. Our boys love to explore the surrounding country, in company with their African friends, and have discovered some hitherto unknown caves with Bushman paintings which date from the Stone Age.*

Chitambo was a paradise for the four of us in school holidays. With our older brothers and some local dogs for protection, we were allowed to wander freely in the surrounding countryside. We often spent the day on our bikes, bumping along paths to remote villages. On one such expedition we wandered into an area of rocky hills beyond the village of Katikulula. The boys had spotted a rabbit and decided to chase it. The frightened creature disappeared through a crack in the rocks, with Doug in hot pursuit. Doug's disappearance was followed by a shout of excitement *"Come and see what I've found!"* We scrambled through a narrow gap and into a cave with unmistakable rock paintings and shards of pottery on the sandy floor. With mixed feelings we told our parents about 'our' cave, and some time later a group of archaeologists from the Livingstone museum came to excavate it, naming the 'Nakakapula cave' a significant site in the transition between the Stone Age and the Iron Age. Our brothers found other cave sites, including a 'fortified village' in the area but they were more remote and the possibility of leopards in the vicinity deterred us from getting back to see them.

Milton continued-

*The medical touring has been taken over almost entirely by Dr. Musk. There is great demand for his visits, especially from some of the further corners of the district, such as Chiundaponde, which is a strong bastion of the Church. Dr. Musk visited there this week and had 140 patients. The Minister and Sister Dyer went too and they all had a very profitable time, and a safe journey despite the heavy rains and flooded roads.*

*We have a new minister now. The Rev. Yaphet Mugara has been transferred back to his home area, Mwenzo, after five strenuous years of faithful service here. He has been a great leader, a wise counsellor on difficult problems, and a great peace-maker in times of trouble. We had a moving Communion service in which he preached his last sermon here. He is succeeded by the Rev. Noah Chulu, a man of a very different character, lacking, perhaps some of the fire of Mr. Mugara, but with great qualities of his own. He is a gentle and humble man, and a great one for travelling round his district.*

*I do not yet have the figures for Chitambo Hospital for 1964 but it must surely be the hospital's busiest year ever. It has been full to overflowing all year through, and we have had many difficult cases which have made heavy demands on the nurses. In my last letter I told of a girl who made a wonderful recovery from sleeping sickness. We have another such patient in the hospital now, a woman who was carried for two days on a bicycle to reach us and was almost dead when she got here. She was semi-conscious for days, but is now up and about, gathering her strength for the journey home.*

*We have had more patients for the cataract operation. Samuel Ntalenga was one. He was sent from Abercorn hospital, in the extreme north of Zambia, to Kitwe on the Copperbelt—a distance of about 500 miles. There happened to be no eye surgeon there so he was sent back to Abercorn. Then he was sent to Chitambo where we were able to do the operations on both eyes. We were also able to give him a pair of cataract spectacles, which had been sent to us from Turriff, Aberdeenshire, so that he was able to read again. More recently two old ladies had their cataracts removed. Neither of them could read so it was more difficult to test their eyes for glasses. The problem was solved by getting them to thread needles in order to find which lenses suited their eyes best. The whole ward cheered them on as they tried to get the threads into the eyes of the needles.*

*In a few days' time there is going to be a great meeting at Kitwe on the Copperbelt to solemnize the union of two more churches with the United Church of Central Africa. The Methodist Church and the Church of Barotseland (a daughter of the Paris evangelical mission) will be joining us, to form the United Church of Zambia. This will be a great step forward, and we hope that it will lead to still further unions. We rejoice in the growing unity of Christians in this country and also in the goodwill of the government towards the Church, and especially towards its hospitals, which are striving to improve the health of the people of Zambia as an integral part of their Christian witness.*

At these words the shadowy trudging figure of Livingstone appears to stop, look round and raise his dusty cap in tribute, before fading again amongst the mopane trees.

## CHITAMBO 1965—THE MOBILE DISPENSARY

By May 1965 the long-awaited new Mobile Dispensary had arrived and Chad was able to take it out around the district. He wrote on 13th May-

*I have just come back from my first trip with the Mobile Dispensary, a gift from the United Church of Canada. Yes it has arrived at last! And a very nice vehicle it is. It is a long wheel base Land Rover with a high tropical roof. There are windows at the back and on one side. Inside, there is a bench seat, a stretcher rest, four tiers of medicine cupboards (a very large capacity,) a wash-basin, bright roof light and powerful examination lamp, fan and large polythene bottles for carrying water. Using the reserve tank and bumper jerry-cans we can carry 28 gallons of petrol which gives us a range of something like 500 miles. A tent extension can be rigged up from the back in a few moments, greatly increasing the work space. The springing seems better than in other Land Rovers I have known, so that it is reasonably comfortable to travel in the back even on bad roads.*

**The Mobile Dispensary**

*It was a pleasure to use. The bottles of medicine travelled well and we arrived at Chibale (120 miles away) with the cupboards just as Mr. Mkandawire, our Senior Medical Assistant, had packed them. Dental instruments, bowls, syringes, dressings etc., all in sterile packs were in one line of cupboards and large stock bottles filled the bottom line opposite. Tablets were above these—I had enough to keep a small hospital going for a week or two. The Mobile Dispensary itself was, of course, a great attraction everywhere and there were at least as many sight-seers as patients. All had to be taken on a conducted tour!*

*What a delight it is to have our own vehicle for this job. With its arrival we begin again in organizing our district work. October to January were busy and very worthwhile months, going round in the station vehicle. However, in February, we were some 70 miles from home in lion country and it was dark. The generator failed; we were lucky to get home. Getting up a new generator took a dismally long time and I had the unhappy experience of not turning up when large crowds were expecting me. There was no way of getting a message out to them. Much of February was lost. I couldn't start giving notice of my next visits until the station vehicle was working again and this cost some more weeks.*

# MOBILE DISPENSARY LOG OF ONE TRIP 1965

## *Monday*

*Ba Maxon who works in the hospital laundry heard of a death at his home village in Chief Kafinda's area. He wanted a lift to the funeral but was not ready on time, left half an hour late. Near Muchinka we met people going to the funeral of a young woman who died in Chitambo on Saturday evening. She had had a retained placenta for 2 days and was exsanguinated when admitted. All the important people knew that the fault was with those who did not bring her quickly. Arrived at Yakobi's village—empty. Everyone at funeral. Went on to guest house (brick, 2 small rooms, tin roof) at Chief Muchinka's village—nobody there. Unpacked and set up medicines, water was eventually brought and a small group arrived. Read and talked on "the lame man at Bethseda." Prayer. Saw patients until about 12.30 pm (40 altogether). No food prepared for us this time. Everyone at the funeral. Left for Kafinda. Saw plenty of monkeys on the way. Arrived at 1.30 pm. Brewed up tea. We were expected here. Started seeing patients and worked til dark. Girl with pneumonia—all left lung involved. Child with severe tonsillitis, plenty of malaria. Rigged up camp bed and mosquito net in dark. Chilufya, our driver, went off to Malupande's village for the evening (he is an ex-TB patient-most grateful). I cooked up a solitary meal.*

## *Tuesday*

*By 6.30 am people were waiting for treatment. Made a start while cooking breakfast. In the middle of cooking, called over to Headmaster's for food. Apologies about the previous night—they had 5 unexpected visitors and not enough relish to go round. This morning we were served cassava porridge and chicken. Returned to work. Girl with pneumonia much better. About 10 am a message that Chief Kafinda wanted to see me before I left. Finished at 10.30 am and packed up. The Chief arrived. He wanted me to visit another centre in his area regularly. Left Kafinda at 11.30 a.m. having seen 68 patients.*

*Arrived at Mpelembe about 1.30pm, dropping Maxon at his village. Land Rover would not start, needed crank handle. Wouldn't start at all after first stop at Mpelembe. Turned out to be only dirty terminals. Crowd of people gathered outside small hut—one door, no windows. Headmaster most helpful.*

*Great welcome from everyone. Tables, chair (initially upholstered armchair), water arrived quickly. Crowd impatient to be home having waited since early morning. Started seeing patients. Eye problems, malaria, dental extractions. David Alexander (Assistant District Secretary from government Headquarters) came in. He was visiting Mpelembe to see self-help building programme. Much activity evident in this place. Worked with patients until dark. Finally a case of smallpox—a child of one year old. Healing but had been severe. Many cases in the area in the previous month the headmaster told me. David called again and saw his first case of smallpox—rather upset. I gave him a telegram to send for me, notifying it (government acted fairly quickly and a vaccination team went into the area and did a thorough job).*

*Left for Chipundu (the Livingstone memorial). Near Chipundu tree was lying over our path. Went off and eventually found village and came back with axes. Tree was logged and removed. Arrived at Chipundu nearly 11p.m. Roused Mr. Malwelwe, the Headmaster. Rigged up bed and mosquito net in Headmaster's office. Mosquitoes very numerous. Malwelwe very helpful in spite of the hour. Bed at last-hot.*

## Wednesday

*School bell at 5.30 am. Immediately after, a wee girl came into the office for books, and I still abed. She continued to go in and out til 6 am. Couldn't get up! Eventually shaved and made breakfast, and shared it with Chilufya and Maxon. Attended school prayers. We were half a mile from the actual spot where David Livingstone died. There is a government Dispensary here. The Medical assistant in charge is a political refugee from Southern Rhodesia and does not like the bush. His medical work was not impressive. We saw a man with a shoulder badly mauled by a leopard (it attacked him while he was bending down filling a bucket at a river). The people did not have much confidence in this dispensary—so often there aren't any drugs, stocks very low at this visit. I supplied what I could. Finished at about 10.30 am. Waited for a blind woman to arrive—cataract in both eyes. Decided to take her to Chitambo. She was subsequently very successfully treated. We also took a man with generalized lymph gland enlargement, another with intestinal amoebiasis, and one with pleurisy for investigation. Heavy rain on homeward journey; road like a river but Land Rover went well. Home between 3 and 4 pm. Saw 70 patients at Mpelembe and 26 at Chipundu.*

1965 saw the arrival of Miss Isabel Richmond to boost the nursing staff. On 1st July Chad and Lily Musk went on leave to Scotland. A Canadian medical student—Dick MacLean arrived in June on a 3-month scholarship funded by Smith, Kline and French. He helped out in the hospital and also with the outreach work in the Mobile Dispensary. His presence eased the load for Milton until Dr. and Mrs. Gordon Robertson arrived, as missionaries from the United Church of Canada.

September saw the departure of Lesley McNair who had been the book-keeper and Administrator of the hospital for four years. Brian Siderman, Bursar of the Malcolm Moffat Teacher Training College at Serenje agreed to visit Chitambo once a month to help with the administration. Just as in Malcolm Moffat's day, the book-keeping was an onerous task on top of the day to day running of the station.

The arrival in March of Mr. Peter Stead as technical officer was very welcome. He began repairs on Dr. Robertson's house, (the original doctor's house built by Malcolm Moffat) installed a diesel electric lighting plant and its housing, for the hospital and electric wiring for the maternity block, built a garage for the hospital vehicles and carried out repairs on numerous hospital buildings and staff houses. He also helped to draw up plans for a new outpatient clinic and T.B. block. The latter was deemed a priority by the Provincial Medical Director. In his spare time he constructed an invisible bridge to Miss Richmond's door and they planned to marry in June 1966.

One of the highlights of 1965 was the employment of Mr. Lovewell Mbebeta, one of Chitambo's own trainees, as a Medical Assistant. Later in the year two more students—Agnes Sebata and Violet Muwamba, graduated as Medical Assistants and joined the staff. The nursing training school was successful in that all its trainees passed their final exams as Medical Assistants. From 1965 onwards the school would train Zambian Enrolled Nurses. 18 new students were taken on, bringing the total number of students to 30. Accommodation for the nursing students became a pressing problem.

Some statistical data for the hospital is included to show how things had changed at Chitambo over the years.

## IN PATIENT STATISTICS FOR 1965

| | |
|---|---|
| Remaining in hospital 31st Dec 1964 | 126 |
| Admitted in 1965 | 1,869 |
| Died | 64 |
| Total in-patient days | 38,499 |
| Daily average of inpatients | 105.3 |
| Number of beds | 82 |
| Total out-patient attendances | 9,666 |
| Daily average of outpatients | 18.9 |
| | |
| Theatre operations | 136 |
| Minor | 41 |
| Major | 41 |
| Caesarean Sections | 18 |
| Forceps deliveries | 6 |
| Total deliveries | 131 |
| Total live births | 121 |

## PREVALENT ILLNESSES

| DISEASE | ADMITTED | DIED |
|---|---|---|
| Pulmonary Tuberculosis | 62 | 6 |
| Other forms of Tuberculosis | 7 | |
| Whooping Cough | 16 | |
| Measles | 78 | 3 |
| Malaria | 165 | 2 |
| Bilharzia | 10 | |
| Trypanosomiasis | 14 | 1 |
| Malnutrition | 34 | 3 |
| Anaemias | 28 | 1 |
| Inflammation of eyes | 117 | |
| Lobar pneumonia | 74 | |
| Bronchopneumonia | 21 | 1 |
| Appendicitis | 5 | |
| Motor accidents | 21 | |
| Burns | 56 | |
| Firearm injuries | 6 | |

Milton comments *There has been a further marked increase in the number of cases of tuberculosis admitted, compared with the previous year. The need for new tuberculosis wards is underlined. Measles was still a prevalent and debilitating disease, even resulting in some deaths. As always the largest single group of patients admitted was that suffering from malaria. Many different kinds of injuries are treated during the year. A growing number of these are due to motor accidents. Every year a number of people are brought in with gunshot wounds, or wounds caused by old muzzle-loading guns exploding in their owners' hands.*

TB patients, whose treatment lasted for up to a year, often ran away from the hospital. In the pre-independence days mission staff would appeal to the local chiefs to help return these patients to the hospital. Later this responsibility was taken over by the Rural Council.

Chitambo was now the main hospital for the district, and recognized by the Zambian government as such with increasing grants. At long last the medical assistants could have salaries similar to their government counterparts. With increased capital expenditure there were hopes of building a special tuberculosis wing, a suitable home for the student nurses and plans for an isolation ward, outpatient clinics and better staff houses. One of the hospital's main benefactors was the Beit Trust. On 15th September 1965 Sir Alfred and Lady Beit came to visit and admire the results of their generosity.

The new diesel generator for the hospital, taken from the old Mwenzo hospital, was much quieter than the petrol engine, which was now reserved for taking x-rays. The petrol generator would wake the whole hospital at night when an emergency Caesarean section was being done. With other parts of the hospital wired, the laboratory could now have some electric equipment, including a centrifuge. An electric clock was donated for the operating theatre and the gift of a new microscope, so important for the identification of tropical conditions such as malaria and sleeping sickness, was a great boon. New shelving in the drug room enabled the drugs to be set out in alphabetical order. The labelling of the shelves was a school holiday job for members of the Currie family, as was the mixing of fortified milk for the orphaned and malnourished babies.

Mr. Lovewell Mbebeta, underwent further training to become a theatre nurse. He also became adept at taking x-rays, relieving the doctors of this additional work. Lovewll was a keen guitarist and singer, leading the church choir and contributing to the musical broadcasts within the hospital.

## THE ROBERTSONS AT CHITAMBO 1965

Daphne wrote-*We arrived at Chitambo in September 1965—Gordon and Daphne Robertson, David 8, Stephen 7, Brian 4, and Kathryn 2. Our trusty green Rover, piled high with bicycles and "stuff" carried us mile after mile into the exciting unknown. All we knew for sure was that the Lord was with us and that he had brought us here.*

**The Robertsons' House**

*Having been told that our house was old and unoccupied we were pleasantly surprised to find a wide airy, brick structure with a large wrap-around brick veranda, the inside freshly whitewashed. It did have character—17 foot ceilings, 4 fire places, 16 doors, and an enormous bathroom. It was not really an architect's dream but we liked it.*

*So what was life like at a bush mission station for the woman of the house? No electricity, no running water, no school. Well—we hired two helpers. Coming from Canada where help in the house is usually a luxury for the wealthy this took some getting used to, but it was certainly necessary. Ba Bernard did the cooking (how I would like to have him now). Chipupu worked outside—chopping firewood, burning it to heat the water in a Rhodesian boiler and then pumping it into water tanks so we were able to have running water in the house. He also cleaned up the garden and planted. We didn't have electricity so paraffin lamps were lit every evening. Ba Bernard also looked after the washing and ironing—the washing done with the stomping of feet in the bathtub. The washing on the line attracted the 'putsi' fly that laid its eggs from which came worms that burrowed under your skin. Hence the necessity of ironing everything.*

*Relationships are very important in a small community. We were fortunate in being there most of the time with Dr. Chad and Lily Musk from Scotland—the home of our ancestors! They were a great support to us, and our children enjoyed playing with their four which remarkably were all the same ages. Friendships have continued over the years with flights between Scotland and Canada. A real joy.*

*The hardest thing we had to do in Zambia was to send David and Stephen away to school—700 miles away. I had tried home school correspondence— unsuccessfully and we had even tried the village school. Eventually we did as others did and sent them to boarding school but it was very foreign to our culture and a big mistake that has certainly affected one of their lives.*

*There were several things I enjoyed doing with the local people. Our large porch lent itself beautifully to sewing classes. The women gathered there with toddlers and babies. This was a social time but they were serious about learning to sew-all by hand and eventually we got a sewing machine. Some material they brought with them and many parcels of cloth arrived from Canada and there was great excitement over choosing new materials.*

*The students came in the evening for Bible study and tea. We used to tease that they liked some tea with their sugar. This was a happy time of discussion and singing. They loved to sing and harmonized beautifully. Another class that was important to me was the literacy class. A few of the old ladies especially wanted to learn to read and they would squat on the floor with their paper on the bench in front and painstakingly print each letter. The whole Bible was printed in Chi-Bemba but very few were able to read. We were excited with them with each step of progress they made.*

*My nursing training came in handy when I taught the nursing students first aid and also when I helped in the hospital when Gordon was ill in bed. Although Gordon got better the mission board decided that we should come home before our furlough was due. It was with mixed feelings that we prepared to leave Zambia—relief at being able to establish the children in good schools and sadness at leaving so much to be done.*

*In looking back on those three years I am reminded of Eugene Peterson saying "Are you going to live cautiously or courageously?" My time at Chitambo would have been richer if I had lived more courageously. It's not the big thing of going off to Africa that requires courage. It's the day to day risk taking in exploring relationships, saying "I'll do it" and daring to put forth a novel idea—the courage to stretch and be all you're made to be—for the glory of God."*

**The Robertsons at Chitambo**

## CHITAMBO 1965-1966, UDI AND SANCTIONS

In November 1965 Southern Rhodesia, under Ian Smith, declared itself independent, without British approval or support. This Unilateral Declaration of Independence (UDI) was the start of economic hardship for Rhodesia, as it was now known, and for the newly independent Zambia who relied on trade routes through Rhodesia for its imports and exports. The United Nations Security Council authorized sanctions against Rhodesia, forbidding most forms of trade or financial exchange with Rhodesia. One of the commodities most affected was petrol. By 1966 petrol rationing was a major problem for Zambia. There were airlifts of oil into the country from Mozambique. Petrol was also brought in by road in huge oil tankers which trundled down the Great North Road past the road end at Chitambo. During the rains, they churned the road up, making it less passable. The Curries managed to buy enough petrol to take the boys to Kitwe for their flight on the VC10 to Britain. They would go to boarding school in Edinburgh for their remaining school years. The journey to the Copperbelt was all the more exciting for the four punctures on the way. Milton was known to stuff inner tubes with grass in order to be able to continue a journey! They were able to visit Bill and Muriel Todd. Bill, John Todd's son was now working at the mine hospital in Chingola.

Back at Chitambo on New Year's Day the two doctors explored the old furrow system which Malcolm Moffat had used for irrigation. They saw in it the possibility of hydro-electric power as there was a drop of about 60 feet from the end of the furrow to the Mabonde stream. The hospital remained busy. They took it in turns to go out on tour, in the Mobile Dispensary, on bad roads and sometimes in heavy rain. Apart from Serenje, the chiefs' villages of Muchinka, Kafinda and Chipundu (at the Livingstone monument) were on the regular circuit. Fortunately they were allowed as much petrol as they needed to run the hospital engine and the outreach programme. There were unwanted trips to Lusaka and the Copperbelt to give evidence in the High Court. On more than one such occasion, a round trip of about 600 miles, Milton was informed that he was not in fact needed in court. He would make the most of the journey by shopping for the hospital and visiting friends.

Milton made plans for his departure on furlough. Because of UDI and the possibility of difficulty going through Rhodesia, he planned to book a sea passage from Dar-es-Salaam, via Suez. The Musks would return to Chitambo for Milton's furlough, as Dr. Robertson was still very new to Zambia, not yet familiar with the language, and it would be a heavy load for him on his own

A group of British and Canadian railway surveyors who were camped at Chitambo in January moved on towards Kasama. The railway would run via Kasama and Mpika, and was due to be started in 1967. It would take about four years to build.

At the nurse training school the course had been reduced by the government to two years instead of three. The implications were a higher turnover of nurses, and a greater number of inexperienced nursing students at any one time. The government stalled on its promise of helping with the building programme. A new TB block and a nurses' home were badly needed. The Chitambo signpost at the end of the road now had the letters U.C. Z. painted on, acknowledging the combined churches of Zambia into the United Church of Zambia.

Milton continued to make regular visits to Chilonga Hospital, a Roman Catholic mission hospital about 90 miles north of Chitambo. The nuns made a great fuss of Milton when he went there and they loved little red-headed Anne. Mother John the Baptist and Sister Josephine came to Chitambo as examiners for the nursing students and stayed with the Curries.

An unpleasant aspect of the work was conducting post-mortems. In Feb 1966 the police brought two bodies—that of a man who had accidentally shot himself in the shoulder while hunting. He had left his gun propped against a tree. A fight had broken out between two dogs and they knocked over the gun which went off, shooting him in the shoulder and severing his subclavian vein so that he bled to death. On hearing the news his wife hung herself. The only consolation to this work was the fee of ten guineas per body.

The Swansons arrived back at Chitambo in February with a lorry-load of building materials ready for the new building project which was expected to last about four years. They also brought a load of furniture, long promised, for the staff houses. There were always repairs to be done to the existing buildings and the hospital sewage system had broken down again due to overcrowding.

Milton x-rayed an old man who claimed to be the son of Malcolm Moffat's cook. The x-ray machine was nearly on its last legs and would need to be replaced. It also needed to be safely 'housed'. An old woman was admitted who remembered being operated on by "the short one" (John Todd). The pot-bellied form of malnutrition known as Kwashiorkor was becoming more prevalent. It was the result of inadequate protein in the weaning diet of babies and young children. These little patients were often anaemic, and blood transfusion was sometimes life-saving for them. Grant Mkandawire, the Medical Assistant, was good at cross-matching blood (from relatives or hospital staff), and Lovewell had learned how to do cut-downs on little veins in small babies who needed blood or intravenous fluids. Disposable transfusion sets had become available, adding to the sophistication of Chitambo medicine.

Milton and Gordon Robertson took turns of weekend duty. In March 1966 Milton had a heavy weekend on with a maternity patient who died, a road accident victim who succumbed from a ruptured liver and spleen, as well as the death of the old woman who remembered John Todd. How heavily these deaths must have weighed on him, and he looked forward to his leave. The Musks wrote to say that they would return for a time to Chitambo.

The nurses' home and the TB block were begun, and a Canadian nurse was on her way. The Roberstons would go on holiday and then Milton would take his furlough. There were more cases of Kwashiorkor which responded well to the nutritional programme that Milton was developing for them.

Milton received a letter out of the blue from a Rev. Dr. Christie Innes, a Presbyterian minister from Pittsburgh, USA. He was the son of Rev. Frank Innes of Karonga (1899), Livingstonia (1906) and Mwenzo (1917-18) who had known Dr. Chisholm of Mwenzo. This was another link which would be of positive benefit to Chitambo.

A boy was brought into the hospital after having been gored by a bull. Milton gave the anaesthetic and Gordon Robertson operated on him. The boy recovered. On the same night Milton was called to an obstructed labour—one of the mission cows! Sadly he was not able to save her and she had to be put down.

The Mobile Dispensary went to Lusaka for servicing and came back with the new Canadian sister Barbara Neidrauer. Meanwhile Milton took the Land Rover out round the district, starting at Serenje and then continuing to Chisomo, right on the edge of the Luangwa Valley. The road wound very steeply down to a hot, humid valley. The Dispensary was run by a Malawian dresser who was doing a good job under difficult circumstances. The next clinic was at Nchimisi School where Milton slept on a camp bed in a house that was being built and had no window panes. There were 83 patients to be seen. He brought back a little girl with possible tuberculosis of the hip.

He stopped back at Serenje for petrol on the return journey and met two Europeans in a Mercedes who said they were surveying for an oil pipeline from Dar-es-Salaam to Ndola. Sanctions against Rhodesia seemed to be having little impact, as the Rhodesians were able to buy petrol from South Africa, the U.S.A. and France. For Zambia, transporting oil by road and air was hugely expensive.

The Curries began the task of packing up for their furlough. Libby and the girls would fly to Australia to spend time with Libby's family before sailing back (via Panama) to join Milton in Scotland. After seeing them off at the airport Milton drove back to Chitambo via Broken Hill, where he met with the Provincial Medical Director—Dr. Bwanausi, a Malawian whose wife was Xhosa. Milton enjoyed the opportunity to speak both Chinyanja and Xhosa with them. Dr. Bwanausi promised a visit to Chitambo to look at the foundations of the new T.B. block and to discuss the grant for them. It was encouraging to discover that the Ministry of Health continued to back Chitambo, and did not want the doctors transferred to Serenje.

With donations from the Lions' Club of Broken Hill and government funding, some new equipment for the hospital was ordered, including a diathermy machine, autoclave and sterilizers. The Church of Canada sent some surgical instruments which could be taken out in the Mobile Dispensary for use in the outreach work.

Milton packed and stored his luggage in Anna Mary's cottage. He would go on furlough to Scotland and then return to help out at Mbereshi for six months.

## THE MUSKS' RETURN—1966, CHITAMBO HOSPITAL HANDED OVER TO GOVERNMENT

Chad and Lily arrived back from furlough in time for the wedding of Isobel Richmond to Peter Stead on 1st June 1966. Gordon and Daphne Robertson were now firmly established at Chitambo after language study at Mbereshi. Barbara Neidrauer from Ontario was the new nursing sister. The hospital was more overcrowded than ever. TB admissions had risen from 50 to 80 since the Musks had gone on leave. There were more than 170 patients for 82 beds. The new 60-bed TB ward was still being built. Isobel had been helping Milton with some office work, but would now be leaving for her new married life, and once again Chad would have all the administration to do. Gordon had taken on the district touring and the Serenje visits.

The nurse training school continued but there was talk of making Serenje hospital the main Teaching Unit and continuing Chitambo as a T.B. hospital. The government introduced workmen's compensation and provident funds (a pension scheme), which improved conditions for employees but increased the administrative load. An increase in grants meant that new equipment could be ordered and patients were better clothed and fed. The nurse training school was short of students because of the poor accommodation and the overcrowding in the hospital.

The Musks had barely returned when all 30 student nurses went on strike. This was followed by visits from the local M.P., the Provincial Medical Officer and the Parliamentary Secretary to the Minister of Health, all of whom delivered solemn lectures to the students and tried to impress on them that medical people should never desert their patients. The Provincial Medical Officer brought with him ten nurses from Broken Hill to relieve in the hospital, but by the time they arrived, the Chitambo students were back. So the Musks had the P.M.O, the MP and a CID man to stay on Saturday night and had 13 for breakfast on Sunday before the dignitaries addressed the students and returned to Broken Hill.

Milton left on 25<sup>th</sup> June in the midst of petrol rationing. He would begin his rounds of speaking at Scottish churches, and raising funds for Chitambo. Paraffin and calor gas became scarce. There were delays in receiving essential goods, as road transport had replaced the trains due to shortages of diesel. UDI was hurting Zambia more than it appeared to be affecting Rhodesia.

Some of the Canadian staff complained about the squalid conditions in the hospital, but their church did not have any spare cash either. Chad pointed out that at least they were providing a basic service for folk in need. The hospital was appallingly busy and so overcrowded that standards seemed to have slipped. There were so many desperately ill babies who needed time and skill to be cared for properly. When Joey Smith and Gordon Robertson were away at the same time, and the midwife, Dares Hara had a day off Chad was left literally holding the baby. It was not often that he was involved in a normal delivery.

The nursing sisters were carrying a very heavy load and morale was low. Jenny Dyer left Chitambo exhausted and depressed. Chad acknowledged that Chitambo was a difficult place. In the midst of these difficulties Grant Mkandawire, senior Medical Assistant and laboratory technician, left for 3 months' leave at his home in Malawi. Another senior Medical assistant, Welton Chavula went to Kawimbe to help out there for a time and they were both sorely missed.

Meanwhile Gordon Robertson had taken two of his boys to boarding school at Sakeji in the Northern Province and he returned with hepatitis. He was off work for 3 months, and suffered from fatigue. Chad visited him every day. Chad was now on his own, attending to urgent calls at Serenje, treating road accident victims, operating until 1 in the morning and having to give evidence in a murder trial at Serenje. While Chad was away a woman was admitted in obstructive labour and needed a Caesarean Section. Gordon had to drag himself out of bed, and successfully performed the Section.

In September 1966 the first VSO (Voluntary Service Overseas) Nurse, Iola Adams, arrived at Chitambo. A big welcome party was planned but early that evening three road accident victims were brought in—an Indian teacher and his wife who were on their way to work at Chilonga Roman Catholic Mission School further north and a German Lay Brother who was driving. The Principal of the school who was also the Mother Superior was killed outright. At 11pm the body was brought in for post-mortem. At 3 am a car full of very upset nuns arrived from Chilonga. After some tea they set off again at 4.30 am, and the following day there were more grieving visitors from Chilonga.

Gordon and Daphne Robertson took two weeks' leave for Gordon to convalesce in Lusaka. Their Rover needed a lot of work to make it roadworthy. Fortunately Gordon was able to return to work on 6th October. Meanwhile the hospital had apparently been condemned by a health inspector and the matter was before Cabinet.

Canadian business Manager Stewart Thompson and his wife Jean arrived in Lusaka and VSO Irene McCloskey arrived by train from Cape Town. Irene was to stay at Chitambo for 6 months. Stewart took over all the administration and Jean helped with accounts. Chad handed it all over to them with great relief. Initially the Thompsons struggled with adding pounds, shillings and pence, but they managed with the help of a new adding machine. They moved into Barbara's house while Barbara, Irene and Iola now shared Anna Mary's "cottage". A new nursing sister, Eileen Searle arrived, and stayed with the Thompsons until Ron Swanson finished the Sisters' flats.

Chad was appointed Secretary of the Presbyterial Medical Committee and the Synod Medical Committee. The SMC sent a delegation to the

Ministry of Health to beg a grant for Chitambo to avoid a take-over by Serenje.

1966 ended inauspiciously with a lightning storm taking out the hospital's electricity supply. The hospital had a small diesel generator as back-up for night lighting and emergency surgery. This had to be kept running all day. Peter Stead, electrician and builder was transferred away from Chitambo before he was able to finish the hospital rewiring. On December 12th Chad wrote *I am impatient with all the difficulties which stinginess and lack of skill and foresight have landed us in. The Hospital smells awful with no sanitation in the main wards. We are still prodding the government for action but have heard no more.*

In January 1967 the Synod of the United Church of Zambia reluctantly agreed to hand over Chitambo Hospital to government. Immediately equipment started pouring in for the new T.B. ward. At the start of the year the wards were full of children with protein calorie malnutrition. Classes were started for mothers of small babies to demonstrate the adding of protein-rich foods to the traditional thin porridge. An Insaka (grass-roofed shelter) was built in the hope of attracting mothers to the infant feeding classes. This was successful, with 20 mothers enrolling, and some student nurses assisting.

The Ministry of Health made 5,000 pounds available for cleaning, painting and tidying each of the provincial hospitals. The Synod clerk met the Permanent Secretary at the Ministry of Health to make the final arrangements for the take-over of the hospital. This was scheduled for 1st July 1967, and a further sum of 50,000 pounds was allocated to get the hospital up to scratch. All the permanent staff had the option of becoming Civil Servants. The Vice President, Simon Kapwepwe visited Chitambo and reassured staff that there was nothing to fear in the government take-over.

The roads were worse than ever, but the Musks were visited by Yugoslav surveyors who were contracted to tar the Great North Road. In spite of language barriers, relationships with the Yugoslavs were cordial and there were many happy encounters with them during the road construction. Mrs. Nikolic, wife of the Chief Engineer spoke a little English and often escorted workmen to the hospital. A source of granite was located near Chitambo and quarrying began, by day and night. In March Eileen Searle was unwell and went to Lusaka for investigations. The new VSO Sister, Irene McCloskey returned to Chitambo after a month of language study in a village. In April a new VSO from Swansea—Helen Meyrick arrived to change places with Irene.

There were plans to build a hydro-electric scheme 60 miles from Chitambo. Local people called it "Kariba" and hoped that it would solve the hospital's power problems. In April 1967 the new Serenje Hospital was opened but had no doctor or midwife, and no theatre or x-ray facilities.

By June 1967 the new T.B. block and the new nurses' home were nearly complete. Barbara would have a little flat at one end of the nurses' home. Eileen Searle returned to Chitambo after surgery and recuperation. She stayed with the Thompsons until Joey Smith's departure, when Eileen would move into Joey's flat. In July the Swanson family left and the hospital was allowed to recruit three tradesmen, though none were highly skilled. Gordon's health remained fragile and Chad was only able to do limited outreach work.

In September 1967 Dr. and Mrs. John Todd were in Zambia visiting their son Bill who was working in the Copper Belt. They visited Chitambo with Bill and his daughter, Heather. They were thrilled with the developments at the hospital, as there had been so many improvements since their last visit in 1964.

A new nursing sister—Helen Chalmers, arrived in September, and Joey Smith returned home. Barbara was able to take a holiday, with Eileen Searle, Jenny Dyer and Helen Chalmers holding the fort. The new Medical Council decreed that a teaching hospital had to have eight nursing sisters.

Gordon Robertson developed a bleeding ulcer and was off sick for another three months. There was no lab technician in October and the work-load in the hospital was heavy. The Musks were due to go on furlough in June 1968. Milton would return to Chitambo in May 1968 from Mbereshi.

1967 ended with a different twist, however, with Chad accepting a job as the Medical Officer in charge of a new Medical Assistants' training School in Lusaka, and Milton coming back to Chitambo earlier than planned.

**Chad, David and Lily Musk (back), Jenny, Elspeth,
baby Gillian and Stewart in Lusaka, 1972**

# CHAPTER 5

# ON LOVING, GIVING
# AND SUFFERING

## CHITAMBO 1968-1969—THE BRIETS' ARRIVAL

In January 1968 Milton, Libby and Anne (aged 4), made the 500 mile journey from Mbereshi back to Chitambo in their Austin A 40. The older girls had already been dropped at boarding school in Lusaka. It was the middle of the rainy season, and parts of the road were at their worst. On arriving at Chitambo, Milton immediately set off again in the 2-ton lorry to fetch their entire luggage. He spent one night on the road, waiting to be pulled out of the mud.

The Musks departed on 11$^{th}$ January 1968. Dr. Gordon Robertson was in poor health, and due to return to Canada in March 1968. Once again Milton was the only doctor in the district. Soon after Milton's arrival the Canadian administrator, Stewart Thompson, and his wife left to take up other duties in Lusaka. The expatriate staff comprised Eileen Searle—Matron and Methodist missionary, and Barbara Neidrauer—Canadian Sister-Tutor and missionary from the United Church of Canada, as well as VSO nurses Helen Chalmers and Angela Moody.

Stewart Thompson had done a great job in organizing the business side of the hospital work and had also been training an African, Jailos Kawonga, to take his place. Jailos, a Malawian from the village of Mulekatembe, near Mwenzo, was well educated and had 10 years' experience as a clerk. He was also a committed Christian. He was quick to learn, and was soon running the hospital accounts and administration with little help. He became Milton's right-hand man—paying the wages, ordering supplies of food, fuel and equipment, filling in government forms and writing official letters, dictated by Milton.

The fact that Chitambo was now a government hospital had many positive spin-offs. One of these was that the government set the wages, and there were fewer disputes from staff who felt under-paid. The church was relieved of the financial responsibility of running the hospital, and the labour of book-keeping was greatly reduced. Goods for the hospital would be delivered to the door, by Central African Road Services (CARS), instead of being left at the Chansa road end for the hospital lorry to pick up. The number of hospital staff increased considerably, particularly cleaning and maintenance staff—so the standard of cleanliness went up. A carpenter and a plumber were taken on, and improvements to water, sanitation, and wiring were eagerly awaited.

While the government still planned to make Serenje the district administrative capital and main hospital, in the long term, they remained committed to extending and upgrading Chitambo Hospital within the following 3 years. Progress was made with tarring the Great North Road. By 1968, 300 miles of the road from Chitambo to Lusaka was tarred-the section nearest Chitambo being undertaken by the Yugoslav company, whose workers came nearly every day to Chitambo for medical help. In return the Yugoslavs were very helpful in looking after the hospital engines and vehicles and Milton applied himself to learning a little Yugoslav in order to be able to communicate with his new patients.

The change to a government hospital would mean the possible appointment of staff who were not Christians and this concerned Milton who was now the only Church of Scotland missionary. The staff, however diverse their backgrounds, remained dedicated in their work.

Milton continued to pray for another doctor for Chitambo. In December 1968 the Ministry of Health appointed Dr. Desai to Serenje Hospital, but there was no house for him, so he was transferred temporarily to Chitambo where the original doctor's house was vacant. He was an Indian graduate and a Hindu. Initially he was rather resentful at being sent out into the bush when he had been promised an appointment in a township, but his attitude changed completely when he heard that eye surgery was being done at Chitambo. He was a specialist eye surgeon, with a Master's in eye surgery from Barodah Medical College. Milton immediately handed over all the eye surgery to him. Dr. Desai would move to Serenje when a house became available but agreed to pay weekly visits to Chitambo to help with eye surgery. Amongst Chitambo staff there was some muted hilarity prior to Dr. Desai's visits, as to whether he was to operate on '*dis* eye or *dis* eye'. Milton, who already had a keen interest in eye surgery, was inspired to learn from Dr. Desai.

The arrival of lady Dr. Bertlesmann-Heinemuller from Germany brought Chitambo suddenly up to 3-doctor status for a short time. She was sent by the Committee of Protestant Churches in Germany. Milton described her as '*a mature and experienced doctor and a most charming personality.*' What's more, there was talk of a young Dutch doctor swelling the ranks at Chitambo, in which case Dr. Bertlemann-Heinemuller would go to Mbereshi in April. Once Dr. Desai's house at Serenje was completed he and his family moved there, only to be transferred almost immediately to another province, leaving Serenje again without a doctor. Such was the fate of government doctors.

On 18th April 1968, Dr. Jan Willem Briet and his wife, Tin and baby boy Joris arrived from Holland. Dr. Briet was young and enthusiastic about touring the district and visiting the remote dispensaries as well as the work in the hospital. The touring work had been abandoned while Milton was the only doctor at the hospital but it was revived and extended with the arrival of Dr. Briet and many more Under-5s clinics were set up in the surrounding villages. This work of preventive medicine coupled with health education became perhaps the most vital contribution to the health of the people, and it coincided with the concept of Primary Health Care, pioneered by Dr. Maurice King of Makerere University in Uganda. Already smallpox, which had been prevalent in the district in previous years, had been eradicated from Zambia. There was hope also of eradicating measles and whooping cough.

The arrival of Jan Willem and Tin Briet greatly eased the medical load for Milton, but more than that—they brought a refreshing enthusiasm and idealism to the work in Zambia. Their willingness to try new initiatives won them the admiration and affection of the Chitambo people. Jan Willem pondered the difficulties that villagers had in getting their sick relatives to the hospital and he concluded that the presence of a sailing boat might expedite the journey from the other side of Lake Lusiwasi. The lake is situated at the junction of the Great North Road and the Chansa Road, (leading to Chitambo). It stretches eastward and covers an area of approximately forty square kilometres. It is situated at a height of 1,554 metres above sea level and provides the headwaters for the Lusiwasi River which flows into the Luangwa River via the Mutinsase. In one of his sketch maps Livingstone showed a lake (Shuia) close to the present site of Lake Lusiwasi. Lusiwasi appears to have been the name since early times, but the lake suffered the brief indignity of being renamed Lake Moir after the brothers who founded the African Lakes Company. Chirupula Stephenson showed his scorn for the re-naming by prefixing it with "the so-called Lake Moir". The name reverted to Lusiwasi in the 1930's. The size of the lake varies considerably. At its greatest extent it occupies fifty square kilometres but it has sometimes shrunk to a few square kilometres at the end of the dry season. Various schemes have been tried to stock the lake with fish, but the appearance of crocodiles in the 1950's dampened enthusiasm for fishing, for a time. The lake is very shallow, with a maximum depth of about two metres.

Jan Willem took measurements from a dug-out canoe and relayed these to his mother in Holland. She bought sail-cloth and sewed the sail to Jan Willem's specifications. When his parents came to visit they brought the sail. One Saturday morning there was an expedition to the lake for the launch of the new sailing boat. All the mission staff were invited and a large crowd of villagers looked on. Jo and I accompanied Milton in a dugout canoe, while Jan Willem fixed up the sail and took the helm of the sailing canoe. A short distance into the lake the sail was caught in a sudden squall and the boat listed heavily and capsized. The water was not very deep and Jan Willem was able to hang onto the boat and to keep his watch out of the water by holding his left arm aloft. The sailing boat never really caught on, and the project was quietly shelved, but it was characteristic of Jan Willem to have given it his best, and he was well remembered for this.

Under the Matron-ship of Canadian Barbara Neidrauer, were four VSO nurses—Angela Moody, Helen Chalmers, Jane Hart and Lisa Molander. Had it not been for VSO, the task of staffing the hospital with qualified nurses would have been very difficult. Margaret Ritchie's arrival in January 1969 swelled the ranks of Church of Scotland missionaries to two. In July 1969 Matron Eileen Searle returned from furlough to take the helm and particularly to help run the operating theatre.

Milton recalled his first outreach trip with Jan Willem:

*Jan Willem and I travelled in the back of the Land Rover. In the front seat with the driver were Sister Margaret Ritchie from Glasgow, and Nurse Dares*

*Hara the midwife from Chitambo Hospital. The first fifty miles of the journey were very comfortable, as we were bowling along on the newly tarred section of the Great North Road that runs through Zambia from Rhodesia to Tanzania. The last 57 miles grew more and more uncomfortable as we bumped over a rough and stony track that led eastwards towards the Luangwa river valley. The last section of the road was so steep that we had to use the extra-low gears of the Land Rover both to go down and to come up again. Our destination was the government Dispensary at Chisomo, which serves the scattered villages in that low-lying valley.*

*Jan Willem is a young missionary doctor who has come to Zambia from Holland to join the staff of Chitambo Hospital. This was his introduction to the medical touring in the district surrounding Chitambo. He and I were both bitten by tsetse flies, the carriers of sleeping sickness, as we went down into the valley, but so far we have not suffered any ill-effects. The jolting of the Land Rover was much more unpleasant than the bites of the flies.*

*The Medical Assistant in charge of the dispensary was not expecting us, because there is no way of sending a message to this lonely spot other than by going there. We found him busy in his dispensary, making the most of his slender resources to meet the needs of the villagers of Chisomo. He had a supply of vaccine lymph, and had been doing a good job of vaccination against smallpox. He had a few inpatients in his pathetically dilapidated wards. Some of them were suffering from trachoma, a destructive inflammation of the eyes, which often leads to blindness.*

*Our main purpose in visiting this remote dispensary was to start a clinic for children under the age of five, to teach mothers how to feed their children, and to give immunization against as many diseases as possible, particularly smallpox, measles, whooping cough and tetanus. The idea of having such a clinic was new to the Medical Assistant, but he quickly caught on to it, and helped in the weighing of children and the giving of injections. Nurse Dares gave a spirited talk to the crowd of mothers who had brought the children to the clinic, teaching them what locally available foods they ought to be giving their children, and following it up with a cookery demonstration for which she had come prepared with pots and foodstuffs. The mothers listened with interest, and afterwards sampled the cooking and tried the various dishes on their children.*

*When the baby clinic was over, I was asked to see a little boy who had been brought to the dispensary by his mother on account of stiffness in the legs. His legs were indeed stiff, and I noticed that when he was lifted up, his whole body was rigid. His trunk was arched backwards, and his face was contorted into the mirthless grin that is typical of tetanus. There was a wound on the face which he had received a week earlier which was the obvious portal of entry of the dreaded germs of tetanus.*

*Fortunately we had in our medical bag some medicines which we were able to give at once, though he had great difficulty in swallowing them. After that I explained to the parents that the boy, Changwe Fwashi, must come to the hospital if his life was to be saved. At this they demurred. Who would look after the garden if mother went to the hospital? The Medical Assistant joined in the argument. Which was more important, the garden or the boy's life? Of course the boy's life was important, admitted the parents, but still it was out of the question for him to go to hospital. Granny, who had come to the dispensary with very sore eyes chimed in at this point. If the boy died, she said, it would be God's will. Some heated discussion followed, in which I had to threaten to report the parents to the local political authorities. Only then did they agree to let their boy come to hospital.*

*The Land Rover was re-packed, and the boy travelled in the front seat on the knees of Dares, with his mother sitting at his side. It was a miserable journey for them all, especially for Changwe who was desperately ill, and for his mother who was unused to motor travel. The journey took three hours and the first fifty miles were frightful.*

*At last Changwe reached Chitambo, where treatment with serum and antibiotics began. Gradually the treatment took effect and the stiffness passed off until at last the boy recovered completely from his illness.*

*Discussing Changwe's illness afterwards with his mother, I reminded her of Granny's words that if he died it would be God's will. I assured her that it was most certainly not God's will that Changwe should die. On the contrary, it was God who had put it into our hearts to visit Chisomo on that particular day. "Yes" said his mother "and it must have been God who put it into our hearts to go to the dispensary that day. There is real gratitude in her heart for the restoration of her little boy's life. As for Changwe himself, he is full of fun and laughter, and he will soon be back with his family and friends at Chisomo.*

*There will be many more medical visits to Chisomo, and the baby clinic, with its preventive injections will save many another boy and girl from getting tetanus and various other infections, and promote the cause of positive health. And maybe the love which Changwe and his mother have found at Chitambo will produce an even greater effect on the people of Chisomo.*

There was disappointment that one of the Chitambo trained Medical Assistants and one of the clerical workers had to be let go, for misappropriation of funds on a grand scale. This was a great blow, as both had been highly trained and trusted, as well as being church members. The question was now asked whether the Church of Scotland had any further role in staffing its former mission hospitals. Mission staff were now faced with the choice of becoming civil servants. While some accepted this change readily, Milton hesitated. Firstly he was concerned about the possibility of being transferred away from Chitambo, and secondly he felt that a Christian influence in the nurse training school would be preferable to a secular approach. For Milton it was important that nurses had a real vocation and were not just holding down a job. At the same time, Milton was prepared to acquiesce to government service if necessary, while continuing to work in the way that he always had.

Medical students played an increasing part in the life of the hospital. Now that the University of Zambia medical school was up and running, Zambian medical students had the opportunity to gain experience in a rural setting like Chitambo. The first two students were Catherine Macpherson (daughter of Myra and the late Rev. Fergus Macpherson) and Alexander Kawayi. Another student was Marjorie Donaldson from Aberdeen University who came on a 3-month 'elective' in her final year of medicine. An aspiring medical student—Isaac Chola, who had just finished secondary school at Serenje, spent his school holidays at Chitambo eagerly soaking up anything he could about medicine.

By the end of 1969 the government had installed a bigger and better electric generator capable of lighting the hospital all night and every night. This was a great improvement, though there were still occasions when the electricity failed and operations had to be performed by lamp or torch-light. Holding a torch or a lamp during operations was one of my first 'medical' jobs, another being the task of swatting flies in the theatre! Although the engine was new, the wiring was in need of replacement. However, in the fashion of the Flanders and Swan song 'The Gas Man Cometh' rewiring would need to be preceded by re-roofing as the old tiled roof was now leaky in too many places. The new roof of corrugated iron would not look as good as the old one but it would protect the wiring better. The re-roofing finally got underway at the end of 1969, in time to coincide with the start of the rains. A bees' nest in the ceiling of the main corridor came down and there were angry bees and the smell of honey to add to the chaos of re-roofing!

Meanwhile on the edge of the Luangwa escarpment about 50 miles from Chitambo, the hydro-electric power station was being built and there were hopes that it would eventually supply Chitambo with electricity. A large labour force was working on the site and once a month an ambulance was sent from Chitambo to provide medical services for the workers, including immunizing their children against the preventable diseases. Measles in particular had taken a heavy toll the previous year.

By the end of 1969 the Great North Road was tarred from Chitambo to Kapiri Mposhi. The entire journey to Lusaka was now on tar. The Yugoslav road builders who had become friends of the hospital now departed. A Chinese company arrived to survey prior to the construction of a railway line from Dar-es-Salaam to the existing terminal at Kabwe (formerly Broken Hill). The railway line would pass close to the Chitambo road end between Chansa and Lake Lusiwasi. The Chinese kept pretty much to themselves. They set up their own clinic and treated their workers—mainly with acupuncture. They also brought sick or injured Zambian workers to the hospital. Communication was limited and Milton, the aspiring linguist, set out to learn as much Cantonese as possible.

The Mobile Dispensary was now on its last legs and the government provided a new ambulance, complete with siren and flashing blue light. The hospital now had a Land Rover and an ambulance. The tarred road was a mixed blessing. The increased volume of traffic quickly led to a rise in the number of serious accidents, many of them as a result of drunk or careless drivers. Many of the injured and dead were brought in to Chitambo. The work of caring for road accident victims was hampered by the breakdown of the hospital's x-ray machine, now in its 16th year. It took 6 months to get a new one.

One of the highlights of 1969 for Milton was the offer, by a German optician by the name of Karl Steudle, to make up one pair of prescription glasses per month. The kindness and professionalism of this offer particularly touched Milton who was developing his own interest and ability in helping people with visual impairment.

1969 also saw the arrival at Serenje of French-Canadian Roman Catholic Father Jean Jacques Corbeil, priest and enthusiastic collector of Bemba cultural artifacts. Father Corbeil had begun his collection of things made by the Bemba people *just for the personal pleasure of knowing more about the people I was living among.* Of particular interest to him were the Mbusa or sacred emblems used in initiation ceremonies of young girls and boys. On a visit to Father Corbeil's small museum at Serenje he treated us to a tour and a demonstration of some of the musical instruments he had collected. Most memorable was his 'playing' of the mouth stones, a collection of small stones placed in the mouth of a young woman and rolled around to give a sound which was said to be attractive to young men—a kind of 'speaking stone'.

Milton ends his 1969 report with—*We go forward into the 1970's with the prospect of considerable material improvements to the hospital. The general state of efficiency of government Departments still leaves very much to be desired, but perhaps that is not a problem peculiar to Zambia. We still see our vocation in trying to help the Zambian people to help themselves. When they are quite able to do that, there will be no more need for expatriate missionaries and technicians.*

## THE BRIETS AT CHITAMBO 1970

In September 1970 Milton wrote: *It is more than high time I wrote another circular letter to my missionary partners and Christian friends, especially as we are due to go on leave on 19$^{th}$ December this year.*

*So much has happened in the past 9 months that it is difficult to compress it into two pages of foolscap. However, here goes. We received two new sisters from the Voluntary Service Overseas Organisation, Susan Goddard and Margaret Stacey, in place of Jane Hart and Lisa Molander who went home. No praise can be too high for these young people who have come here to help us, and without whose help the United Church of Zambia could not have met its undertaking to staff this hospital. Our greetings go to all the Volunteers who helped us in the past, and are now back home. We are tempted to say to them "Will ye no come back again?" In March our Sister Tutor Barbara Neidrauer went home to Canada and has not been replaced, so we have since then been one sister short. We have, however, received two Medical Assistants, Mr. Kabinga and Mr. Myanda, who, between them, act as 'Sisters in Charge' of the male ward, and are doing a very good job. They are both Catholics, but they do attend morning prayers which continue to be a regular part of our day's work.*

*This leads me to mention that the Sunday services held in the wards are being led mostly by Chitambo church members, but we have had, and* accepted, offers from some Roman Catholic teachers from Mabonde School to conduct services on some Sundays, and I have personally been impressed by the way in which they did so, and the absence of any sectarian slant. I hope this does not shock you. To my mind it is a movement of the Holy Spirit. I would add that our friendship with the staff of the Catholic hospital at Chilonga 90 miles to the north has grown stronger with the years, and we continue to work in close harmony.

In the church at Chitambo the congregation has been growing, and a feature has been the number of new places around Chitambo where small congregations meet on most Sundays, led by local preachers. Only on certain Sundays do all the people come in to Chitambo. Another feature has been the recent introduction of drumming into church worship. Drums would have been taboo in earlier days because of their association with heathen practices—just as organs once were in Scotland! One musical minister, the Rev. Ronald Ndawa, has made a great impact on the church with many truly African hymns he has written, which form regular choir pieces every Sunday. Ronald was at church at Chitambo a few weeks ago, and his rich bass voice led the singing. At the end of this year, we are losing our minister, Rev. Noah Chulu, who is being transferred to Kasama, and we are getting a newly qualified minister Rev. Augustine Chibende.

Turning to the hospital—we had a tragedy in May when two of our workers, Harry Million and Patrick Kunda were killed in an ambulance which crashed on the road to the Livingstone Monument, which they were going to visit. Harry Million is particularly missed in the church where he was an outstanding elder and preacher. We are trying to do what we can for the families of these two faithful workers. A new carpenter has been taken onto the staff to replace Patrick. I should like to mention another hospital worker, Hamilton Malwita, whose job is to pack and sterilize syringes. He has recently been received into full church membership, and is a faithful member of the choir. A number of other workers on the staff take a regular turn in conducting morning prayers.

In my last letter I mentioned motor accidents. These continue to bring us much work. In most cases they are due to drink, and this is one of Zambia's greatest problems these days. Just to remind us that we are in Central Africa we have in the hospital at the moment a man smashed up by a buffalo, another gored within a fraction of an inch of his heart by a buck, and another man bitten by a hippopotamus.

*This is the worst year I can ever remember for cases of asthma. We have a certain number of martyrs to this complaint who arrive at Chitambo regularly at the beginning of the rains, and who have to spend several months of each year in hospital. Some of them have been very resistant to treatment, and one of them died in spite of all our efforts. I think I would rather have leprosy than asthma!*

*Talking of leprosy-we had an old leper couple sent to us from Fiwila Anglican Mission 150 miles away. After 25 years of treatment they are cured of their leprosy, though disfigured and maimed, but the old lady was also blind. I found that she had cataract in both eyes, and operated on her. To our joy the operations were successful and the old couple went home rejoicing. We hope to visit Fiwila Mission for our first time next week. I was able to provide the old lady with spectacles from my collection. Earlier this year I got a gift of 700 pairs of spectacles from the Basel Mission in Stuttgart, Germany. They have greatly added to my collection. In addition, I continue to get the most valuable help from my friend—Herr Steudle, of Adelsheim/Baden in Germany who makes up prescriptions of glasses for my more difficult cases.*

*This year for the first time in my life I saw two cases of rabies. I don't ever want to see any more! We had an outbreak in this district and treated many cases who had been bitten by dogs. We saved all who came to us in good time, but once the disease is established, there is absolutely no cure for it, and the patient dies in agony.*

*A perpetual problem in this country is that of epileptics. They all invariably get burnt sooner or later by falling into the fire. But the main problem is to get them to come regularly for supplies of medicine which would keep them free from fits. Many of them are mentally abnormal, and are not responsible enough to take their medicines regularly, and their relatives are too lazy to come and get the medicines for them. The same applies to many cases of mental illness. They could be kept in good health if they would take their medicines, but again the problem is to get the relatives to take responsibility. I couldn't help laughing one night when an epileptic mental boy got loose in the female ward when the lights failed, and all the female patients ran screaming out into the rain until we got the boy under control. One mental patient who came to this hospital for a while this year is accused of having killed two people. The problem is a serious one. The answer is not easy to find.*

*June 14<sup>th</sup> was a great day for Chitambo when President Kaunda paid us an official visit. Never was there such a cleaning up of the grounds and buildings, and bulldozing of roads. All the trees were whitewashed and we had* to prepare to feed mobs of people. The visit was a great success and we were most impressed by Dr. Kaunda's pleasant and friendly manner and genuine humility. One lovely little incident occurred when I was showing him round the female ward. I introduced him to a very nice little girl who had been given a doll from our collection of gifts. I asked what food she fed her baby on, and having heard me repeatedly lecturing the mothers on what foods they should give to their children, she recited the whole list of protein foods, much to the President's amusement. Maybe it was because of his visit that the Post Office has agreed to bring a telephone line to Chitambo. We haven't got the telephone yet-various government departments are still wrangling about who is to pay the fee of 2,400 Kwachas for its installation—but it will come some day, and improve our contact with the outside world.

Meanwhile something that <u>has</u> come is a radio transmitter from the Zambia Flying Doctor Service, in reply to an appeal of mine to Dr. Derek Braithwaite, an old friend of mine, who has recently been appointed head of that service. We are now in direct communication with Ndola 250 miles away and we can call for help whenever we have an emergency that is beyond our resources.

Other improvements are coming slowly. The new hospital roof is on. The new wiring is not yet begun. New toilets built 4 years ago by Ron Swanson are only now being completed. A new engine is promised but not yet here. The hydro-electric scheme 50 miles from here is at last working and sending electricity to Serenje. We shall be connected to it someday.

We rejoiced in the birth of Dr. and Mrs. Briet's second son here at Chitambo—on 1st April, poor chap. Dr. Briet's parents paid us a visit soon after that and delighted us all. Another very welcome visitor was Miss Helen Massie, a medical student from Aberdeen who spent 2 ½ months with us, as did Marjory Donaldson last year.

Our youngest daughter Anne is at boarding school 700 miles away at Sakeji, leaving my wife and me alone in the house with the dog, the cat and the kitten. Never mind, we hope to be a reunited family in December, and we look forward to seeing very many of our friends in Scotland soon.

Libby and the three girls left Chitambo at the end of the school year, en route for Scotland. Jo and I would then remain in Scotland, along with our brothers, to complete our education, while Milton would return to Zambia ahead of Libby and Anne.

# TRAGEDY AT CHITAMBO 1971

Milton's "furlough" was shorter than when he was a Church of Scotland missionary. By September 1971 he was back at Chitambo and his letter of 9th October 1971 speaks for itself

*Dear Friends,*

*In this first newsletter to you from Chitambo I would have been telling you of the welcome I received back to Zambia from the moment I arrived at Lusaka airport, and of the many friends I began to meet as soon as I got to the city of Lusaka. But all this has been completely overshadowed by a terrible tragedy which happened exactly a week after I got back to Chitambo.*

*I arrived on Friday 10th September in a new car which I had bought in Lusaka together with a hitch-hiker whom I had picked up on the road at Kapiri Mposhi and I was given a rousing welcome by the Briets and the other members of staff. On Tuesday morning Dr. Briet and his family set off for Lusaka in their little car so that Dr. Briet could give evidence in a case at the High court in Lusaka. On the way home on Friday 17th Dr. Briet attended a meeting in Kabwe and then set off for Chitambo in the afternoon, breaking his journey to visit some Dutch friends at Mkushi. It was at 10.40 pm a few miles south of Serenje that he met a van on the wrong side of the road, driven by a drunken driver with undimmed lights. There was a head on collision in which Mrs. Briet and their elder son, Joris aged 3 were killed outright. Dr. Briet and his second son Ernest escaped with fractured femurs and cuts and bruises. The driver who had crashed into them was unhurt and sufficiently sober to get a lift to Serenje to summon help. The Police and the Indian doctor from Serenje were soon on the scene with an ambulance, and got Dr. Briet and Ernest first to Serenje and then to Chitambo.*

*I was called at 2 am by our engine attendant, who told me that there had been an accident involving Europeans. I'm sure he knew who had been involved but could not bring himself to tell me. I went over to the hospital hoping to myself that Dr. Briet had got back from Lusaka and could help me with the accident cases when I was stunned to be told by a weeping Medical Assistant that it was Dr. Briet and his son who were injured, and Mrs. Briet and Joris were dead. Dr. Gopinath, the Indian doctor from Serenje soon arrived to help me deal with the broken legs. I want to place it on record that I have never seen a braver man than Jan Willem Briet in the face of such an overwhelming tragedy. He has astonished us all by his courage and cheerfulness.*

*There has been a tremendous outpouring of sympathy throughout the district. The new telephone, which had been installed only four days before, was ringing repeatedly with messages of sympathy from as far afield as Lusaka. There was a constant stream of visitors to see Dr. Briet and his little boy. Poor little Ernest is only 17 months old, and still says from time to time "Mummy gone away", and looks thoughtful; but mostly he is full of spirits and his broken leg will be healed very soon.*

*The funeral was on Sunday, and was conducted by our new Minister, the Rev. Simon Mutambo, who himself had been here only ten days. He was assisted by the Rev. Don Nicol, a Canadian minister who is Chaplain to the Malcolm Moffat Training College at Serenje. The church was absolutely packed that morning for the morning service, and again in the afternoon for the funeral service. Jan Willem asked to be taken to the graveside in the ambulance for the committal, and his dear wife and little boy were laid to rest in the Christian burial ground by the side of the road to Katikulula. There was a great crowd of sympathisers.*

*I think it is only at a time like this that one realizes how much the people here care about those who have come here to help them. We know now how much the Briets were loved, and how much they had become involved with the people of this area. This outflow of sympathy and love has been a great uplift to us all, not least to Jan Willem himself.*

*We were deeply thankful when a few days after the accident Jan Willem's mother arrived from Holland. She has been here comforting him and Ernest, and we have all delighted in her friendship. She went home just today.*

*As it happened, when this disaster occurred, our Matron, Eileen Searle had just gone home on holiday to England, and we had only two Sisters in the hospital—Margaret Ritchie from Glasgow and Margaret Stacey, V.S.O. They rose magnificently to the occasion, and kept the hospital going while at the same time helping and supporting Jan Willem. We had also with us Rosalind Bulmer, a medical student from Aberdeen University, who was a great help to us at this difficult time.*

*Two Sisters who had been posted to Chitambo by the government were on holiday when the accident happened, Ethel Hamilton and Audrey Anderson from Northern Ireland. They arrived back on Wed 22nd and brought our complement of sisters up to full strength for the time being, but Margaret Ritchie and Rosalind Bulmer left us on 30th September.*

*I came back with high hopes of working happily again with Jan Willem, until such time as he would be relieved by another Dutch doctor. Now it is a matter of trying to carry on the medical work single-handed as regards doctors, but well supported by sisters, until the new Dutch doctor comes. A new V.S.O. sister Deirdre Rogers joined us on 28<sup>th</sup> September, so our present sisters comprise two V.S.O.s and two government Sisters. Matron is expected back in a few weeks.*

*I came back to find many material improvements to the hospital. A new kitchen is in the process of being built, and two new staff houses are nearly complete, while a third one is under construction. A new kitchen and dining room are being added to the Nurses' Home. A bore hole has been sunk for water, and new high-level water storage tanks have been erected, with an engine to pump water. The telephone is very useful when it works. There is no word of re-wiring the hospital yet—after four years of asking for it. We can still have an engine failure in the middle of an operation, as happened last week with disastrous results. Among valuable new items of equipment are a cine projector and an epidiascope (opaque projector) which we have been using with great pleasure, as well as a baby incubator and a lot of new books. Some of the latter came from UNESCO and some from the Christian medical fellowship. A pair of magnifying spectacles which I brought from Scotland and a tubal insufflation apparatus have already made themselves useful. We have a supply of Christian film strips for the film strip projector and new ones that I have brought out with me have been used with good effect.*

*A Christian conference was in progress here last week. I was too busy with the medical work to be able to attend any of the meetings except the big communion service last Sunday when Mr. Mutambo was formally inducted by the Moderator of our Presbytery, Mr. Makumba. The church was once again packed. I have never seen so many there for Communion before. As usual when there is a big gathering of Christians here at Chitambo, the old folks among them take the opportunity to come to me for eye testing and once again I was able to help many of them with spectacles.*

*Today I saw a patient on whom Dr. Briet had operated for cataract in my absence, and I had the pleasure of handing over to her a pair of spectacles from Herr Karl Steudle in Germany and of watching her pleasure as she put them on and could see clearly. Dr. Briet's operation had been a great success.*

*There is one patient still in hospital who was here when I left in December. Indeed he has been here over two years. He is a lad called Ifo, who was absolutely desperately ill with trypanosomiasis, ("sleeping sickness") so ill and emaciated* that he was covered with bed sores despite all efforts to nurse him carefully. At times we despaired of his life, but when I came back here I found him fat and flourishing, and I even have hopes that we shall get him walking soon.

It is good to see the Christian witness of the hospital going on faithfully. Mr. Mutambo takes his turn in conducting services in the wards and so do many of the humble workers of the hospital.

The fact that I am now a government servant makes no difference to my work here and it seems clear that the government will welcome other Church-recruited staff for Chitambo. We look forward to the arrival of the new Dutch doctor-Van der Hoeven, sometime in January, if not sooner. I of course look forward to the arrival of my wife and Anne in January, but meanwhile I am fully occupied just keeping the hospital ticking over. I do ask for your prayers, especially for Jan Willem and his little boy at this time and for all of us on the staff that we may be given the power to keep going and to keep witnessing to the love of God through Jesus Christ our Lord.

# JAN WILLEM BRIET'S REFLECTIONS ON 1969-1972

**Jan Willem Briet**

Jan Willem Briet reflected on his time at Chitambo in the following words:

*It is with mixed feelings that I think back on our stay at Chitambo. Several of my memories are quite negative. Despite that, the final picture is not one of disappointment. The loss of my wife Tin and our first-born son Joris by an accident on the Great North Road threw a shadow over our lives for several years. But the continuing support of Tin's two sisters and brothers, our family and friends, and the sharing of our life with Mienke, whose husband died of cancer, when her son Olivier was only one year old, made all the difference.*

*Acquaintance with death and grief brought me nearer to the Zambian people at Chitambo. They knew better than I what it means to lose husband, wife, child or parent. I was and am grateful and surprised whenever I look at the photographs of the women with their white head-dresses, and many others following Tin and Joris from the church to the graveyard at Chitambo. With their hands they pressed down the sand on the graves.*

*Ernest and I stayed at Chitambo for nearly five months afterwards, although the surgeons with whom I trained in Amsterdam offered to take us back to Holland for operative treatment of our fractures. Physically this might have been better, but I think we made the right choice, feeling that we belonged in Chitambo, receiving the best available treatment and surrounded by people who knew our situation. I read Kubler-Ross. Someone gave me Bonhoeffer's "Letters from Prison". Some days after the funeral when my mother and Tin's brother arrived, Milton Currie led a service. I remember he chose airs from the Messiah: 'He was despised' and 'I know that my redeemer liveth'. And Psalm 23. Yes I felt acquainted with grief too. After this experience Milton and I had too much in common, and he taught me lessons for life.*

*More directly related to medical practice he had shown me how to perform cataract operations, using the cryophake, and he introduced me to the reality of tropical medicine. He liked to say that hearing the clatter of hooves does not always mean a zebra. A paratonsillar abscess is not necessarily a Burkitt's lymphoma. If a skinny man comes from Chiundaponde (a village near the Livingstone monument)—look for trypanosomes (the parasite of sleeping sickness) in his spinal fluid.*

*He taught me how to start the engine for the hospital generator, and how to take x-rays when Roger Sikazwe wasn't around. Mr. Mweetwa showed me how to do urgent laboratory tests and how to collect blood from student donors of the Malcolm Moffat Teacher Training College in Serenje. Mr. Mkandawire* was the chief of the outpatient department. I should have left more to him, trusting his experience. He knew how to reposition a dislocated jaw when I failed.

With my 28 years I was as green as Dutch grass, too inexperienced to be in charge of a hospital during Milton's year-long leave. I regret certain decisions I had to make. Milton was once asked by visitors from abroad "What are the main problems you encounter?", expecting, perhaps, to hear about malaria and malnutrition. But the answer was: <u>human relationships.</u> There are also painful memories of failed treatments and operations followed by insoluble complications.

I think in a country like Zambia curative medicine needs the continued support of expatriate nursing sisters and doctors as long as the country cannot supply them in the necessary numbers. The accent, however, should be on prevention, not cure. And that is what Milton could not do when he was alone, but soon after our arrival the Under-Fives clinics were re-started. Every month we went to Kasuko, Muchinka, Chisomo, Chiundaponde, Mpelembe, 15 places altogether. Mothers kept the cards of their children, on which vaccinations and weights were noted. In 1970 I compiled the weights of all Under-Fives. 1260 were below the lower warning line (10th centile). There were 1627 first attendances and 5305 in total. So the percentage of underweight children was between 25 and 60%. We were happy when malnourished children who needed admission recovered and left Chitambo in better shape and spirit, but were saddened to see several of them back with the oedema and enamel skin of Kwashiorkor. Then you realize that agriculture, schooling, transport, clean water and sanitation are far more important than the medical technology imported from Europe.

So what has been the benefit of our presence? For the Lala people I am not sure, although many individual persons have been cured of infectious diseases and lives have been saved by caesarean sections. Preventive and curative medicine can go hand in hand. I never heard the critical opinion of a villager on this matter, but I think they might agree, as, at the time of writing, Chitambo has survived 100 years.

Since 1988 I worked in a teaching hospital in the Netherlands. Several of our residents went to Zambia, Namibia, Zimbabwe and Tanzania, two of them with no intention of returning to our affluent society.

And finally: we cherish the friendships founded in our Zambian days. Not only exchanging Seasons Greetings, but meeting each other when the chances occur. In conclusion: I do not regret those unforgettable years in Zambia.

# THE VAN DER HOEVENS AT CHITAMBO 1971-1972

Dr. Frits van der Hoeven and his wife Marjolijn and their children, Catelijne (aged 3) and Christiaan (aged 1 ½) arrived at Chitambo in November 1971. Their first impressions were mixed.

Frits wrote: *After years of preparation we were ready to leave for Senanga Hospital in Western Province, Zambia. The car was on the boat to Beira, the sea luggage to Cape Town. Only a last course at the Royal Tropical Institute in Amsterdam. But then, unexpectedly there was this very sad telephone message from "Service Abroad", the organization which was sending us out. "Could you leave as soon as possible for Zambia? Not to Senanga in Western Province but Chitambo Hospital in Central Province. There has been a terrible road accident involving the Briet family. Tin and the eldest son Joris are dead. Dr. Jan Willem and his younger son Ernest each sustained a fractured femur and have been admitted to their own hospital."*

*So we packed and left, by Portuguese Airways via Lisbon, Portugal, Luanda, Angola, to Beira, Mozambique. There we picked up our car and drove through Southern Rhodesia to Zambia—through so-called colonial civilization to the somehow chaotic, but stimulating and refreshing freedom of Zambia.*

*We arrived at Chitambo with mixed feelings—relief at reaching our destination and deep sorrow for Jan Willem and Ernest, bedded in the small side ward in the so-called 'old block', with their legs in traction and Plaster of Paris. We met the Currie family—Milton, Libby and Anne. Milton was evidently happy that we had arrived.*

*Our subsequent immersion in the warm bath of the African culture was such a refreshing and stimulating experience. The contrast with our own hurried, materialistic society was remarkable. People took their time to greet one another extensively. I remember that President Kaunda once arrived half an hour late to address Parliament. He apologized and explained that on the way to Parliament he saw, on the sidewalk, an old man from his own village. "Of course I had to get out of my car to greet him and enquire about his health". Imagine a similar situation in Europe! Time in Africa and thus in Chitambo, was a relative thing. Once a week, usually on a Friday, the bus would arrive from Kabwe on its way to Mpika, with a stop at Chitambo. Because no-one ever knew what time it would arrive, passengers gathered at the roadside from the early morning. They often had to wait for many hours. Sometimes the bus did not arrive at all. No frustration, no anger, no scolding. They would sit and talk, sometimes the women would sing and dance. And when the bus had not arrived by dusk they would go home to return the next morning. To experience this aspect of the African culture was in itself already enriching.*

*Our house was a marvelous house, built in 1910 by the nephew of Livingstone. A real Scottish mansion with a wide verandah practically all round the house, the rooms with high ceilings and open fireplaces. The kitchen was a dark hole with a wood stove. The ingenious but primitive Rhodesian boiler—a combination of three oil drums on top of each other, which had to be filled by a hand-pump and heated by a small wood fire below the lowest drum. It did produce warm water, though of a rather brown colour, to the disgust of my father when they visited us and wanted to take a nice warm bath after the long, dusty trip from Lusaka. When it rained we placed dozens of pots and pans in the bathroom and kitchen to catch the water from the leaking tiled roof. The plaster came down from the walls, but we did not mind at all. It was the most wonderful house we ever stayed in. Highlights were when our friends from Serenje, Mkushi or Lusaka chose to have their baby in our hospital and then came directly to our guest-room with its cozy wood fire in the winter. Or when we had parties with spectacular games, for instance using all the floor-space in the house for a game of "Goose" and everybody, including Sister Margaret Ritchie and Rev. Chirwa had to use a contraceptive (packet of pills or a condom) as a marker! Great fun!*

*Chitambo remains a historical place. There are still a few of the original buildings. Milton Currie who had already worked there for thirteen years, as Medical Officer in charge had managed to raise the quality of health services provided to a remarkably high standard. Though Serenje Hospital was supposed to be the District Hospital, in reality Chitambo was its referral hospital. People came from great distances to Chitambo for treatment. In fact all over Zambia "Chitambo Mission" had a very good reputation.*

*And all of this despite rather primitive hospital structures. The laboratory, with Mr. Mweetwa as the laboratory technician was very limited in the range of lab investigations. The same went for the x-ray machine, though we did try to do intravenous pyelograms (IVPs) and even x-rays of the oesophagus and colon using contrast fluid—if available. Questions or concerns about radiation from the x-ray room, with its wooden door, were never raised.*

*The theatre was like a small museum with an assortment of antiques—an operating table which one could raise to the appropriate height by pumping a pedal. However, during operations, due to a leak in the hydraulic system, the table would sink lower and lower until the surgeon had to bend forward more and more. For a tall man like me this became uncomfortable towards the end of the operation. Milton came up with the ingenious solution of placing a wooden stick under the table.*

*Above the table there was a most extraordinary operating light (installed by Dr. John Todd)—an old search-light from a British torpedo boat, with home-made pulleys and counter-weights. And it worked! Unfortunately we could not get spare bulbs, so slowly the quality of light faded to a dangerously low intensity. However, we managed to raise funds in the Netherlands for the purchase of a new operating table and theatre light. Caledonian Airways provided free transport for it because of the forthcoming centenary of Livingstone's death.*

*Night lighting was a constant struggle—with Tilley and Aladdin lamps. The small generator was only used for x-rays and the big one for the hospital and compound, but only from 6 to 10 p.m. Quite often the big generator was out of order due to shortages of spare parts or poor maintenance. But how romantic: our third child, Jesse, was born in the flickering light of an oil lamp.*

*Until the early 1970s the hospital kitchen was a nightmare: a black hole full of smoke. Food was cooked on an open fire. Through an opening in the wall firewood was pushed in from outside. The cooks constantly had tears in their eyes, as had President Kaunda when he visited the hospital kitchen in 1970. He immediately ordered a new kitchen to be built. This was done—a nice yellow building, completely equipped with all electrical appliances, but without electricity. That was not to come until 1975.*

*To work as a doctor in a rural African hospital was tremendously challenging, rewarding and medically interesting. The pathology and morbidity were so different from the situation in a country like the Netherlands. The major diseases were malaria, tuberculosis, schistosomiasis, sleeping sickness and also asthma, skin infections, syphilis and gonorrhoea. The children suffered from measles, gastroenteritis, all kinds of worm infections, pertussis, meningitis and malnutrition. We realized that the majority of these potentially fatal diseases could be prevented. That was the reason that all of the staff spent a lot of time on health education both in the hospital and in the district.*

*There were also a few cases of rabies. The worst case was a young woman with a baby. The baby had been bitten by a rabid dog and developed rabies. Because the mother was breast-feeding she also developed the disease. Both died after a protracted and agonizing illness. Then there were the accidents: lots of burns, fractures, wounds resulting from fights or wild animals, snakebites etc.*

*The range of operations done was rather impressive. The most frequently performed procedures were the Caesarean section, tubal ligation, circumcision, hernia repairs and wound care. Less frequent were amputations, prostate and thyroid surgery, abdominal surgery for intestinal obstruction, hysterectomy and appendicectomy. Milton Currie had also developed an interest in eye surgery. Patients with trachoma were treated and cataracts were removed successfully. It was wonderful to see these men and women, who, a couple of days previously were brought to the hospital completely blind, and who would leave by themselves, with spectacles and a bible clutched under their arm.*

*Chitambo Hospital operated a remarkable outreach programme which was set up by Chad Musk, Milton Currie and Jan Willem Briet, and subsequently expanded over the years. Hospital staff visited more than 20 different Under Five Clinics (UFCs), some of them, like Chipundu, next to where Livingstone's heart is buried, more than 100 kms away. They also visited the Lusiwasi power station, on the edge of the Luangwa Valley with its cable car railway to the valley floor. There were UFCs in the areas of Chief Muchinka, Chief Mailo and Chief Serenje. Thousands of children were vaccinated and hundreds of pregnant women received ante-natal care. Seriously ill patients were usually transported back to the hospital. The weak link in this vital outreach programme was, of course, the ambulance. Hospital transport was often a big problem. During good times we had two Land Rovers—one for hospital business such as collecting pay-checks and groceries from Kabwe, or collecting mail from Kanona and firewood from the surrounding district, while the other was used for the UFCs and for emergency calls. But most of the time there was only one ambulance. This sometimes led to difficulties when the ambulance was expected at a UFC but was required elsewhere, with no way of getting a message to the waiting mothers. Some of those women would have walked for hours to get to the UFC.*

*Despite all this preventive activity, the under-five mortality rate was dramatic. 40-50% of all children under five died directly or indirectly as a result of malnutrition. In the children's ward there were always several cases of Kwashiorkor (protein energy malnutrition) and many of these children with their swollen bellies and their thin reddish hair would die in spite of intense nursing care. A mother with a malnourished child received daily bed-side teaching from Milton Currie—a favourite activity. Only when they could mention the five most important nutritional ingredients they had to give to their children: eggs, fish, beans, milk and ground-nuts were they allowed to be discharged.*

*Despite this bed-side nutrition education the young mothers would seldom change their feeding practices at home—partly because of superstition and partly because of lack of knowledge. When a child improved during its admission this was often attributed by the relatives to medication and vitamins, and not to the intensive feeding programme.*

*At the under-five clinics we used to sell small bags of dried kapenta—a tiny fish which was a favourite relish for the local people. When we accidentally discovered that it was the men who were eating it we pounded the kapenta into a powder, and asked the mothers to mix it into their babies' porridge.*

*One day a rumour went round that a lion was roaming about Chitambo. Its tracks had apparently been seen. People said that it had snatched a baby from its mother. Morton Chisulo a well-known local farmer who used to walk around with a golf-club, organized a hunting party, but to no avail.* (Morton's daughter Dezzy, the youngest of eight, started her enrolled nurse training at Chitambo, but had to move to Mansa when the Chitambo School closed in 1992. She now works in England). *No lion was found. However, during my time at Chitambo several people were mauled by lions. More frequent and often fatal were the injuries caused by buffalos that destroyed the villagers' maize fields. The farmers tried to chase them away or shot at them with home-made guns, often with disastrous results. Because of the 'chitemene' system of slashing and burning, the fields were often very far away from the villages. It sometimes took two days before the patient was brought to hospital.*

*Then there were the snakes! The beautiful but lethal 'boomslang' in the oleander next to the verandah of our house, the spitting-cobra who spat in the eyes of the sisters' cat, the grass-snake that bit Marjolijn in our sitting room, the puff-adder I nearly stepped on at Kundalila Falls. A number of severe and sometimes fatal cases of snake-bite came to the hospital—often far too late for anti-serum, when it was available.*

*There were millions upon millions of soldier ants that once took over our house and on another occasion the female ward, forcing us to evacuate all the patients. In the rainy season there was the amazing sight of the flying ants, emerging from the earth only to be caught by birds and hungry villagers who loved roast ants. We watched pregnant women walk in single file from the maternity ward to the huge ant-hill near our house to eat chunks of earth, probably because of its mineral content. And finally the world-renowned Chitambo delicacy: the caterpillar. Raw or roasted, people loved it. In November people would arrive from as far away as the Copper Belt, and harvest large jute sacks full of caterpillars, on which they made a great profit in Ndola or Kitwe. It was indeed quite a remarkable sight—these trees full of hundreds of thousands of juicy green caterpillars.*

**The van der Hoeven family—Marjolijn, Catelijne, Jesse, Frits and Christiaan**

## MARGARET RITCHIE 1972

In June 1972 Margaret was back at Chitambo for a second three year tour and she took over the Matron's job from Eileen Searle who had to go home because of ill-health. In a letter to her missionary partners in Scotland she described her life at Chitambo-

*I have now settled into a house just next door to my previous one, and my cook is now Ba Ali, very much older than Ba Smart whom many of you will remember from my slides. However, as Ali used to work as a chef in an hotel in South Africa, his cooking has that extra class about it. My little dog, Buci, was looked after well in my absence and we now enjoy the same comradeship as before. Simba, the Siamese-looking cat has not been seen for many months, but I keep hoping someday he will return.*

*With the administrative work I have been kept very busy and sometimes the days are not long enough, but this should improve through experience. It was very nice to see familiar faces again and all the nurses could say was "You are SO fat!" It was nice too, to meet new faces—the Dutch doctor who has taken the place of Dr. Briet, and his wife and family of two; we have also a recently arrived Dutch theatre sister, a VSO sister, two New Zealand sisters and an English sister, who is doing the teaching—so we are very much in the Common Market.*

*The new buildings I mentioned are now completed, but not yet used as there is no electric power. Morning prayers continue as usual, as do the Sunday English bible-study and service, although there are fewer people inclined to lead them. Two things that pleased me on returning were that I had not forgotten the little language I knew, and to be recognized by former patients. Not long ago we had twins in the hospital—born two days apart—James was born two days after John!*

*I should say too that the nurses' bible study is still held on a Wednesday. Last time Dr. Currie had a Brains Trust and it was surprising the very deep theological questions that were raised. They certainly enjoy singing from the new praise books I brought with me.*

*We have two orphans at present and in a way we will be sorry to part with Justina-a ten month old infant, whose father said he would take her home this week. The under-fives clinics have been increased and there is a revival of numbers to the clinics.*

*By the time I write another letter, the senior students will have gone after their exam in August-there are six sitting it this time. Also at that time there will be an overlap of eleven expected new students, some of whom I will have chosen. As this is all done by letter, one wonders if one has chosen wisely! On top of this it is also holiday time for the First Years, so it is a time full of changes.*

*I look forward to all your letters. Thank you for your concern for the work here and I will remember you in thought and prayer, Margaret.*

## CHITAMBO 1972—AFTER THE BRIETS

In June 1972 Milton wrote *I am glad to say that Jan Willem is safely back in Holland with little Ernest, and has started work again. There has been an almost complete change of European staff at Chitambo since my arrival last September—such is the rapidity with which 'expats' come and go these days.*

*We are delighted to welcome Dr. Frits van der Hoeven, Marjolijn and their children from Holland just a few days before Christmas. Together we spent a very happy Christmas Day, made all the happier for the patients in the hospital by many gifts of toys from friends of the Round Table in England. Very many thanks to all of you who contributed. I don't think we ever had so much to give at any previous Christmas.*

*We said goodbye to our Irish Sisters—Audrey Anderson and Ethel Hamilton in January. I took them down to Lusaka when I went to meet my wife and Anne on 8ᵗʰ January and bring them back to Chitambo. Later in January Libby took Jan Willem, Ernest and Margaret Stacey to Lusaka on their way to Holland and England respectively. Libby returned with two new government sisters—Liz Gillott and Janet Mahoney from New Zealand. A few days later we welcomed a new V.S.O. sister, Cathryn Fathers from England. Our next new arrival was Susan Goddard who had been here before as a V.S.O. and had come back as a government Sister. Susan took over the work of lecturing the student nurses which no-one had been able to do full-time since Barbara Neidrauer left two years earlier. We welcomed Margaret Ritchie back from Scotland, on 5ᵗʰ April, this time as a government servant like myself, but still in the spirit of a missionary of the Church of Scotland.*

*The latest recruit from overseas is Miss Gerie van Urk, a nursing sister with theatre experience who arrived from Holland on 7ᵗʰ May. She was recruited by Dienst over Grenzen, the Dutch Missionary Organization, and therefore very much a missionary at heart, though she comes here on a government contract. This is the new pattern of service at Chitambo Hospital and many other hospitals that were formerly Mission Hospitals. A few days later we farewelled Deirdre Rogers, V.S.O. Sister and then Eileen Searle who had been Matron here since 1966. Eileen had to leave a little early for health reasons and is now back in England. Our good wishes go to her for a speedy recovery and our thanks for all she has done for Chitambo. Margaret Ritchie is now acting as Matron.*

*For me it was a joy to have my wife and little daughter with me again, but within a week we had to set out on the long journey to the boarding school at Sakeji in the extreme North-West corner of Zambia, a distance of well over a thousand kilometres—Zambia now having gone metric. It was a two day journey on very bad roads, and it was my first time to see that part of Zambia. Since the school is so remote, they only have two terms a year, so they are long terms, with a long holiday in between. We returned to Chitambo, just the two of us, bereft of all our children. But not for long—because in March our son Douglas flew out for his Easter holidays from Edinburgh. Jet travel is fantastic: in Edinburgh one day and in Chitambo the next. It was a great pleasure to have Douglas with us and he very much enjoyed being back in the land of sunshine. He has gone back to his studies in Edinburgh but meanwhile our second daughter, Marion, has flown out to us and is with us now. Not long after she arrived we made the journey back to Sakeji to bring Anne home, so we have two daughters with us at present, and the place seems much more like home.*

*At Easter we had a very happy visit from the Rev. Neil Bernard, Africa Secretary of the Church of Scotland, and his wife and Miss Betty Hares of the Methodist Missionary Society, and they shared in our services of worship, including the big Communion service on Easter Day, when the church was packed.*

*Our new members of staff seem to get on pretty well together though they come from such different backgrounds. It is a joy to have a medical colleague again and to see his enthusiasm to learn the very different pattern of medical work from what he had known in Europe. In the past two months we have had two cases of diphtheria, a disease which is rare, even in Zambia. Fortunately we were able to save them both.*

*Another rare disease of which we have seen a few cases this year is typhoid. One case was admitted with signs of peritonitis, but when we operated we found the characteristic signs of typhoid, and were able to save the boy by medical treatment. Some of these cases have been sent to us by the doctor at Serenje Hospital 80 kilometres away. There is a new Indian doctor at Serenje hospital but he has very few facilities there and a very small staff. He sends all his more serious cases to us. For a few weeks he has had with him a medical student from Lusaka University—Francis Khama, who has come out frequently to Chitambo with ambulance loads of patients, and has sometimes stayed to watch operations. Knowing that he had never seen a cataract operation we invited him out one day when we were due to do one. It was on an old man called Bin Ntebetela who had already had one eye operated on in the big hospital in Kitwe, on the Copper Belt. For some reason he came to us to have the second eye operated on. It was a complete success and in due course I was able to give him two pairs of spectacles from my collection—one for general use and one for reading. When he first looked out on the world with his new spectacles he was almost speechless with surprise and joy. "Ma, ma, ma, ma" he cried and many other exclamations of joy.*

*When, however, he was given reading glasses, and a Bible in Chi Bemba was put into his hands, his joy knew no bounds as he discovered that he could once again read small print. He at once wanted a Bible to take home with him, and he was given one from my office. A little later he found a motor car going in the direction of his home and he set off on the hundred mile journey armed with his spectacles and his Bible, calling down all the blessings of heaven on our heads. Do you wonder why we find this job so rewarding?*

*Unfortunately this year we are not able to have a medical student from Aberdeen, partly through lack of funds for the air fares and partly due to lack of accommodation here at Chit ambo—the penalty we pay for having a much larger expatriate staff than we used to. Zambia's economy is in difficulty due to the falling price of copper and the disaster in the Mufulira Mine two years ago. Although Zambia is still a relatively wealthy country by African standards, we are all feeling the pinch. It does mean, however, that the help we get from overseas friends is still valued.*

*The influence of China in Zambia is much in evidence these days. Many Chinese goods are on sale in the shops, to help pay for the vast loan from China for the Tan-Zam Railway. Chinese bicycles have completely replaced British ones in the shops—to the dismay of many Zambians as the quality does not compare. Many Chinese railway workers are among us. I met some a few days ago who had brought some Zambian workers for medical care. I was able to speak to them a little, in Chi Bemba. I have not yet treated any Chinese patients. They have their own doctors and are quite independent.*

*Chi Bemba is one of the major languages of Zambia. The local dialect of this district is Chi-Bisa-Lala, from which you will gather that there are two variants of even the local dialect. (Bisa and Lala). The New Testament in Chi-Bisa-Lala has just run out of print and a decision had to be made whether to make a new translation or two new translations, one in Bisa and the other in Lala. A conference here at Chitambo voted overwhelmingly for a revision of the New Testament in Chi-Bisa-Lala, so as to obtain the maximum possible circulation. This is in progress now. Whether we shall ever get the Old Testament in this dialect remains to be seen. Meantime we read the Old Testament in Chi Bemba. Bibles are still much in demand and when our friend Ted Dennison from Christian Council Outreach comes with his book-van he is quickly sold out. We buy copies of the Revised Standard Version (RSV) in English to give to our student nurses when they complete their course of training here. We continue our weekly Bible studies with the student nurses. Last week for a variation we had a Brains Trust, which brought many interesting questions to light. So we continue to strive to keep the Christian witness alive in the secular setting of a government Hospital.*

Working with Frits van der Hoeven was immensely satisfying for Milton. There was light relief from the relentless demands of the job. With the help of eldest son, David, who was visiting with his new wife Esther, Milton constructed a canoe of canvas stretched over a wooden frame, and took Anne and the van der Hoeven children out in it, on the fresh-water quarry created by the Yugoslav road-builders. David, a final year medical student at Edinburgh University, helped out in the hospital and gained some experience.

Another diversion from medical work was the arrival at the Curries' house of a man who introduced himself as Professor Rutahirwa, (Prof of Economics and Political Science) who had come to Zambia as a political refugee from Burundi. He had been helped across the northern border by Rev. Mugara of Mwenzo and he hoped to apply for asylum at the department of immigration in Lusaka.

He was not well received in Lusaka, however, and was told to leave the country within 72 hours or risk extradition to Burundi where he would be executed. He had been given Milton's name as someone who might help him. Disappointed at the response he received in Lusaka, he enjoyed some hospitality at Chitambo on his return journey to Tanzania.

At the end of 1972 Frits van der Hoeven wrote-:

*The longer I lived and worked in Africa, the more I realized how little we white expatriates understand the African mind, culture and tradition. I once met a White Father on the Copper Belt who was writing a book called "Compartmentalization of the African Mind" about the apparent fact that many Africans lived in two worlds at the same time: the so-called Western world, as well as the indigenous African world, and how easily they could switch from one world to the other.*

*For example the story of Mr. Grant Mkandawire, our very reliable Malawian senior medical assistant, who had worked at the hospital for more than twenty years. He was an elder in the church, a regular preacher and a prominent member of the Chitambo community. One day one of the labourers cursed him "that the fire from heaven will come down upon you!" He was shocked and came to see me to tell me that he would leave Chitambo immediately. It took me all I had to convince him to stay, appealing to his Christian faith, his wisdom etc. etc. Finally and reluctantly he agreed to stay.*

*But two days later, on 26th December, lightning struck a tree near his house, passed through the wire washing line which was attached to a water tap and went straight through the copper water pipe, through the wall of his house, and into the armchair which he had just vacated. It took the intervention of Chief Muchinka as well as the Provincial Medical Officer in Kabwe, and the immediate dismissal of the labourer who had cursed him, to convince him to stay.*

# CHITAMBO 1973

In January 1973 Milton was still in discussion with Grant Mkandawire, who had been very unsettled by the lightning episode, and felt that people at Chitambo were against him. Lightning (according to Kenneth Kangende in *"Zambian Myths and Legends of the Wild"*) is a dreaded witchcraft tool which can be manipulated by certain individuals to their own ends.

*For good measure* wrote Milton, *the lightning knocked out the main generator, and the wards have been in darkness since then. This is equally credited to the man's witchcraft, since he is alleged to have made threats about the lighting plant too. I notice that lightning has splintered a whole lot of Chinese wooden telephone poles. I wonder if the man has put a curse on China too. We've got a new generator all ready, but it is not in use yet, as the cement under it is still setting. Indeed we have two new engines: one for the nurses' kitchen and dining room, not yet installed.*

*Libby went recently to the Livingstone Monument for the first time, with Margaret and Mary Ritchie and Isobel Smith, and enjoyed being there. They went in a VW so the road must be much improved. Talking of Livingstone, Libby and Anne visited the Bollens at Mkushi. Nancy Bollen is the daughter of Sir John Moffat and recently when they were visiting the old Moffat house at Kalwa, they uncovered some old trunks, which Nancy decided to clean up and keep. She found some lettering on one of them, and as she cleaned it up the initials "D.L." (David Livingstone) came to light. What a find!*

1973 was a special year for Chitambo for several reasons, starting with the installation of a reliable telephone line. The two doctors' houses and the Matron's house each had a telephone. The number for Chitambo was Kanona 3. This meant that the staff could phone each other, but there was no phone yet in the hospital. It took hours or even days to get through on the phone to Kabwe or Lusaka.

In February 1973 the van der Hoevens' baby Jesse Clement was born. There was rejoicing all round that the birth had gone well, in spite of the absence of night lights in the hospital. The big diesel engine was mended a few days later and the lights came on again for the first time in a year. Milton celebrated by spending an evening in the hospital x-ray room developing and printing photographs. The smaller engine, the one that had been cursed and struck by lightning, was also restored to normal function.

There were visits from Doyce Musunsa and Jackson Mwape, General Secretary and President respectively, of the United Church of Zambia, and a Miss Margaret Harvey of the British Council who came to see the conditions in which the VSO nurses lived and worked.

Milton continued to tackle eye surgery. His repertoire included cataract removal, iridectomy and, occasionally, enucleation of eyes. He dispensed spectacles from a collection sent by the churches of Aberdeenshire. He relied on Herr Steudle for prescription glasses for more complex cases, and he derived some of his greatest satisfaction from restoring sight.

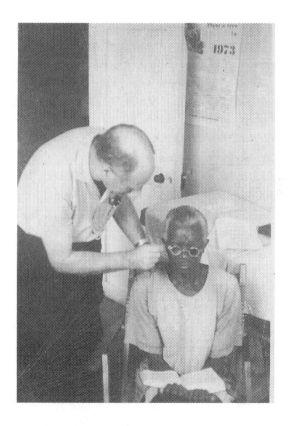

**Milton Currie at Chitambo 1973**

The hospital now had large tanks for the storage of petrol, diesel and paraffin. The ambulance was out of action for four months, having repairs in Lusaka. The only backup vehicle was the Land Rover which also had to make trips to Kabwe and Lusaka for supplies, to collect new staff and pick up the wages. On one such trip Medical Student Catherine Macpherson from the University of Zambia came back to Chitambo for a clinical attachment. Catherine's father, Rev. Fergus Macpherson, originally a Church of Scotland missionary was the first Dean of Students at the University, and later the research historian of the Kenneth Kaunda Foundation.

There was a surprise visit from Mr. and Mrs. Livingstone Armstrong who had come to visit the Livingstone Monument and to prospect for the group of about 12 Livingstone descendants who would come for the commemoration of the centenary of David Livingstone's death on 1 st May 1973. The Livingstone Armstrongs were distant relatives who lived in Switzerland. They were surprised to know that there were already plans afoot to commemorate the day. Rev. Kingsley Mwenda, Secretary of the Christian Council also visited to discuss the plans for the celebrations.

Milton loved small practical jokes. A little boy came into the hospital, having lost his glass eye in a river. Milton fitted him with another one, and then called some nurses to tell him what was wrong with the boy's eyes. When none of them spotted it, Milton poked the boy in the glass eye with a pencil, much to the horror of the onlookers. Milton chuckled over interesting names. A boy called Fly was admitted from Spider Village. VSO sister Catherine Fathers was replaced by Jennifer Daddy. At the same time, student Catherine Macpherson was given a lift back to Lusaka by a couple with the surname Pater!

Milton and Libby escaped for a long weekend to Sir John Moffat's old house at Kapanda, near Mkushi, the Moffats having moved to New Zealand. Milton described the house *as a wonderful old house, with all mod cons, including electric light from a lovely old Lister diesel engine of a pattern I know as well as it is like my old Mwenzo one. There is an old servant looking after the house—an old faithful somewhat like old Jacob at Mwenzo.* The Curries visited David Moffat (Unwin's son) and Rob (Sir John's brother) and Margaret Moffat at Mkushi, thus continuing the Moffat-Chitambo connection.

# ZAMBIA HONOURS LIVINGSTONE—1973

Plans began in earnest for the Livingstone centenary celebrations. A large gathering was expected to take place at the Livingstone Monument, but there were concerns about the health hazards of allowing people to camp there. In some respects little had changed in the hundred years since Livingstone's death—the threat of malaria and sleeping sickness remained, and the heavy rains made travel difficult at that time of year. The plan was to transport as many people as possible to Chipundu, to spend no more than one night there.

Milton recorded the occasion for friends and family in an article for the Church of Scotland magazine—"Life and Work."

*A throb was heard in the sky over Chipundu, and a thousand people who had gathered round the monument to David Livingstone craned their necks to catch a glimpse of the helicopter which was bringing their President, Dr. Kenneth Kaunda. They had met to attend the great gathering to commemorate the 1ˢᵗ of May a hundred years earlier when Livingstone died at that very spot, which was then Chief Chitambo's village.*

*It is a lonely, desolate spot today, surrounded by marshes, and difficult of access in the wet season, when the narrow dirt road leading to it degenerates into a series of mud baths. A mile away from the monument is the little cluster of houses comprising a school, a dispensary and a few scattered dwelling houses known as Chipundu. Chief Chitambo's village is no more.*

*Many plans to celebrate the centenary had been made and scrapped. The initiative in planning the memorial services had been taken by the Christian Council of Zambia, and in particular by its General Secretary, the Rev. Kingsley Mwenda. The government of Zambia showed sympathetic interest, but left the planning in the hands of the Christian community. The final decision was to hold a service at the spot where Livingstone died, and Dr. Kaunda agreed to attend it and be the principal speaker, thus making it a national occasion.*

*The transporting of crowds of people to Chipundu was no small feat of organization. First of all the road had to be repaired, and it was fortunate that the rains had ended early this year (as they had not done for Livingstone in 1873), giving the roads department the chance to fill in the pot-holes and make the road passable. Lorries, buses and Land Rovers were mobilized from government Departments, schools and traders. It was emphasised that this was to be a Christian gathering and priority was to be given to Christian people to attend the ceremony. No beer was to be carried to Chipundu—a wise road—safety precaution.*

*The Christians of Chitambo Mission, 50 miles away from the original Chitambo's village, under the leadership of their minister, the Rev. Simon Mutambo, were charged with the responsibility of setting up a shelter for the President and special guests, and preparing a camp site for the hundreds of people who would spend the night of the 30ᵗʰ April at Chipundu. This they did a few days earlier.*

*On the evening of 30ᵗʰ April, a lorry load of Christians from Chitambo set off for Chipundu, the women of the Guild in their scarlet blouses and white head-scarves, and the choir members to lead the singing. All day they had waited for the lorry, and they disappeared singing into the gloaming. Other lorries were carrying people from many other centres in the district, from distances of 100 miles or more. Those who lived within a radius of 10 miles from Chipundu went there on foot.*

*Meanwhile people from much further afield were converging on Chipundu in cars, vans and mini-buses—people from the Copper Belt and Lusaka, and visitors from overseas. Prominent among them were members of the Caledonian Societies of Zambia, complete with kilts and bagpipes. Many of them camped in the bush by the roadside for the night of the 30ᵗʰ. One group from overseas was led by Mr. Livingstone Armstrong, who is descended from an uncle of David Livingstone. In his party were two daughters of Owen Stroud, the man who built the monument to Livingstone in 1902.*

*A spectacular dawn at about 5 a.m. heralded the 1ˢᵗ of May, the eastern sky flaming with rose-tinted clouds. Was it on such a morning that Livingstone was found on his knees at his bedside, his journey ended? The crowds, among whom were people of many different Christian denominations and many races took up their positions around the concrete obelisk surmounted by a cross. The choirs began to sing the truly indigenous Christian songs which are a feature of modern Zambian church services. Loudspeakers amplified the singing to the crowds. In the audience were brothers, Sir John and Rob Moffat, sons of Malcolm Moffat.*

*The first helicopter to arrive brought, not the President himself, but Mrs. Elspeth Murdoch (who was born at Chitambo) and her sister, Mrs. Mary Dicksmith, great grand-daughters of David Livingstone, and daughters of Dr. Hubert Wilson who served at Chitambo Hospital from 1914-1928. The Presidential party arrived at 10.30 and the service was conducted by the Rev. Jackson Mwape, President of the United Church of Zambia, who gave the* opening address. He stressed Livingstone's role as a freedom fighter and he declared that his real work did not end at Chipundu: it began there.

Next there was a short and charming speech by Mrs. Murdoch, expressing thanks for the privilege of being present at this great event. Her speech was followed by one from Mr. Livingstone Armstrong. Finally there was a long speech by Dr. Kaunda, laying stress on the love and humility which had made Livingstone truly great. Livingstone had understood Africans as no other white man of his time had done, and his sympathy had endeared him to Africans everywhere.

What was most impressive about the whole gathering was that it was a truly African tribute to Livingstone. Granted that there were many expatriates present, some of whom had helped with the organization, the meeting was a spontaneous expression of the love and respect which is still accorded to Livingstone by the people of Africa, among whom he had lived for 30 years, and on whom he had for long periods been totally dependent. Few if any other white men have ever been held in such high esteem by the people of Africa as Dr. David Livingstone. Altogether the service lasted until about 1 pm, which was about as much as the crowd could stand of the heat of the sun.

A new plaque unveiled that day on the Monument reads :

**"After 100 years, the love of God and the memory of David Livingstone has so animated his friends of all races that they gathered here in thanksgiving on 1ˢᵗ May 1973 led by Kenneth David Kaunda, President of the Republic of Zambia."**

## MATRON MARGARET RITCHIE 1973

In June 1973 Margaret Ritchie wrote to her missionary partners in Scotland—:

*Greetings again from Chitambo to you all. Thank you again to all those who remember the work here in the hospital and church and who also keep me in the picture of home news.*

*I wrote before with the comfort of a log fire in the hearth and today was really cold enough for one. However, the sun was out to give the huddled group of patients warmth. There are many youngsters and old people glad of woolen clothing and knitted blankets which we have been able to give out from our stock.*

*Come September I will be half way through the second 3-year tour, but over two months were spent being ill (tick fever) and recuperating. However, while any illness is not greatly appreciated, I discovered the many good friends I had to aid my recovery and am all the more thankful to have my health again.*

*In November I handed over the teaching department to our first trained Tutor. Sister Deva Bethapudy is from South India and, being a Christian, joins in our various activities. She shares a flat with a fellow Indian sister who joined our ranks in March. Our numbers at the New Year were somewhat increased when not only the Dutch doctor's relatives were here but my sister Mary and the Principal from Kapeni College visited from Malawi. I was able to personally chauffeur them as I acquired a second-hand Volkswagen last year. One of the trips I took them was to the Livingstone Monument at Chipundu and we were the first to sign the visitors' book for the centenary year of his death.*

*On May 1st Miss Bethapudy and I, with two students, set off just before dawn, joining the other pilgrims on the way to Chipundu for the special centenary service to be held at the monument. The place was looking trim and much busier than I have ever seen it when I used to go for clinics there! While we were waiting on President Kaunda appearing, a lonely kilted piper circled the monument as he bagpiped 'Scots wha hae', which drew all the amateur photographers present at the gathering. The President of the United Church of Zambia, Rev. Jackson Mwape, conducted the service during which he said in his address that Livingstone's heart had not just been buried where the monument now stood, but that it had been planted, and that we Christians today were left to make the great man's work and witness grow and bear fruit. President Kaunda, who had flown in by helicopter, said during his speech that he wished to pay tribute to a man who proved to be a true friend of the men and women he had come to serve. The day ended memorably when we at Chitambo were invited to meet two great grand-daughters of David Livingstone, one of whom had been born in the house where the late Rev. Mackenzie and his wife used to live.*

*I now have our newest VSO sister sharing a house with me and I am pleased to have her company. She is Jennifer Daddy from Essex and she replaces Catherine Fathers!*

*The next final exams are due in a few weeks' time and as we have had 100% pass rate in the last two exams, let us hope this trend will last. With new people come new ideas and renewed enthusiasm and as a result we now have a proper Paediatric ward, and other ward rearrangements and improvements. The Dutch doctor, Dr. van der Hoeven and the VSO sisters carry on the important work of Under-Fives clinics. When I had occasion to do a clinic recently I was shocked to see one of our past orphans in a malnourished state and so I hope we can still help Chibuye.*

*Simba the cat did reappear but only to assure me that he was glad to visit us and then disappear again as he could obviously look after himself and survive the great outdoors. Buci still pays the odd visit to the nurses' bible study!*

*I hope you have a refreshing and enjoyable summer break.*

*With love from Margaret.*

## CHITAMBO AFTER THE LIVINGSTONE CENTENARY

During 1973 the medical work remained very heavy in spite of there being two doctors at Chitambo. The presence of a new government doctor at Serenje did nothing to ease the load. In fact his presence increased the workload considerably, as he regularly sent ambulance loads of patients to Chitambo. While some of these were indeed serious cases, some were minor and could have benefited from the appropriate treatment at the right time. Milton's knowledge of the people and their languages was a great asset in getting a clear history and making a diagnosis. Also of concern was the Serenje doctor's disinterest in outreach clinics in the Serenje district, and they all gradually closed down. Milton was up regularly in the night operating, and was often exhausted. He and Frits continued to provide regular medical services for Chilonga Hospital, the busy Roman Catholic hospital 90 km north of Chitambo. This took Milton away from administrative duties which piled up in his absence, but he was thoroughly spoiled by the nuns, who greatly appreciated his visits and who adored little red-headed Anne.

From Chilonga he went north to Mpika for petrol, and saw some changes since the start of the railway building programme. *There are big sheds which will be for engine repairs, and there are Chinese everywhere. The Crested Crane Hotel is still going strong, but does not sell petrol any more. I had to go to the Boma—the house which used to be occupied by Mr. and Mrs. Henwick when he was the D.C. It is now occupied by the District Governor and his five wives. The only petrol pump at Mpika sold only regular petrol, but the Indian store-keeper opened his heart to me and sold me enough Super for my needs. While I was buying it I was hailed by an African man who told me he was Aggrey Sikalangwe, who used to be the carpenter when I was at*

*Mwenzo. He had changed a good deal as I must have too, but he recognized me at once and came over for a chat, expecting me to still be able to speak Chinamwanga. Another Winamwanga came over to greet me and we talked about old times.*

In June 1973 Milton looked forward to the arrival of Chilonga's new Dutch doctor, and to a holiday with Libby and two of the girls—Anne and Marion. A weekend expedition to Kundalila Falls with the girls provided some light relief even though Milton described the water as *like the North Sea in winter*. In July, while Frits held the fort at Chitambo the Curries went on holiday to Malawi, stopping at Milton's birthplace in Blantyre, and old haunts in Zomba, Mulanje Mountain and Lake Malawi. Milton was in his element—speaking Chichewa again and meeting up with many old friends and acquaintances of the Currie family. This was his holiday of a lifetime. The return journey was via Luangwa Game Reserve where we saw an abundance of game including lions, which Milton had never seen before in the wild, in all his years in Africa.

Both of us accompanied Milton on ward rounds, and were allowed to watch selected operations before Anne returned to boarding school and I to medical school in Edinburgh.

By September 1973 work had begun on the power lines which would bring electricity to Chitambo from the Lusiwasi power station. At the same time progress was being made on the Tanzam railway. The line had already entered Zambia from Tanzania and clearing already extended for a hundred miles south of Chitambo. The work was expected to take another year to complete. Work was in progress on another improvement for Chitambo: a water filter, reservoir and pumps to pump the existing furrow water to high-level tanks which were erected three years previously. These tanks had never been used because a scheme to sink bore holes for water proved a failure. The original furrow, created by John Howie remained the only water source for Chitambo and towards the end of the dry season it started running low, causing an acute water shortage for both the hospital and the houses. The pump houses were still under construction.

For the first time Milton mentions his future plans in a circular letter dated 29/9/73: *Our final departure from Africa is expected about this time next year. Dr. van der Hoeven hopes to do a second tour at Chitambo, so he should be my immediate successor here. No one is yet in sight to work with him here. I would ask your prayers that someone will be found to carry on the*

*Medical work at Chitambo in the Christian tradition of David Livingstone, and his grandson Hubert Wilson and many others who have followed.*

## CHITAMBO 1974—TRAGEDY

In January a new minister—Mr. Chirwa arrived with his wife and five children. He was a Malawian, who had grown up in Zambia. The rains went on longer than expected to make up for the drought of 1973. Progress continued on the power lines but there was still no date for rewiring the hospital. New doors were fitted to the new x-ray room, and a new theatre lamp was promised from the Lions of Chililabombwe in the Copper Belt. One of the wards built by Dr. John Todd was being renovated as a Laboratory." The Cottage" had a kitchen added to it.

The local MP visited Chitambo in February and asked if there was anything he could do to help. He was begged to push for the rewiring of the hospital and houses. There was a surprise visit from a group from Multimedia, bringing a film they had made about Livingstone, including some shots of Chitambo Hospital. The Chitambo nurses screamed with delight when they saw themselves. Milton's eldest daughter, Joan, who was training as a nurse with the South Edinburgh School of nursing looked forward to a trip to Zambia in the Scottish summer of 1974.

Milton made plans to specialize in Ophthalmology, and he studied as much as he could in the little spare time that he had. He also occupied himself with trying to find a replacement doctor. The most promising was an Italian from a Waldensian church background but who did not consider himself a believer. Milton also tried to find a replacement for Sister Gerie van Urk, who planned to marry Serenje teacher Alan Buckle in May. The Provincial Medical Director phoned to say that money had been made available for the rewiring of the hospital.

In February Frits van der Hoeven struggled in vain to try to save a man who had been accidentally shot. A week later Milton had to do a post-mortem on the man who had done the shooting. He had hung himself! The medical work continued relentlessly, with acute admissions and calls in the night. Four children died of various causes. Milton was called to a maternity case who collapsed and died on the table before he could begin the caesarean section. It was a most depressing time.

There was some light on the horizon. The Lions Club of Chililabombwe sent a delegation ahead of the new theatre lamp. A theatre table for Chitambo was being assembled in England. Recently qualified Dr. Catherine Macpherson came to spend a few days at Chitambo, which greatly cheered Milton. The power lines to Chitambo were complete but new transformers were required before the hospital could be electrified. The new hospital kitchen that had never been used was to be demolished and rebuilt to different specifications.

In March a little girl with rabies was admitted from Serenje, where she had waited for ten days for anti-serum. Sadly she died, but before doing so she bit her mother, who then required treatment. Four other children were admitted with dog-bites and treated prophylactically for rabies.

Milton postponed his departure from Chitambo to the end of 1974, so that Frits could take leave in September. He made plans to take Joan and Anne to Kafue national park. In March there was the possibility of another Dutch doctor coming to replace Milton—an older man who came from a town near Frits' home. He would come in February 1975. Milton applied to the Church of Scotland for a furlough house and he wrote to Professor Faulds in the Ophthalmology department at the Eye Pavilion in Edinburgh about the possibility of taking up a training post.

The new hospital laboratory was up and running and a new x-ray room was being refurbished. An extra children's ward had been created but was already full to overflowing. March was the peak month for admissions. While the heavy rains were welcomed by the farmers, they also brought more cases of malaria, some of whom had cerebral malaria and needed quinine infusions.

Milton had a visit from an evangelist named Rudi Lack who belonged to a mission involved, amongst other things, in smuggling bibles into Russia. He had come up the Great North Road, dropping off gospels in Chinese at the various railway camps. These were made to resemble "little red books"! As soon as he arrived at Chitambo he was arrested by the Military Police and taken off in a Chinese lorry for interrogation. The Chief of the Military Police discussed the matter with Milton, and the man was eventually released, much to the annoyance of the Chinese leaders. Meanwhile the Chinese railway team pumped the Chitambo quarry dry and started blasting out the granite, without any consultation with the Chitambo Church to whom the land belonged.

On 13th April 1974 Milton wrote a long and chatty circular letter to the family. He had been on duty for nine days continuously, as Frits was away. The hospital was exceptionally busy and in the midst of it all Milton was informed that they had run out of diesel. It turned out that someone had left the tap of the diesel tank running twice in the previous week, so that gallons were lost. This meant that the hospital had to rely on Tilley lamps again at night, and had to borrow diesel from Serenje. They waited patiently for the hospital to be rewired.

Three Zambian students of engineering, on their way to Dar-es-Salaam and China, were involved in a car crash and were in the hospital, each with a fractured femur. Milton wrote *Although they are champion grumblers their legs are doing quite well.*

There was an opening ceremony for the new laboratory, and the local M.P. came. Milton was asked to write his speech for him. Milton *"took the opportunity to put in some praise for Malcolm Moffat and Hubert Wilson, and some propaganda for blood donors. I felt a bit of a fraud applauding when the speech was over."*

The Curries now had the firm offer of a Church of Scotland flat in Glasgow for the first five months after their return from Zambia. They eagerly awaited more news of the new Dutch doctor.

Sometime between 13th April and 26th April 1974 a delegation of local chiefs came to see Milton. They had heard that he planned to return to Scotland and they came to beg him to stay. As was customary they asked him to remain amongst them until he died, so that they could bury him with their own hands. They also wrote a petition to President Kaunda pleading for his intervention to convince Milton not to leave Chitambo. How his heart must have ached, as he reflected on the 29 years he had spent serving in Africa, and as he considered his very uncertain future.

On 23rd April he went to the hospital to do his usual evening rounds at about 8 p.m. By 1 am Libby realized that he had not come back, and she went to the hospital to look for him. She found him lying unconscious on the theatre table. By the time she had summoned help from Frits van der Hoeven, Milton had died.

Immediately they heard the news, Dr. Bill Todd and his wife Muriel left Kabwe and reached Chitambo at b 9.30 am. During that day people gathered from far and near—five nuns and one white father from Chilonga, the Morrises from Luanshya, with Peggy Hiscock, the Wilkies (from Mwenzo), the Rev. Doyce Musunsa, who had just arrived back from overseas, Rob Moffat from Mkushi, Margaret Liddell from Isoka, The Mackenzies from Mporokoso, recently qualified doctor Catherine Macpherson, from Lusaka, a Cabinet Minister, Mr. A. Kunda, representing

Dr. Kaunda. Also present were the Provincial Medical Director and the hospital Superintendent and his wife from Kabwe General Hospital. Chitambo Hospital staff including Margaret Ritchie and Dr. Frits van der Hoeven were there.

Bill Todd wrote:

*The ceremony started at 2 pm in the church. There was no weeping and wailing and indeed it was most moving and yet triumphant. Five ministers took part including Doyce, Mr. Sikawe, Mr. Chiwale, and others. The President sent Libby a very fine letter which was read by Mr. Kunda. There was no coffin. Milton was wrapped in an African bamboo mat covered with black cloth and white cloth. Doyce spoke about how fine a man Milton was and that it was typical of his humility to be buried in this simple way. The grave is in a little glade surrounded by trees on the road towards the cave that the children found. The women, dressed in their red and white sisterhood clothes, patted the mound flat, singing hymns and then pressed in a flower each, all round the grave. Libby had a simple little bunch of flowers which she placed on last. Bill (Mackenzie) was beside Libby there and I think he was a great comfort to her. The doctor from Holland was a tower of strength. He looks a fine person and is a beautiful singer. Three chiefs were present and one spoke after the grave ceremony. At Libby's request "Thine be the glory" was sung by us all at the close of the graveside service.*

*Somehow we didn't feel sad for Milton. He had completed his work at Chitambo and loved Africa, and he's buried beneath the African soil he loves so well. Libby is flying today to Sakeji to see Anne. Mr. Moffat has kindly arranged a flight in a small plane belonging to one of the Mkushi farmers.*

# CHAPTER 6

# ENDINGS AND BEGINNINGS

## GIRLS ON A MISSION 2003

So that is how we came to be here, the three of us Joan, Marion and Zanna (Anne), standing by our father's grave in the gentle August sun, surrounded by the kindly faces of the Chitambo church congregation. After the short and moving grave-side ceremony we walked back up the road towards Chitambo in the company of two of the last people to see him alive—nurses Agnes Sebata and Violet Mumbwa, who were trained at Chitambo. They had passed Milton as they were going off duty, and he was coming into the hospital. They had greeted each other as always and gone their separate ways. There was nothing unusual about that encounter, but the memory of it must have haunted them for years to come.

Now we were ushered back to the van for a drive to Chief Muchinka's village on the other side of the Mabonde stream. Visiting the chief was a last-minute item on the agenda, for which we were ill-prepared. We were embarrassed that we had not brought a suitable gift, but we were graciously received all the same and we knelt in front of the chief in his small brick house, in the customary manner, to pay our respects.

On the return drive to Chitambo we took a detour through the village of Ba Jameson, who had worked as our house servant. There was Ba Jameson, outside his house, looking remarkably similar to our memory of him, and pretty sprightly. With shrieks of joy we hugged each other, and caught up on family news. Ba Jameson was disappointed that the boys had not come with us and we promised to encourage them to come back to Zambia too.

Our next stop was the hospital, where we were given a comprehensive tour by Dr. Kanku, a recently qualified young doctor from the Congo.

In his office was a familiar picture of Grandpa John Todd about to do a chest x-ray on a young boy. We were ushered through the wards and laboratory, and we were shown the dilapidated equipment with which the hospital had to make do. When we reached the theatre there was a hush as we peeped in the door of the room where, in reference to our father's death they said 'the accident' had happened on that sad day in April 1974. The theatre looked bright and well-equipped with a sophisticated looking anaesthetic machine. The laboratory needed a new centrifuge, the x-ray plant had broken down, and the maternity wing desperately needed infant resuscitation equipment and incubators. The list went on.

We walked round the back of the hospital, past the original 1908 hospital building, of brick and tiles, now an administrative block. The hospital ambulance, a land-cruiser, was parked nearby. It was battered and broken, and barely roadworthy, we were told. They desperately needed a new one.

Our day at Chitambo ended in a meeting with community and church elders in the hospital classroom. Dr. Kanku made an impassioned speech, thanking us for visiting and requesting financial help for re-equipping the hospital with essential items. I'm not sure quite what possessed us but we said yes, we would help. After a brief refreshment stop at Rev. Chilongo's and a quick photo stop at our old house, 'Cabana', we drove out into the night, each mulling over our experience of the day. Rev. Chilongo had gone ahead of us to Chansa and had arranged for someone to 'find' petrol for us. There's a roaring trade in 'off the tanker' petrol, and for a price we were able to fill up. It was a relief to reach Kasanka and to roll into bed.

## MARGARET RITCHIE 1974

At the end of 1974 Margaret wrote to her Scottish partners-:

*Dear Friends,*

*Chitambo is now clothed in rich shades of greens and reds, the colour of the trees which amaze many people here as, although the cold season is now over and the warmer weather has set in, there has been no rain since April.*

*In my last official letter to you (alas more than a year ago) I wrote about the Centenary of the great man Livingstone's death. Well I did not know David Livingstone personally but in this letter I want to pay tribute to a great medical man that I did know personally until his sudden passing on 24th April—Dr. Hamilton Currie. Chitambo Hospital and Dr. Currie went together—he lived for the hospital and gave himself unsparingly to the service of the people as a doctor and also as an elder of the church. We will miss his wise counsel and remember his great devotion to duty and dedication to God. He fought the good fight with all his might; Christ was his strength and Christ his right; Christ was the way and now Christ is his prize. Let our prayers be especially for the future of Mrs. Currie and daughter Anne.*

*Dr. van der Hoeven took up the reins as Medical Officer In Charge, so hastily thrust upon him and is doing a fine job. Recently another doctor from Holland—Dr. A. Hodde from Amsterdam came to assist for a number of months and is to relieve Dr. van der Hoeven when he goes for a short leave in December. Our Dutch sister was married to a teacher from Serenje (Alan Buckle) in June at Chitambo, and she has not been replaced.*

**Alan Buckle, Gerie and Frits van der Hoeven, Chitambo 1974**

*In fact at one time our Zambian staff complement was very poor but we now have sufficient staff. Our Under Five clinic programme was severely curtailed for a time due to lack of transport fund allowance and to the constant breakdown of the one Land Rover we had left at our disposal. In fact it was not unknown for Dr. van der Hoeven and myself to use our own vehicles for the sake of continuity of some of the clinics at least.*

*We now have a proper water plant with mechanical pump and chlorination but unfortunately it does not always work properly. The old system has still to be used to keep hospital and house with enough water. With the road into Chitambo are now a line of telegraph poles. This leads to a transformer, where the power stops. This comes from the Lusiwasi power station opened a few years back in the Luangwa Valley. Since last December we have been hopefully awaiting a contractor to rewire the hospital and wire the houses but so far no-one has accepted the tender yet. A fairly recent advent has been a bus service which goes twice a day to Serenje, which has proved an asset for nurses, patients and relatives.*

*The nurses' fellowship continues under the leadership of a Chairwoman and secretary from their own ranks and our programme each week is now including local Christians who are invited to participate in Bible study. One Sunday a nurse led the church service, another nurse prayed and did the Bible reading, the nurses' choir sang. I gave the children's talk, Dr. van der Hoeven gave the sermon and the Rev. Chirwa, our Minister, translated—very much a joint effort.*

*This week I have been asked to address a church district conference, the theme being "In His Hands". I hope to talk about the Christian parents' responsibility towards the mental and physical development of their children. I hope to include an outline of the new Nutrition Unit which is to be built in memory of the late Dr. Currie.*

*I took over the book-stall from Mrs. Currie. The number of bibles, gospels and Christian literature in demand shows a healthy interest and meets a worthwhile need. They are sold to hospital patients and at every communion Sunday at the church. Rev. Chirwa also sold an appreciable number last time he went on tour and of course the attenders of this week's conference will also be supplied I am glad to say that many of the books are geared for Zambia but few are printed in any of the local languages.*

*We had a tragedy a few months ago when two of our student nurses were killed in a road accident, so the carnage on the roads continues.*

*I started this letter about trees, and end with the comment that I acquired 76 trees—pine, spruce and eucalyptus—which have been planted by whoever agreed to water the tree every day until the rainy season comes. They are planted near the hospital and there is a disc on every tree with the name of the person who adopted it. So in years to come, Chitambo should have more shade, shelter and I hope beauty.*

*Today I had a walk around where the relatives of patients in the hospital stay. I was delighted to see that they had changed the name of this place-'Kabulanda'—the place of weeping, to 'Ubucetekela'—the place of hope.*

*Thank you all for keeping in touch with me so faithfully and for your continued interest and prayers for the work and Christian witness here. Hoping you will have renewed fellowship and inspiration with the coming winter activities.*

*Love,*
*Margaret.*

## FRITS VAN DER HOEVEN 1975-1977

Dr. Frits van der Hoeven wrote:

*A hospital with 129 beds, a nurses' training school and an extended outreach programme, requires at least two medical doctors. It was for me a great experience to have, in the first years, Milton Currie as my colleague, counsellor and tutor. His wealth of experience of medical care in developing countries was an indispensable source for me. His knowledge of the Bemba language, the African mind and culture was quite amazing, his humour refreshing. Not always the easiest man! I remember how he poured buckets of water over a couple of student nurses who were found sleeping on night duty! And how Scottish: he told me how he had calculated the exact number of razor-blades he should bring with him from his furlough in Scotland, not one too many! I believe he used one blade for four weeks.*

*His sudden death on 24th April 1974 came as an unbelievable shock. Chitambo lost a dedicated, experienced doctor, loved by the people. His funeral was a tremendously impressive and moving event, where the church was packed to capacity, and church ministers from all over Zambia came to pay their last respects. Everybody realized how much he had contributed to the development of Chitambo Mission, its hospital and community. He was buried in the soil of his beloved Africa, next to the graves of Tin and Joris Briet. It took more than eight months before a replacement doctor was found: Jaap and Francien*

*Thijs from Holland, with their two children Willem and Bart, arrived in February 1975.*

*I lost a friend and dear colleague. From one day to the next I had to cope without his support and advice. My first task, as Medical Officer in charge was to order the slaughter of a cow for the funeral celebrations. My second decision was to dedicate the planned Nutrition Rehabilitation Centre (NRC) to Milton Currie. Its realization became possible because of generous donations from the UK, Australia and the Netherlands.*

*The NRC was a small compound next to the hospital, comprising three tiny brick houses, plus a house for the housemother, Lily Mambwe, a lecture room and a traditional, thatched roofed kitchen. A maximum of six mothers and their children could be admitted for a period of three weeks. During these weeks they would, under supervision of Lily Mambwe, and in the absence of doctors and nurses, prepare the food for their children and themselves. Next to preparation of food, lectures were given in nutrition, hygiene, first aid and family planning. Mothers would tend the vegetable garden and learn simple activities like mat-weaving and sewing. The first course for six mothers began on the 4$^{th}$ August 1975.*

*On principle no medication was given in the NRC, nor were any special nutrients introduced. The mothers had to be convinced that the improvement of their child was due to the diet that they prepared for their child, which they could do just as easily in their own homes.*

*Things were difficult at the start. The NRC had been built before local people told me that it was too close to the mortuary and that women would therefore refuse to be admitted. We had to demolish and rebuild the mortuary further away!! Initially it was hard to convince mothers to stay at the NRC for three weeks, but things improved when people saw the very positive results. Follow-up visits were made during Under Five Clinics to mothers who had followed the course. Our assessment was not entirely positive: we realized that though the knowledge of the mothers had substantially improved, and the child recovered, the situation and circumstances in their own village had not really changed i.e. the negative influence of grandmothers who still believed in witchcraft or the poverty which made it difficult to prepare a well-balanced diet. Our conclusion was clear: poverty eradication and income generation remained essential elements in the prevention of malnutrition. Health and development are inextricably bound to one another. Therefore development support by the international community remains crucial.* (Is there an echo here of Livingstone's "Commerce and Christianity"?)

One day a witch-doctor passed through Chitambo on his way from Zaire to Malawi. He asked me if he could have a séance in the evening. Since he was a colleague, though a traditional one, I agreed. That same evening the hall was packed full and there he was behind the table, with his glass bowl and all the other paraphernalia belonging to his profession. One of his clients was a relative of the hospital carpenter who had died the year before in an accident with the ambulance during a trip to the UFC at Chipundu—the Livingstone Monument. Both the carpenter and the bricklayer had been killed when the ambulance had skidded during a tropical downpour. As usual such an unnatural death was attributed to witchcraft. So the relative wanted to find out who was responsible for this.

After consulting his smoking glass bowl he stated—according to the translator—that a local leader was the culprit, and after some hesitation he even mentioned the name: Boston Chisenga—the village Headman of Chitambo. A hush went through the audience. Since he was not present, a delegation was sent to his homestead to collect him. Confronted with the evidence he denied any involvement. Then he had to undergo a test: the witchdoctor prepared a concoction in a bowl, using all kinds of ingredients. He, as well as two volunteers, took a sip of this mixture. After a few moments, only Boston Chisenga's eyes started to roll in their sockets, foam appeared at his mouth, a seizure overtook him and he collapsed to the ground. Realizing it had happened under my jurisdiction, I wanted to intervene, but was restrained by others.

After two minutes Chisenga regained consciousness and immediately confessed to his 'sin': because he suspected that the bricklayer had an affair with his wife, he himself had prepared a concoction and had smeared that on the four wheels of the ambulance the evening before it left for Chipundu, since he knew the bricklayer would join this trip. This, together with a curse on the fate of the bricklayer was the cause of the accident . . . For all present this was apparently a totally acceptable explanation. After further payment by the relatives, my flamboyant colleague prepared another mixture: the crucial medication which Chisenga had to drink. The verdict: the next time he used his knowledge to bewitch others, he would die. Everybody, to my amazement, was satisfied with this. There was no blaming or punishment whatever. The therapy was sufficient, and Boston Chisenga remained the village headman.

At the end of 1974 President Kaunda decided on a boycott of Rhodesia and South Africa because of their apartheid policy. This was a courageous decision given the fact that Zambia depended on road and rail transport of *copper through Rhodesia to the ports of South Africa. It meant that from 1975 onwards all exports had to be transported up the Great North Road to and from Dar-es-Salaam and Mombasa and via the Bangweulu line to Angola. These were costly decisions and the economy suffered. The people of Chitambo felt the pinch. Only 30-40 % of their grocery orders such as coffee, tea, and tinned foods materialized. Petrol was in very short supply again and had to be rationed.*

*Near Chitambo there was a secret training camp for Angolan refugees and freedom fighters from Rhodesia and South Africa. It was supposed to be very hush-hush. For us they were known as "box 16 people", after their post box at Kanona post-office. All kinds of rumours went around. They were rather invisible except when they came to the nurses' hostel, carrying guns and often 'under the influence', to 'visit' the student nurses.*

*The completion of the Tanzam railroad, built by the Chinese and finished at the end of 1975, meant a slight boost to the economy. From then onwards freight trains would carry the copper bars to Dar-es-Salaam. There was also a passenger train. It was a great day when Marjolijn took the children by train from Kanona to Serenje and back.*

*The Chinese were a peculiar lot. They were completely self-sufficient, brought most of their labour force with them and replaced them every five to six months. Yet they did care about the Zambians who worked for them. Whenever one of them was admitted to our hospital, usually because of an accident, they would come to visit him and bring some food. One day I was called to do a post-mortem on one of their Zambian workers who had been killed in an accident. When I arrived the next day at the Chinese camp they took me, despite my objections, to the kitchen. There in the large freezer was the deceased, next to the pork and other perishables. They had not known when I would come. I had to come back the next day after the body had been defrosted! The local people, however, preferred the Chinese to the Yugoslavs who had built the Great North Road. The latter were apparently slave drivers and could not keep their hands off the local women.*

*During 1975 and 1976 the Zambian economy collapsed. The 1973 oil price rise was followed by a slump in copper prices in 1975 and a reduction in export earnings. While in 1973 the price of copper accounted for 95% of all export earning, this halved in value on the world market in 1975. By 1976 Zambia had a balance of payments crisis and rapidly became massively indebted to the International Monetary Fund. Unfortunately the government had failed to take the necessary measures in time to develop alternative industries. The Independence slogan "One Zambia, One Nation" sounded hollow. Due to the recession people started to protest and political opposition in this one-party democracy grew day by day. The President reacted by declaring a state of emergency, which had a profound impact on the nation. From then onwards the political, economic and social situation changed dramatically and government institutions like Chitambo Hospital suffered due to stringent economizing measures.*

*For me the years in Chitambo were unforgettable, instructive, challenging, turbulent, but overall very very valuable. Of course it was only possible for us to stay there because Marjolijn took the responsibility for teaching the children. This was not an easy task in a context where there were daily interruptions by unexpected guests and household matters, but she managed very well in her double role of mother and teacher. Apart from that she set up sewing classes for the student nurses, which resulted in a request from the local women that she set up a sewing class for them too. After some time quite a number of women walked around proudly in their home-made dresses. Just before we left, this Women's Club was officially registered by the National Women's Guild in Lusaka. Another activity was the children's club she organized with one or two of the Sisters, where scores of boys and girls played games and developed all sorts of creative activities. The appreciation of the local people, especially the women was further expressed by the fact that she, as one of very few white people, was asked to join the KKBK, the fellowship of women of the United Church of Zambia. There was a very moving dedication ceremony for Marjolijn.*

*Memorable also were the church services, some of which were quite lengthy affairs! The choir, dressed in beautiful purple gowns donated by the parents of Francien Thijs, made every service a joyful happening. Our weekly bible studies were a very valuable aspect of our Chitambo fellowship.*

*Living and working in Africa has a tremendous impact on one's life. Values have to be redefined. Material wealth has a different meaning. Time is much more relative. And how amazing to experience the vitality and endurance of these people, despite all their hardships, the high morbidity and mortality, the constant struggle against poverty—and yet their laughter, their sense of humour. Amazing. And what a tremendous privilege it was for all of us to be part of the Chitambo community during all these years. We realized this all the more so when, on our way back to the Netherlands, on the last day in Africa, we lost our dear son Jesse in an accident on the beach near Mombasa. How we missed the consolation and fellowship of the people from Chitambo. Our Jesse, born in Africa and buried in its soil like Milton, his first wife(Nancy), his child(Catherine), Tin, Joris Briet and the countless other children who died in Chitambo hospital while ours were thriving. All of a sudden, we painfully realized we were no longer outsiders, for now we shared something essential. We left a part of our life, our heart, in Africa.*

*Dear people of Chitambo: Natotela sana, shalenipo, mutende!* (Thank you very much, goodbye, go in peace.)

# CHITAMBO 1977-1979

In 1977 Dr. Jaap Thijs and his wife Francien Boer came to Chitambo from Holland. After them, in 1979 also from Holland came Dr. Hans Doornbos and his wife Mieke. By 1979 the hospital had 12 wards and 128 beds, including John Todd's "old block" built in 1953, the Maternity Wing (1962) and the 'new' male and female wards of 1967. Although Serenje was continuing to develop as an administrative centre, Chitambo retained its reputation as the better equipped and staffed hospital. Once again the fate of Chitambo Hospital hung in the balance. Should it be reduced to the status of a rural clinic or should it be further developed as the main district hospital?

Discussions between the Minister of Health, the Hon Kunda, provincial, district and local authorities resolved the issue. Chitambo would retain its status as a treatment and preventative centre, and this would require maintenance and extensions to the existing buildings.

The Ministry made funds available to pay off all the hospital's debts, improving relationships with the suppliers and restoring confidence in the Local Purchase Order system. The hospital was able to stay within budget for most items other than fuel costs which were affected by the extensive outreach programme of the hospital.

Chitambo continued to provide training for Zambian Enrolled Nurses. There was one Principal Tutor and one Clinical Instructor. In 1979 there were 36 students in four batches. 19 students sat their final examinations and 13 passed. The nursing school was relocated into more spacious rooms, including a library and tutor's office.

Malnutrition, particularly in infants remained a major cause of hospital admission, with about 40% of all children at Under Fives Clinics below the 10th Centile for weight. The Nutrition Centre, built in memory of Milton Currie, now had a resident housemother (Lily Mambwe), an assistant housemother and Nutrition Co-coordinator. Financial support for the centre came from Holland. Measles too accounted for many admissions, but in 1979 at least there were no hospital deaths from measles, a change from previous years, and probably attributable to improved vaccine uptake. Malaria raged unabated in spite of all efforts to control it. While scabies was not usually a life-threatening condition there were severe cases, and the treatment of choice, Benzyl Benzoate was out of stock for long periods. Sexually transmitted diseases also placed a heavy burden on treatment resources.

The hospital garden provided some relish and supplies were supplemented by a weekly delivery of vegetables from the old Kalwa (Baptist Mission) Farm. This would have pleased Malcolm Moffat! A Chitambo grinding mill enabled a local supply of maize-meal for the hospital. Eggs and broilers were supplied by the local Production Units at Chitambo and by Mkushi River Ranch. The Dutch government sponsored the import of necessary items for the laboratory and operating theatre. In 1979 a new Land Rover station-wagon was provided as a gift from the Simavi-Wild Geese Foundation in Holland, and a Land Rover trailer was donated by Mr. Shrosbree, Chairman of the Mkushi Commercial Farmers. An orchard and six fish-ponds were in the early stages of development in late 1979. All hospital employees were encouraged by the government to grow their own maize, lima beans, millet and ground-nuts.

Donations from Holland also enabled new houses to be built for Maternity and Nutrition centre staff, and an office for a Traditional Healer. The original doctor's house had some repairs to the floors and roof. More staff houses were needed as well as a cold storage building and an isolation ward. Repairs were successfully made to the water pumping system. At the end of 1979 it was evident that Chitambo Hospital continued to attract patients from afar.

## HANS AND MIEKE DOORNBOS 1979

*Dear parents,*

*At this very moment: thunder, lightning, wind and rain. Enormous grey clouds, waving elephant grass and now a thundering noise begins on our corrugated iron roof on which the shower in all its violence erupts.*

*I am sitting in my freshly furnished study at the back of our house with a large window, viewing the garden. It is glorious and impressive weather.*

*Every now and then I look out of my window and continue writing my first homeward bound letter. I am in the mood to describe the view and my feelings, so full of impressions that I have to share with someone. I will get my wife Mieke out of her room to help me because I can't quite paint the right picture for you. Well then Mieke has been sitting on my knee for some time and is now shutting the windows, which are fully exposed to wind and rain and returning with some soaked blankets to dry in my study.*

*In about an hour we expect the hospital staff for coffee. Just as in the past in rural areas in Holland you asked visitors from the neighbourhood only on moonlit evenings, it is obvious that in Chitambo you start making coffee after the rain has stopped. No problem, time is a relative notion over here. We expect some 20 people—administrator, nursing staff, laboratory and administrative staff, matron, teachers etc. Mieke, with the help of Greenwell our out/indoor worker and Ineke, my colleague's wife has been cooking for days and baking buns and bread. I'm looking after beers and lemonade. I wonder how it will be and maybe tomorrow I'll report to you.*

*Anyhow after having settled for one month now we wanted to invite to our house the upper ten of the Chitambo (mission) hospital staff. Firstly because we feel indebted to the people who gave us a very warm welcome here. Secondly for Mieke, who is curious to meet the people she hears so much about from me.*

*Well the weather is more quiet now and I'll begin a more systematic report of my experiences up to now. Daily life is more or less familiar to you thanks to Mieke's frequent letters.*

*Here we go: My first encounter with the hospital was at midnight after our arrival on that evening and it was strange and a bit depressing. We were having late coffee with my colleague Leen and his wife Ineke, when the news : "red ants in old block", arrived. The old block is the oldest part of the hospital housing children's and maternity wards. Armed with torches and ant poison up to the old block. Very old indeed with paintless wards, patients in rags in steel beds or on the floor. A heavy smell and the humming of countless flying ants (not the small types as in Holland, but double winged) and on the floors countless biting red ants. Crying children with their mothers in beds. A watchman and patients in the corridors. No window screens and more insects inward than outward bound. Patients catching them and after removing wings eating with gusto. And in between all this a sweating Dutch doctor spraying foul smelling ant poison.*

*At the moment 24 hours have passed, the feast is over. Because rain did not stop for the whole day the attendance was not overwhelming (13 people*

*altogether), but with so much food everyone was happy. Even to us after sober
weeks it all tasted very good.*

At present it is pouring cats and dogs again This afternoon we made a trip
by car to Kundalila Falls. We took the wrong road, still a beautiful ride with
grass-thatched villages, friendly people, bush chickens etc. We had a picnic in
a sunny place and encountered very bad weather on the return journey. We
parked the car on a height, the water came in waves along the road and we
waited with a book and some groundnuts for better times.

Regarding finance we just heard of again a devaluation of the kwacha
with over 20% and a general price increase of 5%. Now again the hospital
impressions. After the first night with the red ants it proved to be not so bad
at all. You are quickly used to dirty, smelling wards, crowded with patients.
Children's wards may be less luxurious than in Holland but admission to the
ward is much less frustrating for the infants. Children are looked after by their
mothers, washed and fed, even brothers and sisters are sometimes welcome. If
possible during the day out you go out in the sun to the market for maize or
mango. Back to the ward in time for medicines, doctors round etc. Of course
the very sick with i.v. drip, steam cabin or high fever stay inside. Quite often
there is warm contact with parent and infants full of trust in you as doctor
and human being. On the evening round: a bed full of sour smelling rags with
warm bodies of mothers and children, you have to pick the sick one. A sleeping
little body making some repelling movements, a mother half asleep pulling her
baby to her breast and I busy with my stethoscope. A wonderful experience.

Sometimes you are too busy to realise all these miracles. Working at the
OPD with patients from far away, who first have been seen by the medical
assistant and if necessary are forwarded to me. Again they wait patiently for
hours for the doctor. Finally after a hard day's work I come for a quick visit to
the OPD: to work away a long row of waiting people

I want to work fast, the patient has been waiting for days to speak a doctor:
a conflict of interests. Sometimes I send patients away without medicines back
to the bush: almost unforgivable. Sometimes I cut them short in their long,
translated stories: again not alright of course.

You understand: too much work for adopting the African working art. If
possible I try to compromise and the contacts and gratefulness are rewarding.
The pure medical side is wonderful. What is nicer after being medically
graduated than to have the opportunity to encounter all aspects of the clinical
practice? This chance is only reserved for tropical doctors and I am grateful for
that every day here.

*Our hobby morning is Thursday—operating day. My colleague and I discuss the indications before and operate on the big procedures together. To make your diagnosis, consider the indications, to give your spinal or general, perform the operation and arrange post-op care is a fine job. Up till now with good results. We have postponed repositioning of fractures, especially elbows because of doubt about the final functional result, so we have not yet started doing repositions and fixations.*

*Maybe I am concentrating too much on medical technical issues. You understand that also disappointments are present. On the whole we do keep up Chitambo's long lasting good name. Anyhow we see many patients from other regions with own hospitals even from the area around Lusaka. Just as in Holland there is a free choice in doctors. However we have a budget for numbers of treatments and patients in our catchment area. So in that relation we fare worse than other hospitals. Not only money, also fuel and drugs are at present a problem. No streptomycin (many T.B. patients), no scabies ointments (many patients), no insulin (diabetic in coma dies).*

*Just now two mating flying insects land on my desk, throw off their wings and walk to my cup of tea. Wild life is amazing. I will stop writing for the time being for I have some business correspondence to work on as well as preparing some lessons for tomorrow. I notice that I can write endlessly not knowing where to start and stop. Mieke has luckily kept her writings from the beginning and I have made a start. She will take over now.*

*I did not think Hans would omit his first caesarean. Leen came to collect him at 2 a.m. and they were busy until 5 a.m. After having delivered the baby (mother was only 15 years old), Leen was busy resuscitating it. Hans did the stitching. While he was busy with the final skin sutures the nurse commented that two swabs were missing, so Hans removed every stitch again (his first cursing in Chitambo Hospital, in Dutch luckily). The theatre nurse made a nice story of this at our welcome party. She is a beautiful woman with five children who play at our house quite often. Praising the infants is the way to the hearts of the mothers. Our party was very amusing—friendly people, easy talking. It is funny. You do not notice any more that they are black and you start to see family resemblances. All the faces are different but almost without exception the women are beautiful. With the party we used up our last flour and have had to eat maize meal three times a day. So far we love it and Hans is actually putting on weight.*

*Ineke is doing fine. She is due in about four weeks. Should it be necessary Hans will do the instrumental delivery (e.g. Caesarean section), with Leen playing the father or the anaesthetist.*

*In our house the cat is expecting so we look forward to some kittens. Is it spring in Holland? We are always anxious for news.*

*Love and greetings,*
*Hans and Mieke.*

## HOSPITAL ANNUAL REPORT 1979

The annual report of 1979 showed just how well the hospital staff were keeping up Chitambo's good name. The figures speak for themselves, and compare very favourably with those of 1965. They show the scope of the work and the progress made in the nature and complexity of cases handled. The figures in brackets are for 1978.

| INPATIENTS | 1979 | 1978 |
|---|---|---|
| Present in the hospital on 1st Jan 1979 | 106 | (82) |
| Total admissions including above | 4,681 | (4818) |
| Total discharges | 4,531 | (4,620) |
| Total deaths | 61 | (92) |
| Remaining in hospital on 31st Dec | 89 | (106) |
| Total inpatient days | 37,113 | (38,768) |
| Daily average in hospital | 104 | (106) |
| Average length of stay (days) | 8 | (8) |
| Occupancy rate | 82% | (83%) |

| OUTPATIENTS | | |
|---|---|---|
| Total attendances | 18,054 | (16,046) |
| New patients | 13,427 | (12,326) |
| Daily average | 50 | (44) |

## SURGERY

| | | |
|---|---|---|
| Caesarean section | 8 | |
| Tubal resection in ectopic pregnancy | 5 | |
| Abdominal hysterectomy | 6 | |
| Laparotomy | 19 | |
| Cataract surgery | 15 | |
| Hernia | 9 | |
| Hydrocele | 9 | |
| Major amputation | 4 | |
| Carcinoma of testis | 1 | |
| Burr hole of skull | 1 | |
| Total major operations | 73 | (66) |
| Incision and drainage | 183 | |
| Excision (lipoma, cyst etc.) | 22 | |
| Circumcision (phimosis) | 10 | |
| D and C | 33 | |
| P.O.P. reposition | 53 | |
| Suturing wounds | 45 | |
| Skin graft | 37 | |
| Amputation | 8 | |
| Removal of foreign body | 20 | |
| Tracheostomy | 3 | |
| Osteomyelitis plus bore hole | 5 | |
| Nail extraction (paronychia) | 12 | |
| Paracentesis | 29 | |
| Lumbar puncture | 13 | |
| Tooth extraction | 257 | |
| Cut down | 16 | |
| Tubal Insufflation | 20 | |
| Insertion of contraceptive loop | 13 | |
| Miscellaneous | 113 | |
| Total minor operations | 886 | (562) |

## OBSTETRICS

| | | |
|---|---|---|
| Total deliveries | 259 | (286) |
| Live births | 248 | (274) |

| | | |
|---|---|---|
| Still birth and postnatal death | 11 | (12) |
| Vacuum extraction | 10 | |
| Forceps delivery | 2 | |
| L.S.C.S.(Caesarean section) | 8 | |
| Manual placenta removal | 6 | |
| Version and extraction | 1 | |
| Decapitation or craniotomy | 3 | |
| Ruptured uterus, on admission | 2 | |
| Maternal death (eclampsia) | 1 | |

| NUTRITION REHABILITATION CENTRE | 1979 | 1978 |
|---|---|---|
| Admissions | 67 | (76) |
| Follow-ups | 52 | (42) |

More than 300 pairs of spectacles, donated by Memisa in Holland, were provided free to patients with refractive abnormalities. The outreach work continued, with 34 centres being visited every two months and all schools being visited twice a year. Vaccinations for childhood illnesses, and malaria prophylaxis were offered regularly. Antenatal care was provided at Chitambo and at the outreach clinics.

## GOING BACK 1980

In March 1980, shortly before graduating, I had the opportunity to do a medical student elective overseas, and, strangely enough I chose to go to Zambia. My family put me in touch with Mr. James Cairns at Katete Hospital in the Eastern Province. On arrival in Zambia I stayed overnight in Lusaka and took the bus the next day to the Eastern Province. The journey took about 9 hours, and I was dropped at the Katete road end, from where I was escorted by a kind villager, my suitcase on her head, to the hospital. I spent two months there gaining insights and experience in the realities of rural medicine in Africa. Mr. Cairns ran a very good hospital and was a strict disciplinarian. There was little slacking for medical students: doctors' meeting at 7 am, followed by ward rounds, operating or outpatient clinics. I was given some responsibility for the women's and children's wards. There were night rounds, and I was called to witness emergency procedures and to assist in theatre. I went down with malaria, but was only permitted time off when I could no longer stand up!

There was little time for relaxation, but I did get away for a wonderful holiday at Lake Malawi with a doctor and nurse friend. We camped at Salima, swam in the ocean-like lake and ate fresh bream grilled over an open fire on the beach. It was idyllic. At the end of the elective I had the chance to revisit Chitambo, with a Dutch friend, stopping en route at Mkushi at the invitation of Sir John and Lady Peggy Moffat. We arrived un-announced at Chitambo and received a warm reception from Hans and Mieke Doornbos who offered accommodation in our old house—Cabana.

Next day we had a tour of Chitambo and the projects that had been started by the Dutch doctors. There were fish ponds, a rabbit farm, and a building project where the cement floors for pit-latrines were being moulded. The Nutrition Centre was impressive and we visited one of the original buildings of the hospital—with the date 1908 above the door. This had become the hospital museum which housed some memorabilia and photos of the hospital's past. I left my father's stethoscope here. We visited his grave—an emotional moment for me and probably the first time that the reality of his death had sunk in. I had his old Zeiss-Ikon camera, ready to take some pictures but sadly it disappeared from the back seat of the car. Hopefully someone else gained some pleasure from it though I doubt if they would ever perfect his art of photography or spend their evenings in the x-ray dark-room developing and printing their own black and white photos.

We camped at Kundalila Falls and swam in its crisp, clear pools before returning to Lusaka and Scotland. It was good to know that Chitambo Hospital was still flourishing. It would be another twenty five years before I would return.

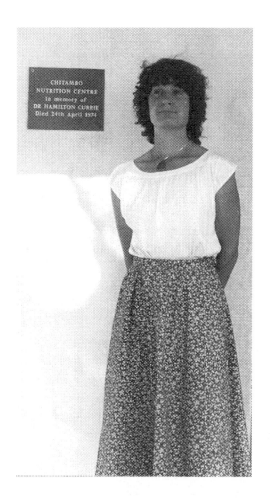

**Marion at Chitambo Nutrition Centre 1980**

# CHITAMBO HOSPITAL 1980-2008

The Dutch organization Memisa continued to send doctors to Chitambo until about 1992. The last two Dutch lady doctors left after a frustrating time. Dr. Frits van der Hoeven met them on his return trip to Chitambo, in 1992 and heard about their plight. They had felt a singular lack of support from the Ministry of Health, and they felt that unless they were constantly pushing things along nothing happened. Their difficulties were compounded by the fact that they had no transport and the telephone connection had been down for over two years. The bus did not call in at Chitambo any more. Food supplies for the hospital were poor as the Ministry did not pay the local suppliers. The hospital suffered from lack of maintenance. It was difficult to attract staff and the nursing school had closed. This was a tough time for Zambia. The price of copper had fallen and there were shortages of many essential items throughout Zambia.

In 1997 my younger sister Zanna was standing in a queue in the post office in her home village of Hathersage near Sheffield. The lady in front of her had a large parcel addressed to Chitambo. Overcome with curiosity Zanna struck up conversation with her. It transpired that the lady's brother was working as a nurse at Chitambo, and his wife was the doctor there. Intrigued, Zanna wrote to Mick and Pip, and received an enthusiastic reply dated 26th March 1997

*Dear Zanna,*

*The world is a small place indeed. We are living in "Cabana" which I presume cannot have changed very much since you lived there. The passion fruit tree is gone but the mulberry bushes are still there as well as mango, avocado, banana palm and frangipani. Descendants of your bees still inhabit the roof and now share it with a large colony of bats.*

*Most of the workers' houses now have electricity—and consequently TV's and hi-fi. Even the female ward has a television set and patients gather every night to watch evangelical programmes and American soap operas (many villagers don't speak English). Next door's children came round the day after we arrived "to watch the video" and we had to show them every room to prove we didn't even have a TV. I'm sure they still didn't believe us. The telephone line which I think existed when you were here is long gone and our only link to the outside world is via radio to Serenje Hospital, where the nurses usually have the kettle plugged in instead.*

*Your father is remembered with affection by the older generation here (the hospital staff have all changed)—when mentioned patients will say "ah yes, Dr. Currie was my doctor." After your father died there were Dutch doctors at Chitambo until 1992 when they pulled out due to administrative problems with Serenje District (the problems still exist). Usually they came out as a couple, with the doctor's partner working as a tutor in the nursing school—the school also closed in 1992 when they left. At present there are plans to re-open the school but no money and the buildings, including the hostel, need extensive renovation.*

*A Nutrition Unit was opened in memory of your father in 1975, consisting of gardens and a shop. Since 1982 these have been run separately from the hospital by MS, which is a Danish aid agency, and has become an agricultural project, taking students from Central Province. Sad to say the unit has had little impact on malnutrition—28% of the children in the area still suffer from Protein Calorie Malnutrition, mostly due to traditional food habits rather than lack of food. When we arrived at the hospital the malnourished children were only receiving the same food as the rest of the hospital patients—nsima* (maize porridge) *and cabbage twice a day, and the mortality rate (amongst children) was horrendous.*

*On seeing what was going on we made this our priority and now the children are getting five meals a day plus fruit snacks(and the very ill get the fortified milk feeds they need) and the mothers are getting the nutrition teaching that the mother&child health unit knew very well they should be having. We've been successful so far but will it last?*

*Apart from the frustrations at the hospital Chitambo is a pleasant place to live and still surrounded by bush. We have walks through the villages and picnics by the quarry pool. The largest wildlife we've seen is a tortoise. It would be nice to have the transport to get away occasionally, especially for Pip who is on call seven days a week. We did manage to get to Kundalila Falls. Mostly our evenings are filled by reading and tapestry. The Danish volunteer at the agricultural project is nice, but a bit of a loner, and because of Pip's status as a doctor the only other people who visit us socially are Chief Muchinka and the Reverend. Occasionally we see other mzungus but it isn't as if we're on a road to anywhere.*

*I had better warn you to beware of short grey-haired old ladies. Pip's mother used to work at the Hallamshire (hospital in Sheffield) and knew several of the consultants as junior doctors. She is now a semi-retired family planning nurse and will no doubt be looking for you, if only to confirm her suspicions that we are living in a terrible place and liable to be eaten by crocodiles at any moment. She is actually very nice and, like you, was born and grew up in Africa until she was ten (in Tanzania). What she is really worried about is HIV and so are we. The official figure for Zambia is that a third of the adult population is HIV positive and I would say it's higher than that. More than half of the adult in-patients at any one time have obvious indications of being HIV positive. Not many are tested for two reasons-:*

1) *We have to buy the test kits, so we reserve them for blood donors and people who request testing (very few)*
2) *The whole country is in massive denial about HIV and AIDS*

*Despite the fact that in all the towns you see health education posters about AIDS, no-one will talk about it. If educated, Zambians refer to it as "that disease" and if uneducated, regard it as witchcraft. Sexual habits are entrenched—one of our environmental health technicians visits the local brothel. Very rarely does a month go by without some quack in Lusaka announcing his "cure" for AIDS and people are paying a lot of money for these.*

*The surgery is a worry for Pip. (She's a G.P.) Mostly she does minor operations—incision and drainage, manipulation and setting of fractures and digital amputations. Now that we have a new District Medical officer at Serenje, we can at least do the major abdomens. He comes out to Chitambo as there is no theatre at Serenje. The obstetrics is interesting. Most of the women have 10 or more pregnancies and as a consequence multiple births are quite common. The midwives are very capable and are teaching me a few things. Pip and I both have babies named after us now! The paediatrics consists mainly of malaria, malnutrition, diarrhoea, conjunctivitis, broken bones and malaria. Plus lots of malaria.*

*The adult wards are full of TB patients, HIV-related disease and the occasional hypertensive. 75% of the TB patients will be HIV positive according to studies carried out in sub-Saharan Africa. I was running the paediatric unit until we got the malnutrition ward fairly sorted out and now am in charge of male ward, as well as being part of the management. We haven't yet been out to any of the rural health centres but we'd love to see them—especially the ones in the Game Management Areas!*

*Well I'd better finish before this letter gets too long, but just a couple of quick things. Do you remember the Waddills of Kalwa Farm? We have a recipe of your mother's via Mrs. Waddill. They will be going back to America this year or next after 27years at the farm.*

*Did my sister tell you that Pip was born in Sheffield (the house where her mother still lives)? Even though we were born within 12 miles of each other and of a similar age, we didn't meet until we were working on an infectious diseases unit in Leicester, which had patients with TB and HIV and the largest single cause of admission was malaria!*

*Hope you like the photos,*
*Take care,*
*Mick Sykes.*

## 2008—THE CENTENARY AND AMBULANCE

In August 2003 my sisters and I returned to our busy lives. The red Zambian dust washed out of our clothes and time passed. We investigated the possibility of buying a new x-ray plant for Chitambo but the logistics were too great. We sent packages of surgical instruments and baby-clothes for the hospital and we kept in touch with Dr. Kanku. From time to time he would send a new wish list and we would scan it for things that we could supply. In one such list he mentioned that the ambulance was 13 years old and would not last much longer. We knew how important it had always been for Chitambo to have a reliable means of reaching people in the outlying district . . . . but how could we provide such an item?

It was Jo's idea. She and a small group of people in her home-town of Penicuik near Edinburgh set up "Penicuik for Africa" in November 2005, with the aim of raising funds for African projects. Chitambo Hospital was the first 'worthy cause' on their list, and it quickly followed that what Chitambo most needed was an ambulance. Then began two years of fund-raising and negotiating, largely by Jo herself to make this dream come true. Whilst this was an ambitious task and there were some inevitable frustrations along the way, there were also many successes including overwhelming generosity, and some large (and anonymous) donations.

By late 2007 Jo's group had raised most of the money required, with a little help from New Zealand, and Jo began researching the best way of buying an ambulance. This was a slow process and there were many considerations about costs of importing and refurbishing, and much red tape to be cut through. Fortuitously, Stewart Musk, one of Chad's sons, was in Zambia in 2007 and was able to visit Toyota Zambia in Lusaka and look at the range of options. The best plan seemed to be to buy a Toyota Land Cruiser that was already in Zambia and have it converted into an ambulance. Jo made many phone-calls to Toyota Zambia to discuss these possibilities, and the plans slowly began to take shape.

Since Chitambo Hospital was to reach its centenary in 2008, it seemed fitting that the ambulance would be a centenary gift, and we now turned our attention to a return trip during which, we hoped, there would be a centenary celebration and the ceremonial hand-over of the ambulance. It is true to say that Jo and I became somewhat preoccupied with this possibility and the Chitambo people responded with a grand plan of their own for the event.

Once again we would make our base at Kasanka Game Park, and Kim and Edmund Farmer offered their support in overseeing the progress with refurbishment of the ambulance. They visited Lusaka regularly and were able to call in at Toyota Zambia to see how things were going. Now the ambulance was a reality, and simply awaited collection. In early July Kim flew to Lusaka with sons James and Dominic, and they drove back to Kasanka in the ambulance, with the siren on and lights flashing some of the time for the boys' amusement! When we saw the pictures of the ambulance parked up at Kasanka we began to feel that we were home and dry. What could possibly go wrong now?

Meanwhile Zanna had been talking to Margaret and Mary Ritchie who were interested to join the expedition, Margaret having been Matron at Chitambo from 1969 to 1978. Twin sister Mary had been a missionary teacher in Livingstone during those years. By co-incidence Jo was doing some work with a freelance medical researcher—Marion Lacey, whose father had been the doctor at Mwenzo before ours. Marion now expressed an interest in coming along. Jo was also involved in discussions with the Scottish Parliament about sending a representative to the centenary event, and the Hon Jack McConnell was approached because of his interest in Malawi and Zambia.

On the other side of the world I was trying to drum up interest in the return trip and I had some e-mail discussions with the author Christina Lamb (*The Sewing Circles of Heart, The Africa House, and Houses of Stone*). In *The Africa House* she had expressed a strong affection for David Livingstone, and I wondered if she'd like to do a Chitambo story. Initially she appeared interested in joining us so that she might write an article for the Times. Subsequently she went to Zimbabwe to cover the elections and we lost touch. Jo and I approached film companies and wrote grant applications for a documentary, but to no avail. There was nothing for it but to tell our own story.

The Chitambo community suggested a date—23rd August, for the centenary celebration. They were now getting quite excited about it and they sent us their proposal. They would invite the six chiefs and they would hire a brass band, and a troupe of majorettes. Four cows and fifteen goats would be slaughtered to feed the people. There would be choirs, dancing, a soccer tournament and speeches. Ministry of Health officials would attend. Invitations were already being sent out. And, by the way, it would cost about five thousand pounds, would we be able to pay . . . . ?

Meanwhile Dr. Kanku had been replaced by Zambian doctor Tiza Mufune, who served at Chitambo for three years before being transferred to Serenje as District Medical Officer. His successor at Chitambo was Dr. Kandolo Nzinga from the Democratic Republic of Congo.

The stage was now set for another adventure. This time we had a fairly clear idea of where we were going, so it was easier to plan and pack. In advance we hired two diesel-fuelled four-wheel drive vehicles from Justin Lubhezi, of Landmark Car Hire in Lusaka so that the seven of us (including Jo's 23 year old son Paul) would be able to travel comfortably, and have some back-up in case of breakdowns. It would also allow some flexibility if we needed to go in different directions. Paul offered his walkie-talkie system for communicating between the vehicles and this was to prove very useful. I felt some responsibility as expedition doctor, and brought along as comprehensive a medical kit as I could muster.

I flew from Sydney to Joburg in the exalted company of the Australian rugby team, the Wallabies, on their way to play South Africa. Unhappily for them and for me we missed our connecting flights from Joburg due to mechanical problems at Sydney airport and the fact that Qantas were now outsourcing repairs to Malaysia. So the Wallabies and I spent a luxurious night at the new, plush Joburg Sun. I was glad of the extra day to rest and prepare for an evening flight to Lusaka.

Arriving at Lusaka airport I was confronted by a choice of three queues—"Zambians", "Visitors" or "VIPs". Having been born and raised in Zambia, I chose the Visitors queue with a pang of nostalgia and wondered idly who qualifies as a V.I.P. No-one from my flight, apparently. Then my sisters were there, steering me past the taxi rank and out into the V.I.P. car park. They had hired two Pajeros and one of them had been bought from a retiring diplomat, complete with diplomatic number-plates which remained valid for five years after transfer. This is quite legal in Zambia, and suddenly people were doffing their hats or saluting as we went by. "Oh now you're regarded as *Untouchables*" said a Zambian friend. I *do* love Zambia!

We spent several days in Lusaka, based again at Jul's guest house, recovering from our journeys and acclimatizing. I had forgotten that Lusaka is at an altitude of 1500m and that mild altitude sickness is quite common in the first few days. Lusaka is a relaxed and friendly city with smart shopping malls and a great craft market at the Arcades shopping centre on Sundays. For variety, quality and prices it would be hard to beat. The Nurse-In-Charge at Chitambo, Levi Chifwaila was in Lusaka for a course at the Medical School and he gave us a tour of the teaching hospital. It was obvious that good care was being provided here with very slender resources. Levi was thrilled with a lap-top that Jo had brought for him.

We were invited to dinner with the Musks' old friends, the Chileshes, who lived in a grand villa near the university. Mrs. Chileshe had gone to great lengths to prepare a wonderful feast, complicated by a power cut of several hours in the midst of cooking. Undaunted she fell back on a combination of a wood stove and a gas primus, and we dined splendidly in the company of the Chileshe elders and some Lusaka ministers. The only shadow over the occasion was the fact that Zambian President Mwanawasa had been taken ill while in Egypt for the African heads of state conference. He had been transferred to an intensive care unit in Paris and his condition remained uncertain.

On the Tuesday morning we stocked up with groceries before heading up-country. We also filled diesel cans, as the fuel situation further north was unpredictable. Travelling with 'the Diplomat' always in front, we were waved through the many police check-points along the way. The villages we passed were mainly built of locally made bricks and thatch. There's a remarkable absence of litter in Zambia. Alternative uses are found for bottles, tins and packets. Old car tyres are turned into shoes, oil cans are converted into banjos and there are a thousand things you can do with a collection of bottle-tops. I was persuaded not to buy a funnel for re-filling the vehicles, when an upturned 1.5 litre plastic bottle cut round the middle will do.

In the late afternoon we called in on David and Christine Moffat on the farm at Mkushi. They were in good form and as welcoming as ever. David Shepherd's elephants still looked down from the living-room wall but David Livingstone's portrait had been moved to a separate room dedicated to his memory and replete with Livingstone memorabilia.

**David and Christine Moffat, Paul, Marion Lacey,**
**Margaret Ritchie, Zanna, Jo and Mary Ritchie, at Mkushi, 2008**

Our destination once again was Kasanka National Park in the north east. This was to be our base for a week while we prepared for the centenary event. The centenary ambulance was parked up here in readiness. Kasanka is a Conservation Trust managed at that time by (Australian) Kim and (English) Edmund Farmer. The small profit from tourism is reinvested in community projects—notably housing, education and health. The accommodation was in thatched chalets or 'rondavels' overlooking a lake. A central lodge served as a dining area and the kitchen staff turned our basic ingredients into a series of feasts. We congregated round the camp fire each night and swapped tales of the day. While there are elephant, hippos, zebras and other large game in the park, Kasanka is renowned for its Black Lechwe (antelopes), Sitatunga (small, furry, splay-hooved, marsh-dwelling antelopes) and Shoe-Bill Storks. It also has amazing bats.

As well as the more traditional guided game drives there are walking or biking safaris, and the option of spending a night in a traditional African village, supported by the Trust. From Kasanka visitors could fly with Edmund over the nearby Bangweulu swamps or out to the Luangwa game reserve. Other sites of interest in the area are the David Livingstone monument and the refreshing Kundalila Falls.

Kim was keen to talk to the local chief about a problem with poachers in the park. We were lucky to get an audience with him too. HRH Chief Chitambo IV, Freddy Chisenga, is the great grandson of the chief who welcomed the dying Livingstone into his village in 1873. His Royal Highness is a colourful character who travels the globe and still exerts a powerful influence over his villagers. We waited outside his palace while a messenger went to announce our arrival. He graciously welcomed us in the traditional way and then insisted on accompanying us to the Livingstone monument.

He showed us the spot where it is said that Livingstone spent his last night, the site of the old *mpundu* tree under which his heart is buried and where the monument with its memorial plaques now stands. The most recent of these was donated by Kingsley Holgate, explorer and raconteur who, with a small group, in 2004, retraced part of the journey of Livingstone's followers as they carried his mummified body to the coast. Chief Chitambo also insisted on showing us the place where Livingstone was carried up from the Lulimala River to his last resting place. There's a village here and its inhabitants had been enjoying some of their own brew when they were surprised by a visit from their chief. They cowered as he called them to order and read the riot act about their intoxication, the state of their village and the fact that they had started burning the grass around their fields too early in the season. We stood by uncomfortably while they gave us quizzical sidelong glances and we replied with small shrugs of apology.

**HRH Chief Chitambo at the Livingstone Monument, 2008**

Back at Kasanka there were visitors waiting to see us—a delegation from the local administration at Serenje. Sadly it had been announced that President Mwanawasa had died following a stroke. For the next three weeks there could be no celebrations. Our centenary event was to be postponed, and the ambulance would be handed over to Chitambo at a later date.

While we were sad at this turn of events we were warmly welcomed at Chitambo on Saturday 23rd August and were shown round the hospital which was run by Congolese Dr. Kandolo Nzinga. There had clearly been much modernization and the facilities looked good. Chitambo Hospital still has a high reputation in the district.

In 2005 Dr. Nzinga came to Zambia from the Democratic Republic of Congo where he had worked as a G.P. On arriving in Zambia he worked at the Arthur Davidson Children's hospital in Ndola for a year and then at the Ndola Central hospital for two years. He was transferred to Chitambo

Hospital in Feb 2008. The top priorities for the hospital for the years 2008-2010 would remain

Malaria
Protein Energy Malnutrition
HIV/AIDS
Pneumonia and
TB

In 2008 staffing was well below the authorized levels for a 130-bed hospital. Nutrition education remained a vital part of the hospital work, and there was a commitment to ensuring that TB and HIV positive patients received their drugs. The outreach work continued, with visits to seven rural clinics including Chipundu where a new clinic had just been built near the David Livingstone monument.

**Ex-Matron Margaret Ritchie at Chitambo Hospital 2008**

We were formally received by the local chief—Muchinka who lives in a small house dwarfed by a huge satellite dish. This time we had an abundance of appropriate gifts! Once again we had the chance to visit Ba Jameson, who used to work in our house. It was an emotional meeting and there were tears of incredulity and warm hugs, as we all struggled to find the right words.

From Chitambo some of us headed out to Kundalila for a quick picnic and swim, while Jo stayed on and spent the night in her old bedroom at 'Cabana', now the home of Dr. Nzinga. On Sunday morning Zanna hitched a ride from Kasanka to Lusaka for her flight home, and the rest of us packed our gear, farewelled Kasanka and returned to Chitambo. (All except Paul who went on a rescue mission to locate a group of Italian tourists who were struggling in an overcrowded vehicle, some 200 Kms off our route.) A great crowd gathered at the old church and we were welcomed in a truly African way with singing, dancing and drumming. The choir marked the occasion with a song they had written about the founders of Chitambo. More tears were shed and childhood friendships rekindled. There was a moving ceremony at our father's grave and some of the old people who remembered him came forward to greet us. Alongside Milton's are the graves of Tin and Joris Briet.

From Chitambo we drove north to Mutinondo Wilderness, a beautiful nature reserve with spectacularly sited 3-walled chalets in the heart of leopard country. We lay under our mosquito nets looking out at the inky sky and wondering what we would do if we were visited by a leopard. The remainder of our journey was a return visit to Mwenzo . . . but that's another story!

All too soon our journey was over and we were back in Lusaka, wishing we had taken more leave. At the time of our departure Zambia was still deeply in mourning for its much-loved president, He is the only Zambian president to have died since independence in 1964. The ambulance presentation took place in January 2009 and Kim was there to represent us and to formally hand over the keys.

**James Farmer and the Chitambo Centenary ambulance**

It is more than three years since our departure from Zambia and Jo has been in discussion with Dr. Mufune and Levi Chifwaila about re-opening the nurse training school at Chitambo. In recognition of her efforts to help Chitambo Jo was honoured in the Scottish Parliament and invited to a reception with ex-President Dr. Kenneth Kaunda when he visited Edinburgh in June 2009. She was able to show him the Todds' invitation card to the 1964 Independence celebrations, and he was moved by this. Our brother Doug and his wife Elspeth, sister Catherine, (nee Macpherson), brother Fergus and Mum Myra Macpherson, also had an audience with the ex-President. Myra's late husband Fergus had been a close friend and biographer for Dr. Kaunda. They enjoyed reminiscing about their time in Zambia and sang some Bemba songs together.

**Jo with Dr. Kenneth Kaunda**

# JAN WILLEM BRIET'S RETURN TO CHITAMBO 2009

In August 2009 Dr. Jan Willem Briet made his first return trip to Chitambo with his wife Mienke and younger son Ernest and his family. In a letter following his visit he writes

*Sunday August 2 2009. To Chitambo. The four letters I had written to Chitambo remained unanswered. When coming home we found an e-mail that we were most welcome. Anyway, we had chosen the Sunday for our visit. We left (Kasanka) before 7 am and arrived just before 10 at the church. Parked the car near the tree with the church bell, still in use.*

*A young man, I think his name is Allan Mutokya, of the church came to shake hands. He did not know of our visit but arranged with some elders a most warm welcome. We met a carpenter, the son of Ba-Mario the night watch, Jonas Mambwe (farmer) and Irene Kapeso who trained as a nurse in our time. Gradually more people arrived until the church was nearly full. We were seated in the front row. After a while we all were invited to stand in front and I could give thanks for the welcome they offered so unexpectedly to us, and also for their empathy shown at the funeral of Tin and Joris. I understood this only long afterwards, from the pictures Dries van der Meulen had taken. Outside the New Israel Church choir started singing and entered the church, finding seats in front, to the left. The senior women's choir in their red jackets and with white headdresses were on the right. They sang with so much energy and so well prepared, solos answered by the choir. The reading was from Deutoronomy 30:15-20 and Hebrews 4:9-12 about not working on Sundays. We could not understand a word but even Madelief was patient. We admired the rhetoric of the preacher, moving his voice up and down, soft and loud. One of the elders briefly explained the order of the service to us.*

*Afterwards they guided us to the cemetery, the elders and a long queue of children. It was not difficult to find the graves, first Milton's, beside him the son of Mr. Mkandawire and then Tin and Joris. The sign on Tin's grave had disappeared but that of Joris was as we left it in 1972, thanks to the efforts of Fergus Macpherson who made them in Lusaka. It was strange but good to be there, especially with Ernest and his son Joris, and with so many people from Chitambo who knew very well about our accident. The meeting with Irene Kapeso touched us the most. She has been working as a nurse until recently, in several places in the country, but Chitambo is her family home, so she has returned.*

*We were shown a brand new marketplace. Much better than sitting under a tree. Our house had disappeared, just as the mango and guava trees beside it. I did not notice the beautiful jacaranda tree. We walked to the hospital and saw the Chitambo Centenary ambulance standing well-polished in front of the new block. Behind it was the new kitchen I had never seen before. We walked through the old block with a male nurse in a very white uniform and met the medical assistant who also does anaesthetics. The equipment of the theatre is a little better than in our days. The labour ward had not changed, nor the room where Ernest was born and where we stayed recovering from our fractures. There was a huge lock on the pharmacy door. The old kitchen which had been blackened by the soot of the wood fire was now the x-ray darkroom, an obvious metamorphosis.*

*We returned to Kasanka and sat by the fire. This had been the aim of our journey. We were happy to have been there at last, and given it a context by approaching it in four weeks by land. Round the camp fire each of us gave a short reflection on our journey together, saying thank you to everybody.*

# DOCTOR LIVINGSTONE AND HIS LEGACY

Did Livingstone ever dream of founding a hospital? He certainly spent a great deal of time on his earlier expeditions searching for a suitable site to establish a mission. In July 1851 he wrote in his diary "*I offer myself as a forlorn hope, in order to ascertain whether there is a place fit to be a sanatorium for more unhealthy spots.*" The prevalence of malaria was the main limiting factor in many of the places he considered. He never found the perfect site. This was left to those who came after him.

Livingstone received greater renown for his exploration than for his doctoring. While a medical degree in 1840 was of somewhat limited use in the face of so many unknowns, Livingstone had an inquiring mind and he used his rudimentary scientific education to a remarkable extent. Biochemistry was in its infancy and bacteriology had yet to be established as a science. The microscope was a primitive tool and the 'humoral' theory of disease was still prevalent. There were few useful instruments, but Livingstone was quick to embrace the recently invented stethoscope. Surgery was performed without anaesthetic, and speed was therefore of the essence. He was one of the earliest doctors to record body temperature with an atmospheric thermometer.

So, by the time he set out for Africa Livingstone had no knowledge of the cause of malaria. What he did know was that quinine was beneficial in treating this perplexing fever, and he went on to write some significant papers on the treatment of malaria. Compared with other explorers in Africa Livingstone lost comparatively few men on his expeditions. His remedy for fever was as follows: "*Resin of jalap and calomel, of each eight grains; quinine and rhubarb, of each four grains. Mix well together and when required make into pills with spirit of cardamoms. Dose—from ten to twenty grains. The violent headache, pains in the back &c. are all relieved from within four to six hours; and with the operation of the medicine there is an enormous discharge of black bile—the patient frequently calls it blood. If the operation is delayed a spoonful of salts promotes the action. Quinine is then given till the ears ring, &c. We have tried to substitute other purgatives instead of the resin, jalap and calomel but our experiments have only produced the conviction that aught else is mere trifling.*" The remedy became known as The Livingstone Pill.

At the same time Livingstone was deeply interested in the culture and practices of the people among whom he lived. He was tolerant and observant of the practices of the traditional healers and he regularly agreed to try their remedies on himself. He also chronicled the kinds of diseases he came across and his attempts at treating some of them. He documented the occurrence of filarial worms in the anterior chamber of the eye, tropical ulcers caused by the maggot worm, the practice of 'geophagy' or clay-eating amongst pregnant women, the prevalence of scurvy, rheumatic fever, smallpox and pneumonia, and the scarcity of tuberculosis among the tribes of Central Africa. He in turn was uniquely tolerated by the tribes amongst whom he travelled and was rarely threatened in any way. In fact he developed a formidable reputation for his clinical abilities.

David Livingstone was the first medical missionary in Central Africa and he set the tone for many of those who followed, notably that their role was to care for the African people and not just for their own missionaries as had happened in other areas of Africa. Most importantly Livingstone loved Africa—with its peoples, vistas, climate, and wild life. It was here that he chose to spend most of his life and here that he chose to die. In this way he also set a precedent that others followed, willingly or accidentally. And what of Commerce and Christianity? Could it be that they have given way to Communication and Collaboration?

Many have questioned the role of missionaries in Africa. The modern, post-colonial world tends to take a dim view of them. So what exactly was Livingstone's contribution, if any to the African cause? Certainly the national outpouring of grief at his funeral, and the honour conferred on him by burial at Westminster set him apart from many other 'great' men. He has been much criticized for his being stubborn, somewhat unconcerned for the welfare of his fellow-travellers, obsessed with discovery, and very hard on his own family. These same qualities enabled him to push boundaries and take risks that would have terrified lesser mortals. His Spartan upbringing prepared him for physical hardship and he expected others to be able to bear the same.

Livingstone's hope was that Africans would accept the Christian gospel if their social and economic conditions were improved. The British government, intent on expanding their economic and political spheres, sponsored Livingstone's Zambezi expeditiion and Livingstone accepted this sponsorship in the hope of promoting legitimate trade in order to combat the slave trade which had fuelled so many inter-tribal wars in the region.

Missionaries alone were not able to protect the weaker tribes and so the missionaries looked to the British colonial administration for assistance. The latter offered limited protection in return for mining and agricultural rights. Meanwhile the missionaries educated the people who then began to challenge colonial rule. Once educated, the African people noticed discrepancies for example, in the amounts spent by colonial government on black and white education. They deeply resented the hut tax which meant that men had to leave their villages and work in the mines or on the railway lines. They were angry at being forcibly removed from their land to make way for railways and farms.

By the end of 1950 in Northern Rhodesia there was a groundswell of support for African self-government. The missionaries, wittingly or unwittingly became instrumental in the African movement towards independence. The Church of Scotland missionaries of Mwenzo, Lubwa and Chitambo were at the forefront of this movement, and this is surely what Livingstone would have wanted. Zambia has honoured Livingstone by keeping a town named after him, when all other European town names were changed. When we asked people at Chitambo what they thought of him the enthusiastic reply was *"He was a good man. He came to help us"*.

# EPILOGUE

Jo returned to Zambia again in May 2010—this time to attend the e-learning Africa 2010 Conference held at the plush Mulungushi Hall in Lusaka. She presented a paper on behalf of her Scottish organisation, NHS Education for Scotland (NES), on scope for re-customising the NHS Scotland Knowledge Network (a sophisticated ICT platform for searching, storing and sharing health-related knowledge and information) as The Africa Knowledge Network (AKN). At short notice, Mr Levi Chifwaila, Nurse in Charge at Chitambo Hospital, presented a second paper on the potential benefits of such 'knowledge exchange' to remote, rural hospitals like Chitambo.

On returning to Scotland, Jo campaigned together with Zambian and Scottish colleagues to obtain grant funding to take knowledge exchange ideas forward. Partners then won a £20,000 grant from the Tropical Health Education Trust (THET), in the UK, for a project on 'Building capacity for e-learning for nurse training in Zambia and Ghana'. This involved 6 international partner organisations in Zambia, Ghana, Scotland and the Netherlands. An early activity was a mini-conference held at MachaWorks, a grassroots internet-providing cooperative based in Southern Zambia. Partners from Chitambo, including Dr Nzinga, Levi Chifwaila, and Matron Hilda Mubanga, attended this confernece and contributed to wide-ranging debate on how e-learning might serve remote, rural hospitals and nurse training schools such as Chitambo. Jo then travelled to Chitambo, with the local team, to see the progress on re-opening the Chitambo School of Nursing. This had long been Levi Chifwaila's dream. Such a move would have profound implications for regeneration of the whole Chitambo community and for meeting the Millennium Development Goals (MDG) for Health. Zambia has a 50% deficit of health workforce, particularly in remote, rural areas such as Chitambo and training of local nurses would go a long way to addressing this crisis and contributing to health improvement for many local people. Jo and PfA campaigned with Levi to realise this dream.

Existing classrooms and dormitories required complete refurbishment and the Zambian government and General Nursing Council of Zambia provided support for this. The Mpepetwe military base, near Kundalila Falls, incorporates a furniture-making factory. Levi and Jo went there and obtained an estimate to completely furnish the classroom and student hostel with beautiful *mukwa*(wooden) desks, chairs, beds, dining tables etc. PfA then worked tirelessly to raise the requisite £9,000 over 2 years, to supply this furniture. The plan came to fruition just in time for the school's re-opening in January 2012. 27 Registered Nurse students were then enrolled. The Government of Zambia has since built extra classrooms and staff accommodation. It is now aiming to double the trainee intake to meet the MDGs for health and a second student hostel is underway. PfA's new 'Friends of Chitambo' sub-group is fundraising both to assist with furnishing the second hostel and with providing training scholarships for deprived student nurses of whom there are currently several.

PfA has also funded a nurse training manikin (Rescusi Annie), which was transported to Zambia by a Scottish Consultant Physician and handed over to Levi at a conference on Maternal and Neonatal Health which both were attending in Lusaka. Levi has personally driven the dream of re-opening the nursing school and has lobbied the Zambian government to the extent that the government has taken notice and has declared Chitambo a new District, with implications for upgrading the hospital to District-level status. Jo is, simultaneously, lobbying the Scottish government, which is proud of its international development reputation (mostly linked to Malawi) on recognising Chitambo's huge historical links with Scotland.

**Dr. Kandolo Nzinga at Chitambo 2011**

Far from the regal grave in Westminster, the statues in Edinburgh, Blantyre (Scotland) and at the Victoria Falls, it is in a remote corner of Northern Zambia that Livingstone's spirit seems very much alive. Livingstone was "of the people", the "right kind of missionary", one who suffered and one who gave himself fully. He certainly began something at Chitambo . . . **and others have carried it out.**

**Mwawombeni Bonse!**

**Levi Chifwaila Chitambo Senior Nurse Tutor**

**Chitambo Nursing School First Intake**

# APPENDIX 1

# Glossary (Bemba or Bisa/Lala: English)

| | |
|---|---|
| Buchizya | The unexpected one |
| Citenge | A piece of cloth for wearing |
| Machila | A Portuguese hammock |
| Mambari | Slave trader |
| Masuku | A wild fruit |
| Milandu | A dispute or argument |
| Mopane | A common tree in southern Africa |
| Mpundu | Fruit-bearing tree, the type near the Livingstone monument |
| Mukwai | Sir or madam |
| Musungu | A European |
| Mutende | Peace be with you |
| Mwawombeni | Well done |
| Nsima | Thick maize porridge, a staple food |

# APPENDIX 2

# Seeking Friends Of Chitambo

**Want to make a difference? Have skills to offer . . . computing (blogging, Twittering, Facebooking etc.)? Fundraising experience? Health professional and/or educational know how?? Or just plain interest and enthusiasm to bring?
Please join us!**

*Background:*

Chitambo, in central Zambia, has major historical links with Scotland. It is where Scottish missionary/explorer David Livingstone died. The link becomes even stronger in 2013, the bicentennial of Livingstone's birth. Penicuik for Africa (PfA) has made major contributions to re-generating the remote Chitambo community, including providing medical equipment and a land cruiser ambulance to the hospital; furnishing the new nursing school and student hostel; and funding a nurse training manikin. All this on minimal resources and much local muscle!

As a result, PfA's Chitambo project is growing exponentially. With so much going on, and PfA's other African commitments taking off, it's time to re-think how best to support our Chitambo partners, at the nursing school in particular. Like many African countries, Zambia is currently suffering a critical shortage of health workforce, including a 50% deficit in skilled nurses and midwives. This has major implications for the healthcare of mothers and children in particular, since maternal and infant mortality remain unacceptably high. The Zambian government is responding by scaling up the rural health workforce and the re-opening of Chitambo School of Nursing in January 2012 is a result. This will make a real difference. However, funds are invariably short and our nursing school partners always welcome some additional help.

*Friends of Chitambo:*

There are many Friends of Chitambo, old and new, around the world, including Zambians abroad (some from Chitambo); doctors, nurses and others who have served at Chitambo Hospital; and local Penicuk and other Scots who have an interest. However, a project like this can never have too many friends. So we are proposing a dedicated Friends of Chitambo group, in parallel with PfA.

Activities might include awareness-raising, including via social media sites (e.g. Twitter, Facebook, LinkedIn etc.); fundraising for specific items (e.g. teaching aids, tyres for the ambulance etc.); sponsoring disadvantaged students; twinning with other healthcare institutions; developing online information blogs; sourcing computers for the school; digging the school well and kitchen garden . . . to name a few! There are also opportunities to contribute to other Chitambo institutions such as the hospital, orphanage, church, local schools and businesses etc.

Alternatively, let us know if you simply want to be kept informed about developments and we will add you to our circulation list.

For more information, and/or to register interest, please contact:

**Dr Jo Vallis (Co-ordinator) Friends of Chitambo**
**Tel: *Home:* 01968 673978; *Mobile:* 07791262918**
**Email address: jovallis@hotmail.com**

# SOURCES

Ballantyne and Shepherd, *Missionary Adventures of Dr. James Henderson 1895-98,* Lovedale Press, 1968.

Brelsford W.V. *The Tribes of Zambia,* Government Printer, Lusaka, 1965.

Buckle A. *A History of the Serenje District,* Unpublished, 1976.

Dugard M. *Into Africa: The Dramatic Retelling of the Stanley-Livingstone Story,* Bantam Press, UK, 2003.

Forster M. *Good Wives? Mary, Fanny, Jennie and me,* Vintage Press, London, 2002.

Fraser D. *Livingstonia: The Story of Our Mission,* Foreign Mission Committee of the United Free Church of Scotland, 121 George Street, Edinburgh, 1915.

Gelfand M. *Livingstone the Doctor: His Life and Travels,* Basil Blackwell, Oxford, 1957.

Gerrard J. *Africa Calling: A Medical Missionary in Kenya and Zambia,* The Radcliffe Press, London, 2001.

Hammarskjold D. *Markings,* Faber & Faber Ltd., London, 1961.

Hobson D. *Tales of Zambia,* The Zambia Society Trust, London, 1996.

Hoch Rev. E *Hippocrene Concise Dictionary: Bemba.* Hippocrene Books Inc. New York 1960.

Hudson J. *A Time To Mourn: A personal account of the 1964 Lumpa Church revolt in Zambia.* Bookworld Publishers, Lusaka, Zambia.

Jeal T. *Livingstone.* Yale Nota Bene, Yale University Press, 2001.

Kangende K. *Zambian Myths and Legends of the Wild,* Minta Publishers, Lusaka, 2001.

Kaunda K. *Zambia Shall Be Free,* Heineman, London, 1962.

Lamb C. *The Africa House: The True Story of an English Gentleman and His African Dream,* Penguin Books, 1999.

Livingstone D. *Missionary Travels and Researches in South Africa,* London 1857.

Livingstone D. *Travels,* J.M. Dent & Sons, Edited by Dr. J.I. McNair, 1955.

Livingstone W.P. *Laws of Livingstonia,* Hodder & Stoughton, London, 1922.

Lyon D. *In pursuit of a Vision: The Story of the Church of Scotland's developing relationships with the Churches emerging from the missionary movement in the twenty-five years from 1947 to 1972,* Saint Andrew Press, Edinburgh, 1998.

McNair J. I. *Livingstone the Liberator,* (undated) London and Glasgow Collins Clear Type Press.

Macpherson F. *North of the Zambezi: A Modern Missionary Memoir,* The Handsel Press, Edinburgh, 1998.

Moffat R.U. *John Smith Moffat C.M.G. Missionary. A Memoir,* Negro Universities Press, New York, 1921.

Pettit C. *Dr. Livingstone, I Presume? Missionaries, Journalists, Explorers and Empire,* Harvard University Press, Cambridge, Massachusetts, 2007.

Ransford O. *Livingstone's Lake: The Drama of Africa's Inland Sea*, Thomas Y. Crowell Company, New York, 1967.

Waller H. *The Last Journals of David Livingstone, In Central Africa from Eighteen Sixty-Five to His Death, John Murray, London, 1874.*

Wilson C. and Irwin A. *In Quest of Livingstone: A Journey to the Four Fountains*, House of Lochar, Isle of Colonsay, 1999.

Young W.P. *Livingstonia: Sketches in the Field,* Church of Scotland, Foreign Mission Committee, Edinburgh, 1947.